BIG BOOK
BABY NAMES
AND
ANNOUNCEMENTS

THE BODY PRESS/PERIGEE

ISBN: 0-399-51710-3
Library of Congress Catalog Card Number: 82-82982
© 1983 The Putnam Berkley Group, Inc.
Printed in U.S.A.

4   5   6   7   8   9   10

TABLE OF CONTENTS

THE BODY PRESS/PERIGEE BOOKS
are published by
The Putnam Publishing Group
200 Madison Avenue
New York, N.Y. 10016

ABOUT THE AUTHOR

Sandra Buzbee Bailey is the mother of four children and an avid researcher of names. Her interest in the subject began when she did a paper on the development of slang for a college class. She became intrigued with variations and derivations of words and names. This fascination led her to genealogy and an interest in incorporating names of past generations when naming new generations.

Before each of her children was born, Sandra read novels, baby-name books and genealogy records looking for the "just right" name. She created so many name lists and became so adept at research that it was natural for her to do the most complete book on the subject. But, all the work was worth it, says Sandra with a smile. Not one of her children has rejected his name—yet!

ABOUT THE ILLUSTRATOR

Darcy Anne Tom moved to Tucson, Arizona, after she completed her education at the Kendall School of Design in Grand Rapids, Michigan. As an illustrator, she has been involved in many projects, including illustrating children's educational books. Darcy is married and recently had the occasion to name a baby—her own little boy!

ACKNOWLEDGMENTS

My sincere appreciation to my mother, Geraldine Buzbee of Herman, Nebraska, for her love and support during the production of this book. Thanks to Dr. Judy Mitchell, who provided valuable assistance in developing a pronunciation guide for the names. Thanks also to my children, Ryan, Elliott, André and Sasha, whose births prompted my search for new and interesting names.

NAMING
YOUR BABY

ABCs Of
Naming Your Baby

How many times in your life do you sign your name? If you sign it once a day and live to be 75 years old, you will have written your name 27,393 times. Many people hear or see your name. It represents you. People get an impression about you from your name.

Studies show a name reflects a certain image. To many people, Judy gives the image of an all-American sportswoman. Dawn gives the image of a sexy, beautiful girl. A name is like a nose—you're usually stuck with the one your parents gave you. And it's there for the world to comment on.

SUCCESS OR FAILURE—IT'S ALL IN A NAME

Research on the psychological effect of a name indicates that it may help make you a success or failure. It depends on the way people react to your name. The sound or spelling alone could land you in jail, get you a job as a college president, or help you become a movie star!

Here's a case in point. A study by two psychology professors, Herbert Harari and John McDavid, suggests teachers are influenced by a student's name when they give out grades. Two groups of teachers were asked to mark essays. Some were told the essays were written by David, Michael, Lisa and Ann. Others were told that the same essays were from Elmer, Sebastian, Adele and Beatrice. The essays by the first group with common, popular names got consistently higher marks than those written by students with older, stodgier names. So if your child gets an *F* on a paper, perhaps you should blame it on the name you gave him, not his I.Q.!

Names that are too hard to pronounce or too offbeat may also doom a student to failure. Studies of 3,000 undergraduates at Harvard University show the highest proportion of dropouts was among those with strange or exotic names.

A NAME IS WORTH A THOUSAND WORDS

The way you perceive a person often depends on his name. How much confidence would you have in a person named John Will Fail or Mary Christmas? They will be joked about and laughed at all their lives. How about uncommon names such as Dwight David Eisenhower, Rutherford Birchard Hayes and Ulysses S. Grant? What did people call these boys when they were young?

How about a name like Cardinal Jaime Sin? There really is a person with this name. He often relates in speeches how he enjoys inviting people to *the house of Sin*. Difficult or humorous names can be overcome—but it takes a lifetime of courage, thick skin and laughing in the face of ridicule. Don't force your child to endure it. Be careful and thoughtful when selecting a name.

Famous people can popularize a name, but be cautious of choosing a faddish name. Names like Tad, Rip and Bo may be in one year, but out the next. Basing a name on the year's most popular TV star or the latest song may seem clever, but the glow may fade later. Don't associate your child with a fad or craze. You don't want your child's name to date him unnecessarily.

WHAT'S IN A NAME?

How significant is the meaning of a name? Meanings vary from one language to another. Often there is uncertainty as to the exact meaning. But you shouldn't assume that all names have lost their meanings, just that some have taken on different or more diverse meanings with the passing of time.

If you name your child Abraham, *Father of the multitude*, does it mean he will have 12 children? Will a girl named Doris, *From the sea*, automatically be a good swimmer? Of course not. The meaning of a name is as important as you want to make it.

In some native cultures, names are considered part of a man's soul. They have a personal effect on the child and how he is treated. In today's modern society, many people don't know the meaning of their names. But a name and its meaning can be important if we make it so. It can give us something to be proud of and something to pattern our lives after. The choice is yours and your child's!

KAMEKO—*Child of the tortoise*

A LASTING LEGACY

One of the lasting gifts you give your child is his or her name. Take time to pick or construct a name that has the dignity, beauty and lasting qualities you want. The right name will bring both of you happiness.

In this book you will find more than 13,000 names, nicknames and variations—Oriental, Egyptian, Russian, Hebrew, European, Latin, Polynesian, American Indian, American, East Indian and Eskimo. Look through the names to find ones you like. Make a checklist and then eliminate them one by one. Another section in this chapter, How To Choose Or Create A Name, beginning on page 15, will help you further.

Take plenty of time deciding on the name to give your child. It will be a legacy he or she will appreciate for a lifetime.

Where Names Come From

HEY YOU THERE!

Thousands of years ago, before the development of formal language, how did one tribe member identify another? One native may have grunted to his neighbor, "Ugg," meaning "Hey you over there!," and that was the beginning of name identification.

History shows early names were coined from a variety of sources: from a circumstance of birth, a physical characteristic of the child or some hoped-for quality parents wanted their child to possess. Early names were borrowed from tribal gods. They were taken from animals, objects, stones and flowers. If the name caught on, it was handed down from one generation to another.

Along the way original meanings were forgotten or combined with other meanings. As nations mixed through trade or war, they borrowed names and added their own pronunciations and spellings. The result was a mixture of names. The trail is sometimes difficult to follow for someone who wants to discover the original meaning of a word or name.

RELIGION DOES ITS PART

Christianity provided a remarkable change in the giving of names. In the Middle Ages, it was decreed by Christian law that a child's name had to contain the first name of a saint or martyr, or the child could not be baptized. The list of eligible names was taken from the Bible and included such names as Mary, Ann, Elizabeth, John, Nathan and James. For this reason, these names have been common in Christian cultures for centuries.

Different sects brought about trends in names. An example is the Puritans. They began using names as an indication of moral or religious worthiness. The outcome was a proliferation of names such as Repentance, Purity, Comfort, Faith, Hope, Charity and Mercy.

GABRIELLE—
God is my strength

MADE IN HOLLYWOOD

In more recent times, the movie industry has done its share of creating trends or vogues in names. The influence of the silver screen has carried over into all aspects of people's lives, including what we name our children. Many children were given names because of a famous Hollywood namesake: Greta, Hedy, Myrna, Joan, Bette and Pearl; or Cary, Charlton, Rex, Boris, Ricardo and Marlon.

Television has been even more pervasive. It influences our thought and speech in more ways than we imagine. From soap operas, situation comedies and made-for-TV-movies, we have been deluged with popular names such as Jaime, Sonny, Erica, Constance, Jaclyn and Derek.

WHICH SMITH?

Have you ever tried to count all the John or Mary Smiths in a big-city phone book? If so, you realize the importance of choosing the right first name to go with your surname. If you have a common surname, consider giving your child a unique and unusual first or middle name.

Another way to avoid problems with common surnames is to select three given names so your child will avoid identity mix-ups. Chinese and American Indians don't have this problem. These cultures frequently give as many as 10 names. But before you go to excess, remember that most application or registration forms provide a space for only three names.

The combination of first name and surname should sound pleasing together. Be careful that the combination doesn't create humor or discomfort. A child may get tired of living a lifetime with unfortunate combinations such as Lovey Good, Goodhue Red, Ham Burger, Lake Trout or I. M. Zamost.

BOY OR GIRL?

There is a trend today to give a boy's name to a girl and, to a lesser extent, a girl's name to a boy. Examples are Terry, Chris, Jerry, Carrie and Billie. Most American-Indian and Polynesian names don't have this problem—their names can be used for both boys and girls. American culture is heading in that direction, possibly because of the equal-rights movement and the tendency for women to assert themselves in all areas of society.

Some names sound the same for boys or girls, but the spelling gives a clue to the sex. In the following names, the first spelling is feminine and the second version is masculine: Carol/Carroll, Leslie/Lesley and Claire/Clair. Unless you see the person, it is difficult to determine the sex. Such mistaken sex identity may prove troublesome to your child. Your son may get women's mail and your daughter may be drafted!

WARREN—*Protecting friend*

NICKNAMES—A WAY OF LIFE

We have a tendency to shorten names. We may be too lazy or too busy to pronounce a complete name. When picking out a suitable name for your baby, consider the shortened form or nickname. If you pick William, be sure you don't mind friends or family calling your boy Bill or Willy. Barbara may sound beautiful to you—but you may dislike Babs or Bobi. You can't entirely predict nicknames, but remember that many people go through life answering to them.

Another shortened form of a name is a love nickname or pet name. Names of endearment are good therapy for everyone. A name that is special between two people helps their relationship. Often these names develop naturally and are difficult to predict. But if your son is named Teddy, don't be surprised if his baby name is Teddy Bear—especially if he's cute and cuddly!

MY HERO!

"My boy is named after the most famous man in history, Abraham Lincoln," said a proud mother. Many cultures have been overly enthusiastic about naming their children after national heroes or heroines. Thousands, maybe millions, of children have been named after George Washington, John Kennedy, Winston Churchill, Joan of Arc, Florence Nightingale and Napoleon. There's nothing wrong with this if the name is not contrived and fits with your surname. Be careful of naming your child after people who are more infamous than famous. Such names as the following generate more negative response than positive: Adolf Hitler, Benedict Arnold and Lee Harvey Oswald.

In many families, it is traditional to name the first boy after his father or grandfather. If the baby is a girl, strange things may happen, such as changing James to Jamie. But is it fair to name only the first child after the father or mother and imply the other sons or daughters are not quite as good or important?

In our family we decided each son would bear his father's name, which is Rickard. So we gave each boy his father's name as a *middle* name. In naming our daughter, we decided on Sasha, which is a derivative of my name, Sandra. So, in our case, both parents' vanity is satisfied.

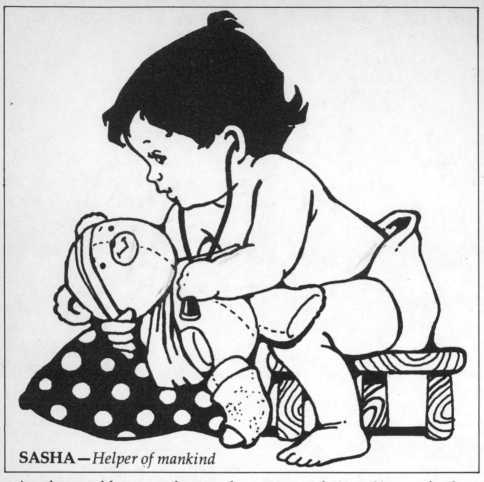

SASHA — *Helper of mankind*

Another problem may be grandparents or relatives. You can't please everyone. You may start a tug-of-war if you consult relatives about names. Make your choice of a name and then announce the happy news—it's less traumatic that way.

Some people want to pass on an ancestral or traditional family name. This often gives children a link with the past and helps you in your search for a name. A common practice is to give the wife's maiden name as a middle name, which helps in genealogical research. There is one caution: Don't settle on an out-of-date name that will be disliked by your child throughout his life.

THE ARTS AT WORK

Books, plays, poems and music have provided many characters from which to draw names. Authors of fiction can create super heroes or heroines and choose names to fit them perfectly. The arts are a great source of names for your child. Remember some of the wonderful and lovable characters that you have enjoyed in reading, listening or viewing. Maybe one of these characters will provide the right name for your baby.

How to Choose or Create a Name

Should your child share a name with anyone? Your boy or girl is unique—why saddle him or her with a common name like Mary or John? Some psychologists believe common names help a child become successful and uncommon names should be avoided. Other experts say the reverse. Some people feel special when they're the only Kaja in the class or school.

One woman confided it was difficult to live with her unusual name. But she said she would not trade it for a common name. It made her feel out of the ordinary—not just another Mary, Jane or Barbara. She also gave her children uncommon names.

The decision is up to you. This book offers you common and uncommon names. If you can't find the perfect name for your special child, use the following helpful hints to create your own.

PRONUNCIATION + SPELLING = NAME

Names are tricky at best. Don't confuse the issue by making it hard to pronounce. Consider the whole name as a unit, not just the first name. The name should sound nice and melodious. How would you like to go through life with the name Chuck Stuck? Say it 10 times. Now do the same with Jonathan Stuck. One name is harsh and abrasive. The other flows smoothly.

Your child's name should sound pleasing. One way to accomplish this is to use the rhythm system. Most phonetic specialists agree that equal numbers of syllables in first and last names sound clipped and dead. Names like Pat Bond, Jeff Call or Stan Green are not nearly as rhythmical as Pat McDonald, Jeff Browerman or Stanley Green.

Next comes the problem of spelling. Have you ever looked at a person's name on paper and been afraid to pronounce it? It's helpful if names are spelled simply and close to the way they are pronounced.

"Teacher, my name is *juh-MEL-uh*. No, it's spelled J-A-M-I-L-A. No, it's not pronounced ja-MIL-a. No, it wouldn't be better with two E's!" By this time, the children in the classroom are all rolling on the floor with laughter. How embarrassing for your beautiful daughter! Maybe a more simple name—one that's easier to spell—would be less confusing and less irritating.

SPELL IT OUT

A letter sent to Ann Landers points out the problem of initials. The man's name in the letter was J.B., with no other given name, just initials. He said not having a full-fledged name was the worst thing a parent could possibly do. Teachers called him a liar, insisting that he must have a first name. He had trouble with insurance companies, military service, voting and opening bank accounts. Giving your child initials for a name may lead him into countless arguments and problems. Friends will always think he's covering up a ridiculous first name!

Juniors or numbers after names can also cause problems. There is a trend away from this tradition. Would you like to be known as "little Bill" or "big Bill"? No one likes to live in someone's shadow. Do your child a favor—give him his own identity.

Consider what your child's initials will spell? If you name your son Peter Ivan Gordon, he will go through life with the initials P.I.G. Look at all aspects of a name before you make a final decision.

YOUR NAME AND MEANING

Create a name with the meaning you want. You may find a name you like but the meaning is not quite right. For example, Katherine means *pure* and Kali means *energy*. By combining them, you can form the meaningful name, Kalerine. This might express your hope for the future—*pure energy*.

Now consider a boy's name. Homer means *promise* and Donald means *world ruler*. By combining and altering them slightly, you can create the name Maldon, possibly meaning *promised world ruler*.

This process can be used many times to develop your own names and meanings. Try different names together and see what you create.

Famous Name Changes

During the last part of the 19th century and early in this century, immigrants to the United States often changed their names. People arriving in this country were encouraged to take new names to fit better into American society.

Today, the practice of changing names is most prevalent among movie stars, show-business celebrities and sports stars. Many hope a more appealing name—and one that's easy to pronounce—will help them attain popularity. It's all part of the art of selling yourself to the public.

Following is a list of people who changed their name to create a better public image or for personal or religious reasons. Their original name is listed opposite their professional name. See which you like best.

PROFESSIONAL NAME	ORIGINAL NAME
Muhammad Ali	Cassius Marcellus Clay, Jr.
Woody Allen	Allen Konigsberg
Julie Andrews	Julia Vernon
Fred Astaire	Frederick Austerlitz
Lauren Bacall	Betty Joan Perski
Lucille Ball	Diane Belmont
Jack Benny	Joseph Kubelsky
Irving Berlin	Israel Baline
Yogi Berra	Lawrence Peter Berra
David Bowie	David Jones
Mel Brooks	Melvin Kaminsky
Yul Brynner	Taidje Kahn, Jr.
Bugs Bunny	Happy Rabbit
George Burns	Nathan Birnbaum
Ray Charles	Ray Charles Robinson
Chevy Chase	Cornelius Crane Chase

PROFESSIONAL NAME	ORIGINAL NAME
Cher	Cherilyn LaPierre
Mike Connors	Krekor Ohanian
Robert Conrad	Conrad Robert Falk
Joan Crawford	Lucille Le Sueur
Bing Crosby	Harry Lillis Crosby
Tony Curtis	Bernard Schwartz
Rodney Dangerfield	John Cohen
Doris Day	Doris Kappelhoff
Sandra Dee	Alexandra Zuck
John Denver	Henry John Deutschendorf, Jr.
Bob Dylan	Robert Zimmerman
Dale Evans	Francis Octavia Smith
Jamie Farr	Jaemeel Farah
W. C. Fields	William Claude Dukenfield
Redd Foxx	John Elroy Sanford
Greta Garbo	Greta Luisa Gustafson
Judy Garland	Frances Gumm
Crystal Gayle	Brenda Gail Webb
Cary Grant	Archibald Leach
Rex Harrison	Reginald Cary
O. Henry	William Sidney Porter
Bob Hope	Leslie Townes Hope
Rock Hudson	Roy Scherer, Jr.
Elton John	Reginald Kenneth Dwight
Boris Karloff	William Pratt
Diane Keaton	Diane Hall
Bert Lahr	Irving Lahrheim
Ann Landers	Esther "Eppie" Pauline Friedman Lederer
Michael Landon	Michael Orowitz
Gypsy Rose Lee	Louise Hovick
Jerry Lewis	Joseph Levitch
Peter Lorre	Laszlo Loewenstein
Bela Lugosi	Arisztid Olt
Paul McCartney	James Paul McCartney
Shirley MacLaine	Shirley Beatty
Karl Malden	Mladen Sekulovich
Dean Martin	Dino Crocetti
Groucho Marx	Julius Henry Marx
Meatloaf	Marvin Lee Aday
Ethel Merman	Ethel Zimmerman
Zero Mostel	Samuel Joel Mostel
Kim Novak	Marilyn Paul Novak
Hugh O'Brien	Hugh J. Krampe

PROFESSIONAL NAME	ORIGINAL NAME
Tony Orlando	Michael Anthony Orlando Cassivitis
Peter O'Toole	Seamus O'Toole
Satchel Paige	Leroy Robert Paige
Gregory Peck	Eldred Gregory Peck
Bernadette Peters	Bernadette Lazarra
Ginger Rogers	Virginia McMath
Roy Rogers	Leonard Slye
Mickey Rooney	Joe Yule, Jr.
Yves St. Laurent	Henri Donat Mathieu
Soupy Sales	Milton Hines
Sissy Spacek	Mary Elizabeth Spacek
Mickey Spillane	Frank Morrison
Ringo Starr	Richard Starkey
Sly Stone	Sylvester Stone
Robert Taylor	Spangler Brugh
Danny Thomas	Amos Jacobs
Rip Torn	Elmore Torn, Jr.
Twiggy	Leslie Hornby
Abigail Van Buren	Pauline Esther "Popo" Friedman Phillips
Nancy Walker	Ann Myrtle Swoyer
Mike Wallace	Myron Wallace
Muddy Waters	McKinley Morganfield
John Wayne	Marion Michael Morrison
Tuesday Weld	Susan Kerr Weld
Gene Wilder	Jerome Silberman
Flip Wilson	Clerow Wilson
Shelley Winters	Shirley Schrift
Natalie Wood	Natasha Gurdin
Cy Young	Denton True Young
Loretta Young	Gretchen Young

MIX IT UP!

PUT LETTERS IN THE MIXER

One way to create a name is to combine mother's and father's names. Do this by taking the given name or maiden name of the mother and the first or last name of the father. Pick letters from each name to form a pleasant-sounding name. For example, Rickard and Sandra form Sandrin. The last name, Kelsey, and maiden name, Martin, combine to form Kelmar. You may want to go back as far as grandparents and great-grandparents for name combinations.

A meaningful word can be used to form a name. The letters in the word *earth* can be switched to Retha. Chastity can be altered to form Sachtity.

If all else fails, use the letter-bowl trick. Choose letters of the alphabet from names of ancestors, from your children's names, from famous people or from the alphabet. Put them in a bowl and mix them up. Make sure you have enough vowels. Play a game with your family by picking out letters to form the ideal name.

ABSOLUTELY THE END

Adding certain suffixes or endings to a name can produce an interesting new name. Try the following endings on masculine and feminine names: *alie, ann, an, and, ana, ald, ane, lee, een, ella, elle, ena, ene, et, ette, etta, ey, ice, ie, illa, ille, ina, inda, ine, inne, itsa, sin, sy, isa, itka, is, ita, ley, lyn, y, yn, win, wina.* On a name like Sabra, drop the *a*, add *illa* and you form the new name, Sabrilla.

You can also modify a boy's name to give the desired touch. The ending *ie* can be added to Ross to form Rossie or turn Ron into Ronnie.

If you want to name a child after father or mother, but don't want to use a junior or second, add a suffix to form a slightly different name. Lew becomes Lewis or Lewan. Jean becomes Jeanene or Jeanetta. Many names in this book can be altered by adding such endings. Possibilities are limitless.

ADD DASH TO THE MIX

Hyphenation is another way to create a name. A hyphen joins two names together and adds style to an otherwise bland name. John-Lee and Lani-Ann are two examples.

A trend today is to give girls their mother's maiden name as part of their name. The two names are connected by a hyphen, such as Mary Newton-Alison. This can be done with a boy's name. Robert Paul Martin-Black is more memorable than Robert Paul Black.

A MISSING LETTER

With a little modification, family names are a source of new names. Grandma's or grandpa's name, minus a letter or two, can produce a favorable name. Harlow can be changed to Arlow and still put a twinkle in grandpa's eye. You may want to rearrange grandma's name to form a more modern and unusual name. Samantha becomes Manthas by dropping one letter and rearranging the others. This way you can give joy to grandparents without duplicating the same name. Think how interesting family reunions will be!

MOTHER NATURE

Name combinations can be found everywhere you look, especially in nature. By using the first letters of Sky, Island, Volcano, Earth and Nature, you create Siven, a name for a child of nature. Use the opposites, Fire and Ice, to make the intriguing name, Firice.

This same approach works by combining letters or syllables. Try combining words from the title of your favorite song, book or poem.

Use any of these ideas to create a new name. Employ your imagination. Experiment and have fun. The most important points to remember while experimenting are:

- Make sure the name sounds pleasing.
- Be certain it's pronounceable.
- Spell it correctly and predictably.
- Be sure you like the name!

Most Frequently Given Names

The American Name Society is a group devoted to the study of names. Representatives from this group recently conducted a poll to determine the most popular boys' and girls' names. The results of the survey are used here with the permission of Kelsey B. Harder, the Society's president.

According to the American Name Society, these are America's favorite names, in order of popularity:

Top American Boys' Names	Top American Girls' Names
1. Michael	1. Jennifer
2. Jason	2. Mary
3. Matthew	3. Karen
4. David	4. Michelle
5. Brian	5. Jessica
6. Christopher	6. Katherine
7. John	7. Rebecca
8. James	8. Deborah
9. Jeffrey	9. Robin
10. Daniel	10. Megan

Astrology—
Just Plain Fun

Astrology originated in 2000 B.C. in Babylonia. It began with the study of heavenly bodies to predict the future. Between 600 and 200 B.C., astrologers developed individual horoscopes.

Interest in astrology declined with the rise of Christianity. In the 1930s, a newspaper in England began publishing a horoscope column and interest in astrology picked up again.

Astrology is based on the belief that heavenly bodies form patterns that reveal a person's personality or future. Most scientists believe that astrology is not a science. Others regard it as fun and harmless. Whether you believe it or not, you can still have fun applying it to naming your baby.

CAPRICORN (Dec. 22—Jan. 20)
Birthstones—Ruby, chalcedony
Flowers—Flaxweed, moss, rush, ivy,
　amaranth
Colors—Dark browns, green, black
Personality—The most conscientious
　children of the Zodiac
Zodiac Symbol—The goat

ARIES (March 21—April 20)
Birthstones—Bloodstone, crystal
Flowers—Buttercup, daisy, starthistle
Color—Brilliant red
Personality—The most brilliant children of
　the Zodiac
Zodiac Symbol—The ram

AQUARIUS (Jan. 21—Feb. 19)
Birthstones—Garnet, amethyst
Flowers—Daffodil, pansy
Colors—Mingled shades
Personality—The most loyal children
　of the Zodiac
Zodiac Symbol—Water-bearer or the
　sage

TAURUS (April 21—May 21)
Birthstones—Sapphire, ruby, diamond
Flowers—Cowslip, daisy, goldenrod, violet
Colors—Red-orange, yellow, cream
Personality—The most popular children of
　the Zodiac
Zodiac Symbol—The bull

PISCES (Feb. 20—March 20)
Birthstone—Amethyst
Flowers—Tuberose, water lily, lotus
Colors—Green-blue, shades of
　lavender, amethyst
Personality—The most imaginative
　children of the Zodiac
Zodiac Symbol—The fish

GEMINI (May 22—June 21)
Birthstones—Agate, sapphire, quartz
Flowers—Marigold, fern, lily-of-the-valley
Colors—Silver-gray, blue
Personality—The most alert children of the
　Zodiac
Zodiac Symbol—The twins

CANCER (June 22—July 21)
Birthstones—Emerald, cat's-eye
Flowers—Lily, white poppy, iris
Colors—Pearl, delicate greens
Personality—The most sensitive
    children of the Zodiac
Zodiac Symbol—The crab

LIBRA (Sept. 24—Oct. 23)
Birthstones—Peridot, aquamarine
Flowers—Goldenrod, violet, cowslip
Colors—Blue, pale yellow, pastels
Personality—The most intuitive
    children of the Zodiac
Zodiac Symbol—The balance

LEO (July 22—Aug. 23)
Birthstones—Amber, topaz, onyx
Flowers—Poppy, sunflower, red rose
Colors—Amber, deep orange
Personality—The happiest children of
    the Zodiac
Zodiac Symbol—The lion

SCORPIO (Oct. 24—Nov. 22)
Birthstone—Topaz
Flowers—Thistle, hawthorne
Color—Deep red
Personality—The most thorough
    children of the Zodiac
Zodiac Symbol—The scorpion

VIRGO (Aug. 24—Sept. 23)
Birthstones—Carnelian, jade
Flowers—Fern, azalea, morning glory
Colors—Yellow, gray-blue
Personality—The most ambitious
    children of the Zodiac
Zodiac Symbol—The virgin

SAGITTARIUS (Nov. 23—Dec. 21)
Birthstones—Emerald, topaz
Flowers—Holly, jessamine, carnation
Colors—Deep violet-blue
Personality—The most independent
    children of the Zodiac
Zodiac Symbol—The archer

BIRTH ANNOUNCEMENTS & HANDOUTS

Birth Announcements

First impressions count! Your baby made quite an impact on you. Use the announcement ideas in this chapter to make an impression on friends and relatives.

There are four categories of birth announcements: surnames, hobbies or interests, professions, and general ideas. Even though announcements illustrate a particular name, many can work for anyone by slightly changing the message. Announcements related to professions or interests may not coincide with your situation, but they may spark ideas or variations that work for you.

Materials for announcements are usually inexpensive and often found around the house. Most announcements can be made from poster board, wood, cloth, writing paper or construction paper. Use felt pens, colored pencils, acrylic paints or watercolors to add color to announcements. To help preserve your message, cover it with clear contact paper before cutting it. Grocery or craft stores carry contact paper and other items for making announcements.

Use the illustrations in this chapter as a guide for creating your announcement. If you want it to be the same size as shown, trace the illustration on transparent tracing paper. Use the edge of a pencil to rub graphite on the opposite side of the design and retrace the design on paper. Or use carbon paper to trace the design onto paper or cloth. If you want your announcement larger or smaller, measure key points on the illustration and enlarge or reduce them to scale on your announcement.

To involve the whole family in announcing a new baby, let older children help color, letter and draw the announcements. They'll enjoy helping announce their new baby brother or sister.

Use the illustrations and ideas in this chapter any way you want. Be creative and enjoy announcing your baby in style!

Surnames

LET'S GO FISHING

The surname Bass was the inspiration for this announcement, but the idea can be used for Trout, Pike, Fisher, Fishman, Finley and other names. Draw and cut out the announcement. Put in a fish representing each member of the family. The smallest diapered fish is the new arrival. Bubbles carry the data of the birth. Color fish gold, green or other bright colors. You can cut the fish, bubbles, fish house and vegetation from colored construction paper and glue them in the scene. This announcement goes over swimmingly with friends!

A TOUCH OF ROYALTY

Here's an idea for surnames that contain the words King, Queen, Duke, Royal or Prince. The idea also works for any family with blueblood. Fold a sheet of paper in half. Cut three sides of the announcement as shown in the illustration above. Use blue, purple and gold to color the crown. Spread white glue on the gemstone and sprinkle with gold or silver glitter to add sparkle to the announcement. Write text in stylish script on the inside. The copy above shows you how to word the message. Now there's an announcement fit for a King—or his son or daughter!

browns
are announcing:

Brooke Marie
NAME
August 4, 1989
DATE
5:53 p.m.
TIME
6 lbs. 9 ozs.
WEIGHT
20"
LENGTH

now we're going to color the town red!

COLOR THE TOWN RED

A large, oversize crayon makes a clever announcement for surnames that contain a color—Brown, Black, Redman, Whitely and so forth. It also works well for any colorful family. Use colors appropriate to the name or choose any bright, bold color. You might add: "Now we're going to color the town red!" Maybe your friends will get the hint and join the party!

HIDDEN MEANINGS

Analyze your surname and come up with a unique word puzzle for recipients to solve. For example, the name *Hartvicson* has several shorter words or sounds in it. *Hart* becomes the heart symbol and *son* becomes a friendly sun. Many longer surnames can be taken apart in the same way. Use an open mouth to tell or shout about your baby. The baby-face sun represents a new baby boy. Fill the lower half of the announcement with important information on the birth. Your friends will get the meaning soon enough!

Hobbies Or Interests

There's a little racket at our house!

JAMIE JOHN JENKENS
SEPT. 16, 1982   10 lbs. 1 oz.
3:57 P.M.   18½"

We're busy playing with our new racket. You're invited to come play with him too!

WHAT A RACKET!

Avid tennis players can have fun with this announcement. Draw or cut out the message in the shape of a tennis racket. Use words that sound alike such as *racket* and *racquet*, or other tennis terms, to convey the idea of the new arrival. The same concept works using a baseball glove, golf putter or bowling ball for other sports. Score this announcement 40 LOVE!

NAME THAT TUNE

Here's an announcement for musicians or music-lovers. Make a sheet-music staff to carry the good tidings. The treble clef becomes the stork. Each note represents a member of the family. The last measure contains facts about the baby. Recipients will appreciate the sound of this announcement!

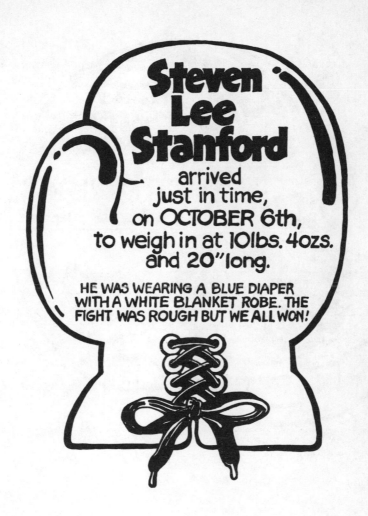

Steven Lee Stanford arrived just in time, on OCTOBER 6th, to weigh in at 10lbs. 4ozs. and 20" long.

HE WAS WEARING A BLUE DIAPER WITH A WHITE BLANKET ROBE. THE FIGHT WAS ROUGH BUT WE ALL WON!

THE CHAMP

Fight-fans can help this new arrival box his way out! Pattern this announcement after a boxing glove. Use brown construction or craft paper for the glove. Punch holes with a hand punch for eyelets. Use short shoelaces to tie the glove. This announcement is a real knockout!

Meet our future quarterback

STANLEY JOHN BAKER

BORN 12·17·89 TIME 5:45 P.M.
WEIGHT 8 LBS, 2 OZS.
LENGTH 19"

PHOTO

TACKLE THIS!

Here's the perfect announcement for football players, coaches or Sunday-afternoon quarterbacks. Cut out a helmet shape from colored construction paper or poster board. Use the colors or insignia of your favorite team to personalize the helmet. Make four diagonal slits as shown to hold a picture of the baby. Don't forget the vital statistics on your little bruiser.

SEAN LYNN BARRET dropped in on the Barret home on the night of Nov. 10th at 2 a.m. She weighed 6½ lbs. and was 17" long!

RIBBON →

DROP IN

Skydivers or daredevils will enjoy sending this announcement. It's a welcome change from printed announcements. Cut out a round piece of cloth from remnants. Or sew together alternating panels of pink and blue cloth. Punch four to six holes around the edge of the cloth. Thread pink and blue ribbons through the holes and attach ribbons to a small plastic baby that can be found at most toy or craft stores. Write a cheery message on the cloth with permanent laundry markers. Mail the parachute in a large Manila envelope or small box. What a nice surprise to drop in the mail to friends or relatives!

Professions

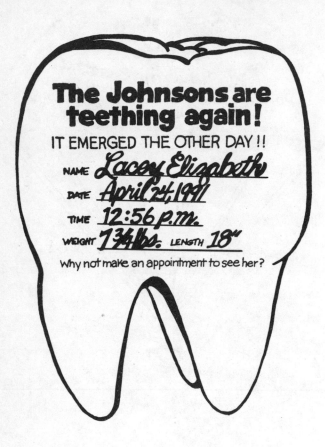

The Johnsons are teething again!

IT EMERGED THE OTHER DAY !!

NAME *Lacey Elizabeth*

DATE *April 24, 1991*

TIME *12:56 p.m.*

WEIGHT *7 3/4 lbs.* LENGTH *18"*

Why not make an appointment to see her?

TEETHING AGAIN

Dentists or dental hygienists appreciate this toothy way to present a new member of the family. Cut out the tooth shape from bright, white paper. Outline it in black, blue or bright pink. The sample copy gives you ideas on ways to word the message. This announcement makes a clever tie-in to your profession and may bring you several visitors—private and professional!

WE LOVE HIM!

What a blooming-good idea! Present your new arrival as a pretty flower-child. Frame a picture of your baby with colorful yellow petals. Attach a straw to the flower and bright green leaves to the straw. Makes a great announcement for gardeners, florists or flower-lovers.

IT ADDS UP!

One plus one doesn't equal two—but three—when you use a calculator to announce your baby. Bankers, loan officers, credit managers and other financial people can give an announcement that adds up to fun. In place of the numbers that normally appear on the calculator, put the date of birth, time born, weight and length. The baby's name reads on the digital display. It's all calculated to get your good tidings out to the world.

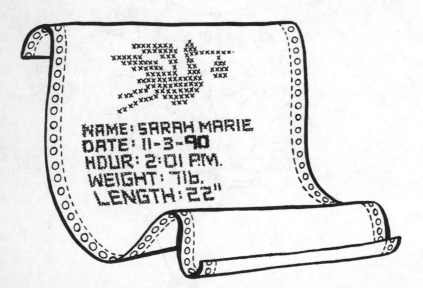

PRINT OUT

Just the ticket for creative programmers or those who have access to a computer. Program the computer to print out a baby symbol such as a stork, bottle, rattle or diaper pin using X's. Let the X's also show vital statistics about the birth. If you're not adept at programming, use a computer or word processor to print the announcement in regular typeface. Box the information in lines or X's. This announcement will compute with technical friends.

General Ideas

The Calls are ringing to tell you about the call they made to the doctor...

TIME
4:02 PM

DATE
3·2·91

WEIGHT
6½ lbs

Elizabeth Jane Call

18"
LENGTH

ONE RING-A-DINGY

This toy telephone announcement works well for any family with a happy message to tell! Put vital statistics in the phone's finger holes. Color the announcement with felt markers or acrylic paints in bright, cheerful colors. Try blue eyes, red lips, pink cheeks, green wheels and a red receiver. This is one call your friends and relatives won't want to miss!

The Andersons Present

PHOTO

Mary Lee

APRIL 5 1983

12:07 a.m.

8lb.

21"

HIGHEST RATINGS

Tune in for the debut of your newest TV star. Cut along the dotted lines at top and bottom of the TV screen to form tabs. Insert a cute photo of baby using the tabs as photo holders. Knobs give information on the date, time, weight and length. Make sure your friends don't miss the best show of the season!

a
baby
tornado
hit the Moore's place
on Saturday May 8!

It weighed 8lbs. 3ozs.
When it hit it was
18" high
It was called
JODY ANN
MOORE.

YOU SHOULD SEE WHAT
SHE'S DONE TO OUR
HOUSEHOLD!

IN A WHIRL!

Here's a fast-moving way to announce your new baby. Tornado shape draws immediate attention when delivered in person to your friends or pulled from an envelope. Cut around the edge of the tornado to emphasize its shape. This is one announcement your friends will remember—as well as all the commotion it caused!

BROTHERLY LOVE

Here's an announcement from a brother's point of view. Too bad the addition was a baby sister and not a new bedroom or playroom! If your family is larger than the one in the illustration, draw a larger house with more rooms. Use felt markers or color pencils to color the boy and the house. This is one way to remember everyone in the family when you announce your new arrival.

We finally got all the pieces together & delivered a baby boy!

Name *Daniel Patrick O'Keefe*

Date *4-16-83*   Time *2:55 p.m.*

Weight *8 lbs. 2 ozs.* Length *20"*

COME SEE OUR CUTE LITTLE PUZZLE!

PUZZLING

What a delightful way to inform friends and relatives about your bundle of joy. Print vital information about the birth on heavy paper or card stock. Cut up the message into pieces similar to a jigsaw puzzle. Place the pieces in an envelope and let the recipient reconstruct it. You can bet friends or relatives won't be puzzled for long!

NO LION!

This announcement catches your eye. Cut the lion's head out of gold-colored construction paper. Draw or print details in black ink or marking pen. The mane carries all the information about the new baby. It's the perfect announcement for families who feel like roaring about their new arrival!

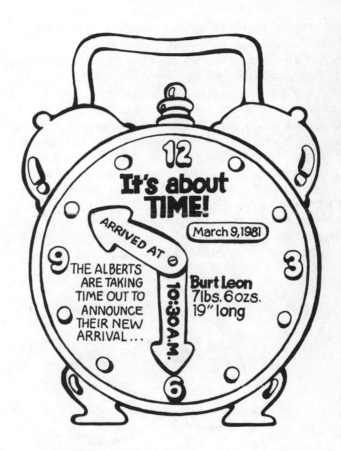

It's about TIME!

March 9, 1981

ARRIVED AT

THE ALBERTS ARE TAKING TIME OUT TO ANNOUNCE THEIR NEW ARRIVAL...

10:30 A.M.

Burt Leon
7 lbs. 6 ozs.
19" long

TIME HAS COME

This announcement is for the woman who thought her pregnancy would never end! Hands of the clock point to the time of birth. Calendar window gives the date. Other information is carried on the face of the clock. Announce your little one with this timely message.

Handouts

Cigars are traditionally handed out by new fathers. Why be traditional? Be creative and non-traditional. Give any of the gifts in this chapter to your friends and associates and they'll remember you as the proud—and original—New Father.

You'll find gifts such as the low-cal toothpick, pet rock and leftover pickle. Proud dads will like *Chip Off the Old Block* or *Blowing Your Own Horn.* If you like to give treats to eat, there's an apple, fortune cookie or Sugar Daddy. To counteract sweets, there's the baby toothbrush to be used regularly three times a day!

If you like one of these ideas as a baby announcement, don't limit it to Dad's friends. Modify the idea and send it to relatives and friends. These ideas and illustrations work in many different ways.

Most gifts are easy to make and economical. Friends and associates will remember the day you gave them an unusual Daddy's gift. Choose one of these creative gifts and let the world know you're a Proud Papa!

LO-CAL TREAT

Many new fathers hand out sugary treats or fattening candies. Here's a low-calorie surprise. Buy a box of toothpicks and attach a message to each one. The message reads: "I didn't want to give you something fattening, so I didn't give you anything at all!" The opposite side of the paper reads: "Our No. 1 Pick" and gives vital information on the birth.

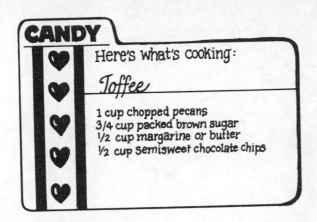

RECIPE COLLECTORS

Here's something interesting to give friends—a favorite family recipe. Business executives may want to give a Recipe for Success. Buy some small recipe cards and decorate them with stickers or illustrations. Print the recipe on one side and information about the new arrival on the other. A candy recipe is appropriate to announce your little sweetie.

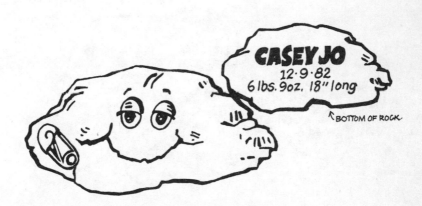

PET ROCK-A-BYE

A pet rock makes an inexpensive daddy handout. Collect smooth rocks from a streambed or get them at a gravel pit. Buy acrylic paint and plastic eyes at a craft store. Paint the rock a bright color. Glue on the eyes with all-purpose glue. Paint statistics on the bottom of the rock.

FLOATING ON AIR

You'll be on Cloud 9 when you deliver this announcement to buddies. Buy a package of balloons at a toy or novelty store. Blow up each balloon and tie a string to temporarily keep it inflated. Use a black marker to write your message on the outside of the balloon. Draw a stork or baby cartoon if you are artistic. Untie the string and deflate the balloon. Your friends get the message when they blow up the balloon!

HAVE A FORTUNE, COOKIE

What a fortunate idea! Make your own fortune cookies or purchase a bag of cookies from a Chinese specialty shop. If you buy cookies, carefully remove the fortune—tweezers work well. Type or print your message on small strips of paper. Roll the paper up and stuff it into the cookie using a fingernail file or thin knife. Give cookies to fortunate friends.

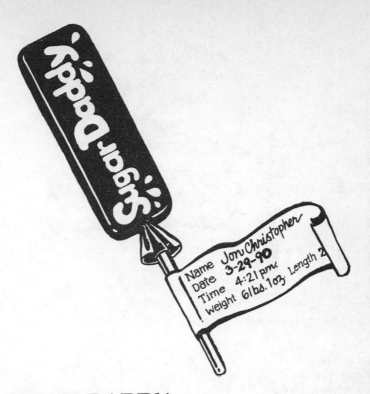

I'M A SUGAR DADDY

A *Sugar Daddy* sucker is a sweet way to boast of your new arrival. Attach a tag with statistics to the handle of the sucker. Gummed or peel-off labels work well for the tag.

APPLE OF MY EYE

Fresh fruit catches the attention of friends. An apple is always a welcome treat. Tape a note, label or clever drawing to the apple to brag about your newborn. Your friends will get the message and munch with pleasure!

NOTHING TO SNEEZE AT

This daddy handout helps with the sniffles. Using permanent markers, draw a stork or other baby symbol on a handerchief. The message might say: "Nothing to sneeze at!" Print pertinent information about the birth. It's a useful and stylish gift to hand out.

NUTS ABOUT MY BABY

Carefully pry apart a walnut shell and take out the nut. Place the message of the birth inside. Tie the shell halves together with a pink or blue ribbon as appropriate. Your friends and associates will think it's a real nutty gift!

CHIP OFF THE OLD BLOCK

Here's one for a proud Daddy. Buy plain toy wood blocks or cut blocks from a 2x2 or 2x4 board. Using the wand from a woodburning set, burn your message into the block. Print on as many sides as necessary. Friends will enjoy turning the block over to read your good tidings.

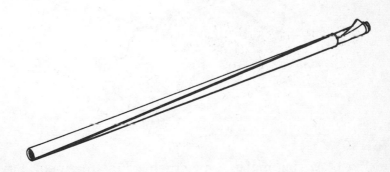

FOR THE STRAW BOSS

Purchase a package of brightly colored straws. Print your new-baby message on a piece of paper. Roll up the paper and place it in the straw. Your associates will agree it's the last straw!

PIPE UP

Here's a way to pipe up to your friends. Buy an inexpensive corn-cob pipe. Print your message on a strip of paper. Roll up the paper and place it in the bowl of the pipe. Smokers and non-smokers will get a kick out of this alternative to the cigar.

BABY KEY FOB

A personalized key ring makes a memorable announcement. Buy key rings and contact paper. Make fobs out of the contact paper. A triangular shape is interesting. Cut the contact paper so it makes a triangular frame. Peel the backing off the contact paper and press a picture of your new baby to the contact-paper frame. Add pertinent data to the back of the picture. Attach fob to the key ring with tape or ribbon.

NO MORE PICKLES

Wrap in plastic wrap all the pickles your wife no longer wants. Tie each one with a blue or pink ribbon as appropriate. Write a clever message on a strip of paper or large gift tag and attach to the pickle. Watch the reaction of your associates!

LITTLE TINKER

Purchase a set of Tinkertoys from a toy or department store. Put two wheels and a stick together as shown in the illustration. Write your message on a long, thin piece of paper. Tape one end of the paper to the stick and roll up the message like a scroll.

FLASH

Flash the news of your baby's arrival. Buy 4-way flash cubes from a camera or department store. Write the message on a strip of paper or label and tape it to the flash cube. Your baby will make news!

IT'S ABOUT THYME!

Everyone will know the time has come when you hand out these clever herb sachets. Use an attractive square cloth and place thyme spice in the center of the cloth. Fold the cloth into a bag and tie with a colorful ribbon. Tag the sachet with information about your new arrival.

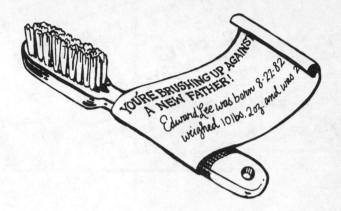

BRUSH REGULARLY

A small blue or pink toothbrush will announce a new mouth in the family! Write your message on a strip of paper or a self-adhesive label. Attach the message to the toothbrush. Tell your friends or associates to brush three times a day and remember your baby!

BLOW YOUR HORN

Go ahead, blow your own horn a little. Purchase party noisemakers as shown in the illustration. Unroll the noisemaker and print your message on the paper. Or write the message on a separate piece of paper and tape it to the unrolled noisemaker. Let the noisemaker roll back up. When the recipient blows the horn he'll discover you're a new Daddy. May even start a party!

TOP SECRET

This file is for privileged eyes only. Use a letter-size Manila folder to hold regular-size sheets of paper. Print TOP SECRET on the front of the folder. Print SECRET FORMULA on top of a piece of paper. List the vital statistics of the baby, such as eye color, hair color, weight, length, date of birth, time born, unusual markings, parents, names of brothers and sisters, baby's name and other information. Use other sheets of paper to list relatives, draw a family tree or provide other classified data. This secret will be hard to keep!

NAMES
AND
MEANINGS

How to Use the Baby-Name List

Names on the following pages are arranged with girls' names first, followed by boys' names. You will find common names, unique names, even exotic names. There are more than 13,000 names to choose from!

Each entry contains a lot of information. Look at the example of the name Antoinetta.

NAME: Antoinetta
PRONUNCIATION: (an-twa-NET-tuh)
ORIGIN: Slovak, Swedish, Latin
MEANING: *Priceless*
FORM, IF APPLICABLE: Feminine form of Anthony.
INTERESTING FACTS:
Literature: *My Antonia*, novel by Willa Cather.
Entertainment: Antoinette Perry, leader of the American Theater Wing.
VARIATIONS OR DERIVATIONS OF THE NAME:
Antonetta, Antonia, Antonie, Antoinette, Antonina, Netta, Netti, Nettie, Netty, Toinette, Toni, Tonia, Tonie, Tony, Tonye

---

Most people are interested in finding out about famous people who share their name. Listings include famous namesakes. Some categories are Literature, Mythological, Historical, Sports and Biblical.

The origin of a name is sometimes difficult to determine. Languages have intermixed and several languages claim names as their own. In each instance, I give the most commonly accepted origin. Where the claim seems equal, I list two or three origins. In some cases, names from different cultures have different meanings.

Names often have many derivations or variations. Although Antoinetta may not suit you, Toinette may fit your child. Go through the variations. This is one of the most helpful features of this book.

To help you say the names, a pronunciation guide is included. It describes how to pronounce each name, so you'll be able to determine if a name sounds right for your baby.

For each name listed in this book, at least one pronunciation is given. Some names have two pronunciations. One pronunciation may be more popular than another. The most frequent pronunciation is given immediately following each name listing, which shows the principal spelling for the name. The following tips will help you use the pronunciation markings more efficiently.

- Words are separated into syllables by dashes. Example: MAR-tin.
- The syllable that receives the most stress appears in capital letters. Example: HEL-un.
- The symbols for vowel sounds may be new to you. Long vowels, those that are pronounced like the names of the letters, are marked with a line over the vowel. Example: The *a* in Jane is marked JĀN. Short vowels have no additional markings. Example: The *a* in Janet is indicated by JAN-it. There are separate pronunciations for long and short vowel sounds. Some vowels are influenced by other sounds around them and are not long or short. They are listed under *Other Vowel Sounds* in the table below.

VOWEL SOUNDS

Long Vowels

Letter	Written Phonetically	As Sounds In The Word	Is Spelled Phonetically
A	ā	ate	āt
E	ē	eat	ēt
I	ī	hike	hīk
O	ō	oak	ōk
U	ū	use	ūz
OO	ōō	ooze	ōōz

Short Vowels

Letter	Written Phonetically	As Sounds In The Word	Is Spelled Phonetically
A	a	at	at
E	e	edge	ej
I	i	it	it
O	o	ox	oks
U	u	up	up
OO	oo	book	book

Other Vowel Sounds

Letters	Written Phonetically	As Sounds In The Word	Is Spelled Phonetically
AIR	air	fair	fair
AR	ar	car	kar
AW	aw	all	awl
ER	er	her	her
OI	oi	boy	boi
OR	or	more	mor
OW	ow	cow	kow
UH	uh	about	uh-bowt

BABY-NAME WORKSHEET

	First	Middle	Last
1.			
2.			
3.			
4.			
5.			
6.			
7.			
8.			
9.			
10.			

RANK NAMES IN ORDER OF PREFERENCE:

First:_____

Second:_____

Third:_____

See pages 283-288 for more Baby-Name Worksheets.

GIRLS' NAMES

Abby (A-bē)
Familiar form of Abigail.
Famous: Abigail Van Buren, *Dear Abby* newspaper columnist.
Abbe, Abbey, Abbie

Abebi (uh-BĒ-bē)
Nigerian— *We asked for her and she came*
Abeni

Abigail (A-bi-gāl)
Hebrew— *Father of joy*
Famous: Abigail Adams, wife of President John Adams.
Biblical: One of King David's wives.
Abagael, Abagail, Abbi, Abbye, Abigael, Gael, Gail, Gale, Gayel

Abra (AB-ruh)
Hebrew— *Mother of the multitude*
Feminine form of Abraham.
Abira

Acacia (uh-KĀ-shuh)
Greek— *Thorny*
Cacia, Cacie, Casey, Casia, Kacia, Kacie

Acantha (uh-KAN-thuh)
Greek— *Sharp-pointed, thorned*
Acandi, Acandy, Candie, Candy, Cantha, Kacia, Kacie

Ada (Ā-duh) or (A-duh)
Teutonic— *Happy*
Latin— *Of noble birth*
Hebrew— *An ornament*
Adah, Adan, Adey, Adda, Addi, Addie, Addy, Adi, Aida, Eada, Eda, Edey

Adabelle (Ā-duh-bel) or (A-duh-bel)
English— *Joyous and fair*
Adabel, Adabell, Adabellie, Adahbelle, Bell, Belle

Adah (A-duh)
Hebrew— *Ornament*
Famous: Adah Menken, 19th century American actress.
Ada, Addia, Addie, Addy

Adalia (uh-DĀL-yuh)
German, Spanish— *Noble one*
Adal, Adala, Adali, Adalie, Adela, Adele, Adelia, Adelle

Adamina (a-duh-MĒN-uh)
Hebrew— *Daughter of the earth*
Adameana, Ademine

Adamma (uh-DA-muh)
Nigerian— *Child of beauty*

Adara (uh-DAIR-uh)
Greek— *Beauty*
Arabic— *Virgin*

ADALIA—*Noble one*

Adelaide (A-duh-lād)
German—*Noble and of kind spirit*
Literature: Adelaide Anne Proctor,
    author.
**Adalia, Adaline, Adela, Adele,
Adelia, Adelina, Adelind,
Adeline, Adella, Dela, Della**

Adele (uh-DEL)
German, French—*Noble*
**Adelaide, Adelia, Adeline,
Adelle, Akela, Aline, Del,
Della, Delly, Hagayah, Heide**

Adena (uh-DĒN-uh)
Hebrew—*Sensuous or voluptuous*
Adina, Dena, Dina

Aditi (uh-DĒ-tē)
Hindi—*Free and unbounded*
Interesting: In Hindi lore, Aditi is
    mother of the Gods.

Adora (uh-DOR-uh)
French—*Beloved*
**Ador, Adore, Adoree, Dora,
Dori, Dorie, Dory**

Adrienne (Ā-drē-en)
French — *Dark one*
Feminine of Adrian.
Adrea, Adria, Adrian, Adriana, Adriane, Hadria

Afina (uh-FĒ-nuh)
Rumanian — *Blueberry*
Afin, Efina

Afra (A-fruh)
Hebrew — *Female deer*

Agatha (A-guh-thuh)
Greek — *Good*
Literature: Agatha Christie, writer of detective fiction.
Ag, Agace, Agata, Agathe, Aggi, Aggie, Aggy, Agueda

Agnes (AG-nes)
Greek — *Pure*
Interesting: St. Agnes, martyred at age 13, is commemorated on January 21.
Entertainment: Agnes Moorehead, actress.
Ag, Aggee, Aggi, Agna, Agnella, Agnese, Agnesse, Agneta, Agnola, Aigneis, Annis, Ina, Ines, Inessa, Inez, Nessa, Nessi, Nessie, Nessy, Nesta, Nevsa, Neysa, Una, Ynes, Ynez

Aida (Ā-duh) or (ī-Ē-duh)
Italian — *Happy*
Entertainment: The opera *Aida,* by Verdi.
Ada, Aila, Aili, Iraida, Zaida, Zenaida, Zoraida

Aileen (ā-LĒN)
Irish — *Light*
Entertainment: Eileen Farrell, Metropolitan Opera star.
Ailene, Alaine, Alane, Alanna, Alayne, Allan, Allen, Allene, Allina, Allyn, Eileen, Helen, Ileane, Ilene, Lana, Lanna

Airlia (AIR-lē-uh)
Greek — *Ethereal*

Ailsa (ĀL-suh)
Teutonic — *Girl of cheer*

Alanna (a-LAN-uh)
Gaelic — *Comely, fair*
Feminine form of Alan.
Alaine, Alane, Alayne, Allyn

Alarice (al-uh-RĒS)
Teutonic — *Ruler of all*

Alberta (al-BERT-uh)
Old English — *Noble or brilliant*
Feminine form of Albert.
Albetine, Albertine, Ali, Alli, Allie, Ally, Alverta, Auberta, Auline, Bert, Berta, Berte, Berti, Bertie, Berty, Elberta, Elbertina, Elbertine

Alda (AL-duh)
German — *Battle, war*
Aldith, Alta, Auda, Edith

Aldea (al-DĒ-uh)
Teutonic — *Rich*

Aldora (al-DOR-uh)
Greek — *Winged gift*

Alethea (a-LĒ-thē-uh)
Greek — *Truth*
Aletha, Alethia, Alithea, Alithia, Alsta, Althea

Aletta (a-LET-uh)
Spanish — *Winged bird-like*
Aleta, Alleta, Alletta, Leeta

Alexandra (al-eks-AN-druh)
Russian, Greek— *Helper or defender of mankind*
Feminine form of Alexander.
Interesting: Alexandria, important city in Egypt.
Famous: Alexandra, Danish princess and queen of England.
Alejandra, Alejandrian, Alessandra, Alex, Alexa, Alexandrina, Alexia, Alexina, Alexine, Alexis, Ali, Alix, Alla, Alli, Allie, Allix, Ally, Alya, Cesya, Elena, Lesya, Lexi, Lexie, Lexine, Lexy, Olesya, Sacha, Sande, Sandi, Sandie, Sandra, Sandy, Sandye, Sascha, Sasha, Sashenka, Shura, Shurochka, Sondra, Zandra

Alfreda (al-FRĒ-duh)
Teutonic— *Wise or diplomatic counselor*
Feminine form of Alfred.
Alfi, Alfy, Allie, Elfreda, Elfrida, Elfrieda, Elva, Freda, Freddie, Freddy, Frieda

Alice (AL-is)
Greek— *Truth*
Old English— *Noble*
Literature: *Alice in Wonderland,* by Lewis Carroll; 1922 Pulitzer Prize given to Booth Tarkington for *Alice Adams.*
Entertainment: Alicia Alonso and Alicia Markova, ballet dancers; Ali MacGraw, actress.
Adelaide, Adelice, Ailis, Aleece, Ali, Alicea, Alicia, Alika, Alikee, Alis, Alisa, Alisha, Alison, Alissa, Alix, Alla, Alleece, Alli, Allie, Allison, Allson, Allsun, Allyce, Allys, Alys, Alysia, Alyss, Alyssa, Elissa, Ilysa, Ilyssa, Lissa, Lyssa

Alida (uh-LĒ-duh)
Greek— *From the city of fine vestments*
Aleda, Alyda, Leda, Lida

Alina (a-LĒ-nuh)
Polish, Russian— *Bright, beautiful*
Adeline, Aleen, Alene, Allene, Alta, Alya, Lina

Alita (a-LĒ-tuh)
Spanish— *Noble*
Adela, Adelina, Adelita, Dela, Lela

Aliza (uh-LĒ-zuh) or (uh-LĪ-zuh)
Hebrew— *Joyous*

Alleen (al-LĒN)
Dutch— *Alone*

Allegra (uh-LĀ-gruh)
Italian— *Lively, joyful, merry*
Entertainment: Allegra Kent, of the New York City Center Ballet.

Alma (AL-muh)
Latin— *Soul*
Arabic— *Learned*
Interesting: *Alma Mater* means nourishing mother.
Entertainment: Alma Gluck, opera star.

Almira (al-MĪ-ruh)
Hindi— *Clothes basket*
Arabic— *Exalted*
Feminine form of Elmer.
Almeria, Almire, Elmira, Mira, Myra

Alodie (a-LŌ-dē)
Anglo-Saxon— *Wealthy, prosperous*
Alodi, Alody

Aloysia (a-LOI-shuh)
Teutonic— *Famous in war*

Alta (AL-tuh)
Latin— *High*
German— *Old*

Althea (al-THĒ-uh)
Greek— *Wholesome or healing*
Altheda, Althee, Altheta, Thea

Alva (AL-vuh)
Spanish, Latin— *White or fair*
Famous: Thomas Alva Edison, inventor of the light bulb.

AMABEL—*Loveable*

Alvina (al-VĒN-uh)
Old English—*Noble friend*

Alvita (al-VĒT-uh)
Latin—*Animated*
Feminine form of Alvin.
**Alivinia, Alverta, Alvinia,
Vina, Vinne, Vinnie, Vinny**

Alyssa (a-LIS-uh)
Greek—*Sane, logical*
Alissa, Ilyssa

Amabel (AM-uh-bel)
Latin—*Loveable*
Amabelle, Belle

Amalia (uh-MĀL-ē-uh)
Polish, Hungarian—*Industrious*
Amelia, Emil, Emili, Emily

Amanda (uh-MAN-duh)
Latin—*Beloved*
Entertainment: Amanda Blake
played Kitty on TV series,
Gunsmoke.
**Amandi, Amandie, Amandy,
Manda, Mandi, Mandie,
Mandy**

Amara (uh-MAR-uh)
Greek— *Of eternal beauty*
**Amaratha, Amarga, Amargo,
Mara**

Amber (AM-ber)
French— *Amber*
Arabic— *Jewel*
Literature: *Forever Amber,* by
Kathleen Winsor.

Amdis (AM-dis)
Latin— *Love of God or immortal*

Amelia (uh-MĒ-lē-yuh)
Teutonic— *Hard-working*
Famous: Amelia Bloomer,
supporter of the American
women suffrage movement;
Amelia Earhart, pilot.
**Amalea, Amalia, Amelie,
Amelina, Ameline, Amelita,
Amy, Emmas**

Amity (AM-i-tē)
French, Latin— *Friendship*
Amitie, Mitti, Mittie, Mitty

Amy (Ā-mē)
French, Latin— *Beloved*
Literature: Amy Laurence Lowell,
Pulitzer Prize-winner in poetry.
**Aimee, Amata, Ame, Ami,
Amie, Amye, Esma, Essme**

Anclin (AN-slin)
French, Latin— *Hand maiden*

Andrea (AN-drē-uh) or
(an-DRĀ-uh)
Latin, Italian— *Womanly*
Feminine form of Andrew.
**Aindrea, Andee, Andi,
Andie, Andre, Andreana,
Andree, Andrel, Andria,
Andriana, Andromeda, Andy**

Anestassia (an-uh-STĀ-shuh)
Russian, Greek— *Resurrection*
**Ana, Anastassia, Anestasie,
Anstice, Asia, Nastie, Nessa,
Stace, Stacey, Stacie, Stacy,
Stasa, Stasya, Tasenka,
Tasia, Tasya**

Angela (AN-jel-uh)
Greek— *Heavenly messenger*
Entertainment: Angie Dickinson,
Angela Cartwright, actresses.
**Ange, Angel, Angele,
Angelica, Angelika, Angelina,
Angelique, Angelita, Angie,
Angline, Angy, Gelya**

Anita (uh-NĒ-tuh)
Spanish, Hebrew— *Grace*
Entertainment: Anita Bryant,
actress and former Miss
America; Anita Ekberg, actress.
Anitra, Ann

Ann (AN)
Hebrew— *Full of grace, mercy and
prayer*
Biblical: Anne was the mother of
the Virgin Mary.
Famous: Anne Hathaway, wife of
William Shakespeare.
Literature: *Anna Karenina,* by Leo
Tolstoy; *Anna Christie,* Pulitzer
Prize-winning play by Eugene
O'Neill; Ann Landers, columnist.
Entertainment: Anna Pavlova,
ballet dancer; Ann-Margret,
Anne Bancroft, actresses; Anne
Murray, pop singer.
**Ana, Anabel, Anabella, Anabelle,
Analiese, Analise, Anet, Anett,
Anetta, Anette, Ania, Anica,
Anita, Anitra, Anna, Annabel,
Annabella, Annabla, Annable,
Annaboelle, Annalice,
Annaliese, Annalise,
Annamariam, Annamarie, Anne,
Annebella, Annelise,
Annemarie, Annetta, Annette,
Anni, Annice, Annie, Annis,
Annora, Anny, Anuska, Anya,
Hanna, Hannah, Hanni, Hannie,
Hanny, Nan, Nana, Nance,
Nancee, Nancey, Nanci, Nancie,
Nancy, Nanete, Nanette,
Nanice, Nanine, Nanni, Nannie,
Nanny, Nanon, Nette, Nettie,
Netty, Nina, Ninette, Ninon, Nita**

Anselma (an-SEL-muh)
Teutonic— *Divine protectress*

Anthea (an-THĒ-uh)
Greek— *Like a flower*
Anthe, Anthia, Thea, Thia

Antoinetta (an-twa-NET-tuh)
Slovak, Swedish, Latin— *Priceless*
Feminine form of Anthony.
Literature: *My Antonia,* novel by
Willa Cather.
Entertainment: Antoinette Perry,
leader of the American Theater
Wing.
**Antonetta, Antonia, Antonie,
Antoinette, Antonina, Netta,
Netti, Nettie, Netty,
Toinette, Toni, Tonia, Tonie,
Tony, Tonye**

April (Ā-pril)
Latin— *Opening*
Aprilette, Averil, Averyl, Aviel

Arabela (air-uh-BEL-uh)
Latin, Spanish— *Beautiful altar*
Entertainment: *Arabella,* opera by
Richard Strauss.
**Ara, Arabele, Arabella, Arabelle,
Arabellie, Arabelly, Bel, Bell,
Bella, Belle, Bellie**

Ardelia (ar-DĒL-ē-yuh)
Latin— *Fervent or zealous*
**Arda, Ardeen, Ardelis, Ardella,
Ardelle, Ardene, Ardent, Ardin,
Ardine, Ardis, Ardra**

Ardith (AR-dith)
Hebrew— *Flowering field*
**Alda, Aldith, Ardeth, Ardyth,
Aridatha, Datha, Edith**

Arella (a-REL-uh)
Hebrew— *Angel messenger*
Arela

Aretha (uh-RĒ-thuh)
Greek— *Best*
Celtic— *High*
Entertainment: Aretha Franklin,
pop singer.
Retha

Aretina (ar-e-TĒN-uh)
Greek— *Virtuous*

Ariadne (ar-ē-AD-nē)
Greek— *Holy one*
Famous: Ariadne, daughter of
King Minos of Crete.
Entertainment: Opera *Ariadne auf
Naxos,* by Richard Strauss.
Ariana, Ariane, Arianie

Ariel (AR-ē-el)
Hebrew— *Lioness of God*
Literature: Prospero's spirit
servant in Shakespeare's *The
Tempest.*
Aeriele, Ariela, Ariella, Arielle

Arlene (ar-LĒN) or (AR-lēn)
Celtic— *A pledge*
Feminine form of Arlen.
Entertainment: TV and radio star
Arlene Francis.
**Aileen, Aline, Arlana, Arleen,
Arlen, Arlena, Arlette, Arleyne,
Arlie, Arliene, Arlina, Arline,
Arluene, Arly, Arlyne, Lena,
Lenna, Lina**

Ashley (ASH-lē)
Old English— *From the ash-tree
meadow*
Ash, Ashla, Ashlan, Ashlen

Astra (AS-truh)
Greek— *Like a star*
Entertainment: Singer Astrid
Gilberto.
Astrea, Astred, Astrid

Atara (uh-TAR-uh)
Hebrew— *A crown*
Atera, Ateret

Athalia (uh-THAL-ē-yuh)
Hebrew— *The Lord is mighty*
Biblical: Queen of Judah.
Atalie

Athena (uh-THĒ-nuh)
Greek— *Wise*
Mythological: Goddess of wisdom.
Athen, Athene, Athenia

Atlanta (at-LAN-tuh)
Greek— *Unswaying*
Atlante

Audrey (AW-drē)
Old English— *Noble strength*
Entertainment: Audrey Hepburn,
Audrey Meadows, actresses.
**Audey, Audi, Audie, Audra,
Audre, Audrie, Audry**

Augusta (AW-gus-tuh) or
(aw-GUST-uh)
Latin— *Majestic, sacred*
Feminine form of August.
Literature: Lady Augusta Gregory,
playwright, co-founder of the
Irish National Theater Society.
**Auguste, Augustina, Augustine,
Austin, Austina, Gus, Gussi,
Gussie, Gussy, Gusta, Gusti,
Gustie, Gusty, Tina**

Auria (OR-ē-uh)
Latin— *The aureate or golden*

Aurilia (aw-RĒ-lē-yuh)
Latin— *Golden*
**Aura, Aurea, Aurel, Aurelea,
Aurelia, Aurelie, Auria, Aurie,
Aurora, Aurore, Ora, Oralee,
Oralia, Oralie, Orel, Orelee,
Orelia, Orelie, Rora, Rori,
Rorie, Rory**

Aurora (uh-ROR-uh)
Latin— *Dawn*
**Aurore, Ora, Rori, Rorie,
Rory, Rota**

Autumn (AW-tum)
Latin— *Autumn*

Ava (Ā-vuh)
German— *A bird*
Hollywood: Ava Gardner, actress.
Avi, Avie, Avis

Azelia (uh-ZĒL-yuh)
Hebrew— *Whom the Lord reserved*
Azelea, Azel, Azela

Babette (bab-ET)
Greek— *Stranger*
Babe, Babs

Bambi (BAM-bē)
Italian— *Child*
Entertainment: *Bambi*, a Walt
Disney film based on storybook
animals.

Barakah (ba-RAWK-uh)
Arabic— *White one*

Barbara (BAR-ber-uh)
Greek— *Stranger or foreign*
Literature: Barbara Cartland,
gothic romance writer; *Major
Barbara*, by George Bernard Shaw.
Entertainment: Barbara Stanwick,
Barbra Streisand, Barbi Benton,
actresses.
**Babby, Babette, Babs,
Barbette, Barbi, Barbra, Barby,
Bobbi, Bobbie, Bonnie**

Barbo (bar-BŌ)
Swedish— *Stranger*
See Barbara.

Bathilda (ba-TIL-duh)
Teutonic— *Commanding battle-maid*
Bathilde

Bathsheba (bath-SHĒ-buh)
Hebrew— *Daughter of the oath*
Biblical: Mother of Solomon.
Batsheva, Sheba

Beata (bē-AT-uh)
Latin— *Blessed or divine*
Bea, Bee

Beatrice (BĒ-uh-tris)
Latin— *Bringer of joy*
Literature: Beatrix Potter, author
of *Peter Rabbit.*
Entertainment: Beatrice Arthur,
actress who plays *Maude.*
**Bea, Beatrisa, Beatrix,
Bebe, Bee, Beitris, Betrix,
Trix, Trixi, Trixie, Trixy**

Becky (BEK-ē)
Hebrew— *The ensnarer*
See Rebecca.

Bela (BEL-uh)
Czech— *White*
Bel, Belia, Bell

Belicia (b̲uh-LĒ-sē-uh) or
(b̲uh-LĒ-shuh)
Spanish— *Dedicated to God*
Belia, Belikia, Belisia, Belita

Belinda (buh-LIN-duh)
Italian— *Wise and immortal*
Spanish— *Pretty*
Bel, Belle, Lindie, Linds, Lindy

Bella (BEL-uh)
Latin— *Beautiful*
Famous: Bella Abzug, New York
Congresswoman.
**Bee, Bela, Belinda, Bell,
Belle, Bellie, Belva, Belvia,
Bill, Billi, Billy**

Bena (BĒN-uh)
Hebrew— *Wise*
Feminine form of Ben.
Benay, Benie, Bennie

Benedetta (ben-uh-DET-uh)
Italian— *The blessed*
Feminine form of Benedict.

Benita (buh-NĒ-tuh)
Latin, Spanish— *Blessed*
Feminine form of Benedict.
**Bendite, Benedetta, Benedicta,
Benedikta, Beneta, Benne,
Benni, Bennie, Benny, Benoite,
Bernetta, Bernette, Bernita,
Binni, Binnie, Binny**

Berenice (bair-uh-NĒS)
Greek— *Bringer of victory*
**Benadette, Bernadette, Bernadina,
Bernardina, Bernardine, Bernelle,
Berneta, Bernetta, Bernette,
Berni, Bernie, Bernice, Berny,
Bunni, Bunnie, Bunny, Nisie,
Nizie, Veronica, Veronika,
Veronique**

Bernadette (bern-uh-DET)
See Berenice.
Feminine form of Bernard.
Entertainment: Bernadette Peters,
actress.

Bertha (BER-thuh)
German— *Shining*
Feminine form of Albert.
**Berdie, Berta, Berte, Berthe,
Berti, Bertie, Bertina,
Bertine, Berty, Bird**

Beryl (BERL)
Greek— *Jewel, precious*
Berri, Berrie, Berry, Beryle

Bessie (BES-ē)
Hebrew— *Consecrated to God*
Bess, Besse, Bessy

Beta (BĀ-tuh)
Czech— *Dedicated to God*
**Alzbeta, Bethany, Betica,
Elizabeta, Elizabeth, Liza**

Beth (BETH)
Hebrew— *House of God*
Bethany, Elizabeth

Bethany (BETH-uh-nē)
Arabic— *House of poverty*
Biblical: Village near Jerusalem.
Beth, Elizabeth

BIRDIE—*Sweet little bird*

Bethesda (buh-THES-duh)
Hebrew—*House of mercy*
Interesting: Bethesda, name of a
  pool in Jerusalem, the waters of
  which became healing when
  stirred by an angel.

Betsy (BET-sē)
See Elizabeth.
Famous: Betsy Ross, maker of the
  first American flag.
Bette, Betty

Bette (BET-ē) or (BET)
See Elizabeth.
Famous: Betty Ford, wife of
  President Gerald Ford.
Entertainment: Bette Davis, Betty
  Hutton, Betty Grable, Bette
  Midler, actresses.
Bettina, Bettine, Betty

Beulah (BŪ-luh)
Hebrew—*She who will be married*
Biblical: Another name for Israel.
Beula

Beverly (BEV-er-lē)
Anglo-Saxon — *Beaver meadow*
Entertainment: Beverly Sills, opera
singer; Beverly Bayne,
silent-movie star.
**Bev, Beverle, Beverlee, Beverley,
Beverlie, Bevvy, Buffy**

Bianca (bē-ON-kuh)
Italian, Teutonic — *White*
Famous: Bianca Jagger, former
wife of Rolling Stones' Mick
Jagger.
**Beanca, Beanka, Biancha,
Bianka, Blanca, Blanche**

Bibi (BĒ-bē)
Arabic — *Lacy*

Billie (BIL-ē)
Old English — *Strong willed*
Feminine form of Bill.
Music: Billie Halliday, blues singer.
**Billi, Billy, Wilhelmina,
Willie, Willy**

Bina (BĒ-nuh)
See Sabina.

Birdie (BUR-dē)
Teutonic — *Sweet little bird*
Bird, Birdella

Birget (BUR-jet)
Norwegian — *Protecting*
Bergette, Bergitte, Birgitta

Blanche (BLANCH)
French — *Fair, white*
**Bell, Bellanca, Bianca, Blanca,
Blanch, Blanka, Blinni, Blinnie,
Blinny, Branca**

Blanda (BLAN-duh)
Latin — *Affable or seductive*
Blandina

Blenda (BLEN-duh)
Teutonic — *Dazzling*

Bliss (BLIS)
Old English — *Bliss or joy*
Blisse, Blissie

Blossom (BLAW-sum)
Old English — *Flowerlike*
Blom, Bluma

Blythe (BLĪTH)
Old English — *Joyous*

Bo (BŌ)
Chinese — *Precious*
Entertainment: Bo Derek, actress.

Bobbi (BO-bē)
See Roberta.
Bobbie, Bobby

Bobett (bo-BET)
See Barbara.
Feminine form of Bob or Robert.

Bobina (bo-BĒN-uh)
Czech — *Brilliant, famous*
Berta, Roba

Bona (BŌ-nuh)
Hebrew — *Builder*
Spanish — *Bald*

Bonita (bō-NĒ-tuh)
Spanish — *Pretty*

Bonnibel (BON-ē-bel)
Latin — *Good and beautiful*
**Bonnibelle, Bonniebelle,
Bonniebellie**

Bonnie (BON-ē)
French, Latin — *Sweet and good*
Famous: Bonnie and Clyde,
bankrobbers.
Entertainment: Bonnie Raitt, rock
singer and actress.

Brandy (BRAN-dē)
Dutch — *Brandy drink*
Brandi, Brandie

Brenda (BREN-duh)
German — *A sword blade*
Entertainment: Brenda Lee, pop
singer; Brenda Lewis,
Metropolitan Opera singer.
Brandon, Bren, Brendan

BRUNHILDA — *Armored woman warrior*

Brenna (BREN-uh)
Celtic — *Raven maid*

Bretta (BRET-uh)
Irish — *From Britain*
Bret, Brit, Brita, Brite, Brittany

Bridget (BRI-jet)
Irish — *Resolute strength*
Biblical: Patron saint of Ireland.
Entertainment: Brigit Nilsson,
  Metropolitan Opera soprano;
  Brigit Bardot, actress.
**Beret, Berget, Biddie, Biddy,
Birgitta, Bitgitta, Bride, Bridie,
Brietta, Brigid, Brigida, Brigit,
Brigitta, Brigitte, Brita**

Brier (BRĪ-er)
French — *Heather*

Brina (BRĒ-nuh)
Slavic, Celtic — *Protector*
Feminine form of Brian.
Breanne, Briana, Bryna

Brittany (BRI-tuh-nē)
Latin — *From England*
Brit, Britni, Britt, Britta

Brooke (BROOK)
Old English — *From the brook*
Entertainment: Brooke Shields,
  model and actress.

Brunhilda (BROON-hil-duh)
German — *Armored woman warrior*
**Brunhilde, Brynhild, Brynhilda,
Hilda, Hildi**

Calandra (kuh-LAN-druh)
Greek — *The lark*
**Cal, Calandia, Calendre, Calley,
Calli, Callie, Cally**

Calantha (kuh-LAN-thuh)
Greek — *Beautiful blossom*
**Cal, Calanthe, Calli, Callie,
Cally**

Calida (kuh-LĒ-duh)
Greek — *Most beautiful*
**Calesta, Calista, Calla, Calli,
Callie, Cally, Calysta, Kalla,
Kalli, Kallista, Kally**

Calla (KAL-uh)
Greek — *Beautiful*
Cal, Calli, Callie, Cally

Caltha (KAL-thuh)
Latin — *Yellow flower*

Calypso (kuh-LIP-sō)
Greek — *Concealer*
Mythological: Sea nymph who
  kept Odysseus captive.

Cam (KAM)
Vietnamese — *Orange fruit or to be
sweet*

Camille (kuh-MĒL)
Latin — *Self-sacrificing*
Cam, Camala, Camel, Camila, Camile, Camilla, Cammi, Cammie, Cammy, Milli, Millie, Milly

Candace (KAN-dis)
Greek, Latin — *Glittering*
Historical: Names and titles of queens of ancient Ethiopia.
Literature: Candace Stevenson, winner of Poetry Society of America Award.
Entertainment: Candace Bergen, actress.
Candi, Candice, Candida, Candie, Candis, Candy, Kandace, Kandy

Candra (KAN-druh)
Latin — *Moon*

Capri (kuh-PRĒ)
Zodiac — *The goat*
Capra, Capre, Capria, Kapre, Kapri

Cara (KAR-uh)
Irish — *Friend*
Latin — *Dear*
Carina, Carine, Carrie, Carry, Kara, Karina, Karine, Karrie, Karry

Caresse (kuh-RES)
French — *Beloved*
Car, Caresa, Caressa, Carissa, Charissa, Karesa, Karissa

Cari (KAIR-ē)
Turkish — *Flowing like water*
Literature: *Sister Carrie,* novel by Theodore Dreiser.
Carrie, Kairee

Carilla (kuh-RIL-uh)
Feminine form of Charles.

Carina (kuh-RĒ-nuh)
Latin — *Keel*
See Karen.
Caren, Carin, Carine, Caryn, Karen

Carissa (kuh-RIS-uh)
Greek — *Loving*
Carrie, Charissa

Carita (kuh-RĒ-tuh)
Latin — *Charity*
See Charity.
Carie, Caritta, Karita

Carla (KAR-luh)
Teutonic — *One who is strong*
Feminine form of Charles.
Entertainment: Carly Simon, pop singer.
Carly, Karla, Karly

Carlotta (kar-LOT-uh)
Spanish, Portuguese, French — *Petite or feminine*
Interesting: Name was introduced to France and England by the wife of Louis XI.
Carla, Carleen, Carlene, Carletta, Carlie, Carlina, Carline, Carlita, Carlota, Carly, Karla, Karletta, Karlina, Karlita, Karlotta

Carmel (kar-MEL) or (KAR-muhl)
Hebrew — *God's vineyard*
Biblical: Mt. Carmel in Palestine.
Carma, Carmela, Carmen, Carmill, Karma, Karmen

Carmen (KAR-min)
Latin — *Song*
Hebrew — *Vine-dresser*
Entertainment: Opera *Carmen,* by George Bizet.
Carma, Carmencita, Carmine, Carmita, Charmine, Karmen

Carna (KAR-nuh)
Hebrew — *Horn*
Carmita, Carniela, Carniella, Carnis, Carnit, Karmen, Karnis

Carol (KAIR-uhl)

French — *Song of joy*
Feminine form of Carl or Charles.
Famous: Caroline Kennedy, daughter of President John F. Kennedy; Princess Caroline of Monaco.
Entertainment: Carol King, singer and songwriter; Carol Channing, actress; Carrie Fisher, actress who plays Princess Leia in *Star Wars*.

Carey, Cari, Carla, Carleen, Carlen, Carlene, Carley, Carlin, Carlina, Carline, Carlita, Carlota, Carlotta, Carly, Carlyn, Carlynn, Carlynne, Caro, Carola, Carole, Carolin, Carolina, Caroline, Carolyn, Carolynn, Carolynne, Carri, Carrie, Carroll, Carry, Cary, Caryl, Chariene, Charla, Charleen, Charlena, Charlotta, Charmain, Charmaine, Charmian, Charmion, Charyl, Cheryl, Cheryln, Karel, Kari, Karla, Karleen, Karlen, Karlene, Karlotta, Karlotte, Karole, Karolina, Karoly, Lola, Loleta, Lolita, Lotta, Lotte, Lotti, Lottie, Sharleen, Sharlene, Sharline, Sharyl, Sherrie, Sherry, Sherye, Sheryl

Caron (KAIR-uhn)

French — *Pure*

Casey (KĀ-sē)

Gaelic — *Brave*
Casie, Kacie, Kasey

Cassandra (kuh-SAN-druh)

Greek — *Entangling men*
Mythological: A prophetess of ancient Greece.
Entertainment: Cass Elliott, pop singer with the Mamas and Papas.

Cass, Cassandre, Cassie, Sandra

Catalina (kat-uh-LĒN-uh)

Greek — *Pure*
Caterina

Catherine (KATH-ren)

Greek — *Pure*
Literature: Catherine Barkley, heroine of Hemingway's novel, *A Farewell to Arms;* Catherine Earnshaw, heroine of Emily Bronte's novel, *Wuthering Heights*.
Entertainment: Catherine Deneuve, Cathy Lee Crosby, actresses; Gymnast Cathy Rigby; Catherine Crosby, wife of Bing Crosby.

Caitlin, Caitrin, Caren, Carin, Caron, Caryn, Cass, Cassy, Catarina, Cate, Caterina, Catha, Catharina, Catharine, Cathe, Cathee, Catherina, Cathi, Cathie, Cathleen, Cathlene, Cathrine, Cathryn, Cathy, Cathyleen, Cati, Catie, Catlaina, Catriona, Caty, Caye, Ekaterina, Kate, Katherine, Kathie, Kathleen, Kathlin, Katleen, Katlin, Katrina, Katrine, Katty, Kit, Kitty, Trina, Trine, Trinette

Cecilia (suh-SĒ-lē-yuh)

Latin — *Blind*
Famous: St. Cecilia, patroness of music.
Entertainment: Cicily Tyson and Sissy Spacek, actresses.
Cecelia, Cecil, Cecile, Ceciley, Cecily, Ceil, Celia, Cicily, Cis, Cissy, Sisely, Sissy

Celeste (suh-LEST)

Latin — *Heavenly*
Entertainment: Celeste Holm, actress.
Cele, Celesta, Celestia, Celestina, Celestine, Celia, Celie, Celina, Celinda, Celinka, Celka

Celina (se-LĒN-uh)
Polish, Latin — *Heavenly*
Cela, Celek, Celestyn, Celestyna, Celinka, Celka, Cesia, Inka, Inok

Chaitra (SHĀ-truh)
Hindi for Aries zodiac sign.

Chanda (CHAN-duh)
Sanskrit — *The great goddess*
Mythological: Name assumed by Devi, the greatest goddess.

Chandra (CHAN-druh)
Sanskrit — *Outshines the stars*

Charity (CHAIR-i-tē)
Latin — *Benevolent, charitable, loving*
Charita, Charry, Cherry

Charlotte (SHAR-lot)
French — *Little and womanly*
Feminine form of Charles.
Literature: Novelist Charlotte Bronte.
Carla, Carleen, Carlene, Carline, Carlota, Carlotta, Carly, Charla, Charleen, Charlene, Charline, Charlotta, Charmain, Charmaine, Charmian, Charmion, Charo, Charyl, Karla, Karleen, Karlene, Karlotta, Karlotte, Lola, Loleta, Lolita, Lotta, Lotte, Lotti, Lottie, Sharleen, Sharlene, Sharline, Sharyl, Sherrie, Sherry, Sherye, Sheryl

Charmaine (shar-MĀN)
Latin — *Little song*
Charmain, Charmian, Charmion

Chastity (CHAS-tuh-tē)
Latin — *Purity*
Famous: Chastity Bono, daughter of Sonny and Cher Bono.

Cherie (SHAIR-ē) or (shuh-RĒ)
French — *Dear one*
Famous: Cher
Literature: Cherry Ames, heroine of novels for young girls.
Cher, Chere, Cherey, Cheri, Cherry, Sherrel, Sherrell, Sheryl

Cheryl (SHAIR-el)
See Charlotte.
Entertainment: Cherylynn La Tiere, pop singer; Cheryl Tiegs, actress and model; Cheryl Crawford, actress.
Cherylynn, Sheryl

Chloe (KLŌ) or (KLŌ-ē)
Greek — *Young grass*
Mythological: Greek goddess of agriculture.
Cleopatra

Chloris (KLOR-is)
Greek — *Pale*
Mythological: Goddess of flowers.
Entertainment: Cloris Leachman, actress.
Chloe, Chlor, Clor, Cloris, Kloris

Christa (KRIS-tuh)
Greek — *The anointed*
Chris, Chrissy, Christabel, Christabelle, Christal, Christel, Christiana, Christiane, Crystal

Christina (kris-TĒN-uh)
Greek — *The anointed*
Feminine form of Christian.
Famous: Christine Brinkley, model; Christina Onassis, daughter of Aristotle Onassis.
Entertainment: Tina Louise, actress; Tina Turner, pop singer.
Sports: Chris Evert Lloyd, tennis champion.
Chris, Chrissi, Chrissie, Chrissy, Christa, Christal, Christiana, Christie, Christine, Chrystal, Crystal, Kristianna, Kristina, Kristine, Tenna, Tina

Cinderella (sin-duh-REL-uh)
French— *Little one of the ashes*
Literature: Famous fairy tale.
**Cinda, Cindee, Cindia,
Cindie, Cindy, Ella**

Cindy (SIN-dē)
See Cynthia.
Entertainment: Cindy Garvey, talk
show hostess; Cindy Williams,
star of *Laverne and Shirley*.

Cipriana (si-prē-AN-uh)
Spanish— *From the island of Cyprus*
Kupris, Sipiana

Clara (KLAIR-uh)
Latin— *Bright or illustrious*
Famous: Clare Boothe Luce,
author, playwright and former
congresswoman.
**Clair, Claire, Clarabelle, Clare,
Claresta, Clareta, Claretta,
Clarette, Clarey, Clari,
Claribel, Clarice, Clarinada,
Clarine, Clarissa, Clarita,
Clarrette, Clary, Cliarra,
Klair, Klaire, Klara, Klare,
Klarika, Klarrisa**

Clareta (KLAR-et-uh)
Spanish— *Brilliant*
Clarette, Clarita

Clarice (kluh-RĒS)
French— *Making famous*
Literature: *Clarissa Harlowe*, novel
by Samuel Richardson.
**Clarisa, Clarise, Clarissa,
Clarisse**

Claudia (KLAW-dē-uh)
Latin— *Lame*
Feminine form of Claude.
Entertainment: Claudia Cardinale,
Claudette Colbert, Claudine
Longet, actresses.
**Claude, Claudetta, Claudette,
Claudie, Claudina, Claudine,**

Clementine (KLEM-en-tīn,
Latin— *The merciful*
Feminine form of Clement.
Entertainment: Song *Oh My
Darling, Clementine*.

Cleo (KLE-ō)
Greek— *The famous*
Clea, Cleopatra, Clio

Clitilde (kluh-TILD-uh) or
(kluh-TILD)
Teutonic— *Famous battle-maiden*
Clothilde, Clotilda

Clover (KLŌ-ver)
Old English— *Clover blossom*
Entertainment: Movie *Daisy Clover*.
Klover

Colette (kō-LET)
Latin— *Victorious*
Collette

Colleen (kaw-LĒN) or (KŌ-lēn)
Irish— *Girl*
Entertainment: Colleen Dewhurst,
actress.
**Coleen, Colene, Collie,
Colline, Colly**

Connie (KON-ē)
See Constance.
Entertainment: Connie Frances,
singer; Connie Stevens, actress
and singer.

Constance (KON-stans)
Latin— *Constancy*
Entertainment: Constance Bennett,
actress.
**Con, Conni, Connie, Conny,
Constancia, Constancy,
Constanta, Constantia,
Constantine, Costanza,
Konstance, Konstanze**

Consuela (kon-SWĀ-luh)
Latin, Spanish— *Consolation*
Literature: Consuelo, heroine in
George Sands novel.
Consolata, Consuelo

CORDELIA—*Sea jewel*

Cora (KOR-uh)
Greek—*Maiden*
Famous: Coretta King, wife of
Martin Luther King.
**Corabel, Corabella, Corabelle,
Corella, Corena, Corene, Coretta,
Corette, Corey, Cori, Corie,
Corilla, Corina, Corine, Corinna,
Corinne, Coriss, Corissa, Correna,
Corrie, Corrine, Corry, Cory,
Kora, Korella, Korie, Korry**

Coral (KOR-uhl)
Greek, Latin—*From the sea coral*
Interesting: Coral was worn by
South Sea Islanders as a charm to
ward off evil spirits.
**Caralie, Coralie, Coraline,
Corallie, Koral, Koralie,
Koraline, Korallie**

Cordelia (kor-DĒ-lē-uh)
Celtic— *The sea jewel*
Literature: King Lear's faithful
daughter.
**Cordelie, Cordey, Cordi,
Cordie, Cordula, Cordy, Coretta,
Corinna, Corinne, Delia, Kella,
Kordella, Kordellia, Kordula**

Corliss (KOR-les)
Old English— *Cheerful or
good-hearted*

Cornelia (kor-NĒ-lē-uh)
Latin— *Yellowish or horn colored*
Feminine form of Cornelius.
**Corinna, Cornela, Cornelie,
Cornelle, Cornie, Corny,
Nelia, Nelie, Nell, Nellie**

Cosima (ko-SĒ-muh)
Greek, Italian— *Orderly arrangement*
Feminine form of Cosmo.

Crystal (KRIS-tul)
Greek— *Brilliantly clear*
Entertainment: Crystal Gayle,
singer and Loretta Lynn's
youngest sister.
**Chris, Cris, Crys, Krystal,
Stell, Stella**

Cybil (SIB-ul)
See Sibyl.
Entertainment: Cybil Shepherd,
actress and model.

Cynara (si-NAR-uh)
Greek name derived from island in
Aegean Sea, now called Zinara.

Cynthia (SIN-thē-uh)
Greek— *Moon goddess*
Historical: Affectionate name
given to Queen Elizabeth I by
Ben Johnson, Walter Raleigh and
Edmund Spenser.
**Cindy, Cyn, Cynth, Cynthie,
Kynthia**

Cyra (SĒR-uh)
Greek— *Lord, ruler*
Feminine form of Cyrano.
Cira, Cyrilla

Cyrene (suh-RĒN)
Greek— *Unknown*
Mythological: Nymph carried by
Apollo to Libya.
Cyrena

Cyrilla (suh-RIL-uh)
Latin— *Lordly*
Feminine form of Cyril.
Ciri, Cirilla

Dacey (DĀ-sē)
American— *Southerner*
Dacia, Dacie, Dacy, Dasi, Dasie

Dagania (dag-uh-NĒ-uh)
Hebrew— *Ceremonial grain*
Daganya

Dagmar (DAG-mar)
Danish— *Joy of the Danes*
Famous: Beloved Danish queen.
Dagare, Mar

Dagna (DAG-nuh)
Teutonic— *Fair as the day*
Dagny

DAMALIS—*The tamer*

Daisy (DĀ-zē)
Anglo-Saxon—*Day's eyes*
Daisey, Daisi, Daisie

Dale (DĀL)
Old English—*From the valley*
Entertainment: Dale Evans, actress
and wife of Roy Rogers.
Dael, Daile, Dailie, Dayle

Dalila (duh-LĪ-luh)
Swahili—*Gentle*
Delilah, Lila

Dallas (DAL-us)
Gaelic—*Wise*
Dalton

Damalis (duh-MAL-is)
Greek—*The tamer*

Damara (duh-MAR-uh)
Greek—*Gentle girl*
**Damon, Damaris, Mara, Mari,
Maris**

Damita (duh-MĒ-tuh)
Spanish—*Little noble lady*
Damite, Damitee, Damitie

Dana (DĀ-nuh)
Celtic— *From Denmark*
Mythological: Dana, mother of the
gods.

Danica (duh-NĒ-kuh)
Slavic— *The morning star*

Daniela (DAN-yel-uh)
Hebrew— *God is my judge*
Feminine form of Daniel.
**Danella, Danelle, Danett,
Danette, Dani, Danice,
Daniella, Danielle, Danila,
Danit, Danita, Danni, Dannie,
Danny, Dannye, Danya, Danye**

Danit (dan-ĒT)
Hebrew— *To judge*
Feminine form of Daniel.
Dania, Danita, Danya

Daphne (DAF-nē)
Greek— *Laurel tree*
**Daffi, Daffie, Daffy, Daph,
Daphle**

Dara (DAR-uh)
Hebrew— *Compassion*
Darda, Darya

Daralis (duh-RAL-is)
Old English— *Beloved or dear*
Daralice

Darby (DAR-bē)
Gaelic— *Free man*
Old Norse— *From the deer estate*
**Darb, Darbie, Darcee, Darcey,
Darcy, Darsey, Darsie, Dercy**

Darcie (DAR-sē)
French, Celtic— *From the stronghold
or dark one*
Darcee, Darcey, Darcy

Darda (DAR-duh)
Hungarian— *A dart*
Hebrew— *Pearl of wisdom*
Dardis

Daria (DAR-ē-uh)
Persian— *Queenly*
Feminine form of Darius.
**Dareece, Darees, Dari, Darice,
Darya**

Darlene (dar-LĒN)
Anglo-Saxon— *Tenderly beloved*
**Daralice, Daralis, Darelle,
Darla, Darleen, Darline, Darlleen,
Darrelle, Darryl, Daryl**

Daron (DAIR-en)
Gaelic— *Great*
Feminine form of Darren.

Davine (duh-VĒN)
Hebrew— *The loved*
Feminine form of David.
**Daveta, Davida, Davita, Davina,
Devina, Veda, Vida, Vita, Vitia**

Dawn (DAWN)
Anglo-Saxon— *Break of day*

Deanne (dē-AN)
See Diana.
Feminine form of Dean.
Deana, Dena, Deon, Deonne

Deborah (DEB-uh-ruh)
Hebrew— *Bee*
Entertainment: Deborah Harry,
singer known as *Blondie;* Debbie
Boone, singer, daughter of Pat
Boone; Deborah Kerr, Debbie
Reynolds, actresses.
**Deb, Debbee, Debbie, Debby,
Debora, Debra**

Dee (DĒ)
Welsh— *Black, dark*
Dede, Deirdre, Delia, Diana

Deedee (DĒ-dē)
Hebrew— *Beloved*
Entertainment: Dee Dee Lewis,
pop singer.
Dee Dee, Didi, Jedidiah

Dehlia (DĀ-lē-yuh)
Norwegian— *From the valley*

Dela (DĒ-luh)
Spanish— *Hope*
Della

Delia (DĒ-lē-yuh)
Greek— *Visible from Delos*
Mythological: Name for the moon goddess.
Adelaide, Dede, Dee, Deedee, Dehlia, Delinad, Della, Didi

Delilah (duh-LĪ-luh)
Hebrew— *The temptress*
Biblical: Companion of Samson.
Dalila, Delila, Lila, Lilah

Della (DEL-uh)
Teutonic— *Of nobility*
Entertainment: Della Reese, pop singer.
Del, Dela

Delora (duh-LOR-uh)
Latin— *From the seashore*
Delores, Deloris

Delphine (del-FĒN)
Greek— *Calmness*
Interesting: Possibly derived from dolphin.
Mythological: Delphine means calm sea in Greek mythology.
Delfeena, Delfine, Delphina, Delphinia

Demetria (duh-MĒ-trē-uh)
Greek— *From fertile land*
Mythological: Goddess of fertility and harvests.
Demeter, Demetra, Demitria, Demy, Dimitria

Deminica (duh-MIN-i-kuh)
French, Latin— *Born on the Lord's day*
Feminine form of Dominic.
Domeniga, Dominga, Domini, Dominic, Dominica, Dominique

Dena (DĒ-nuh)
Hebrew— *Vindicated*
Feminine form of Dean.
Deana, Deena, Dinah

Denise (duh-NĒS)
Greek— *Wine goddess*
Denice, Denni, Dennie, Denny, Denys, Denyse, Dinnie, Dinny

Derora (duh-ROR-uh)
Hebrew— *Flowing brook*
Derorice, Derorit

Desdemona
(DEZ-duh-mōn-uh)
Greek— *Girl of sadness*
Demona, Desdamona, Mona

Desiree (dez-i-RĀ)
French, Latin— *So long hoped for*
Desire

Deva (DĒ-vuh)
Sanskrit— *Divine*
Interesting: Hindi goddess of the moon.

Devi (dē-VĒ)
Sakti— *Goddess*
Interesting: Hindi goddess of power and destruction.

Devora (de-VOR-uh)
Russian— *A bee*
Debora, Deborah

Diana (dī-AN-uh)
Latin— *Divine*
Mythological: Roman goddess of the hunt, moon and fertility.
Biblical: Temple of Diana at Ephesus was one of the Seven Wonders of the ancient world.
Famous: Diana, Princess of Wales.
Literature: Dian Thomas, author and TV personality.
Entertainment: Diana Ross, pop singer; Diahann Caroll, Diane Keaton, actresses.
Deana, Deane, Deanna, Deanne, Dede, Dee, Dena, Denna, Denne, Di, Diahann, Dian, Diandra, Diane, Dianna, Dianne, Didi, Dyan, Dyana, Dyane, Dyann, Dyanna, Dyanne

Dianthe (dī-AN-thuh)
Greek— *Divine flower*
Diantha

Dinah (DĪ-nuh)
Hebrew— *Vindicated*
Biblical: Daughter of Leah and
Jacob, known for her beauty.
Entertainment: Dinah Shore,
singer; Dina Merrill, actress.
Dena, Diane, Dina

Dionne (DĒ-on)
Greek— *Divine queen*
Feminine form of Dion.
Mythological: Mother of
Aphrodite.
Entertainment: Dionne Warwicke,
pop singer.
Diona, Dione, Dionis

Disa (DĒ-suh)
Norwegian— *Active spirit*
Greek— *Double*
Lisa

Dixie (DIKS-ē)
American— *Girl of the south*
Interesting: Term for the American
South.
Famous: Dixie Lee Ray, former
member of the Atomic Energy
Commission and governor of
Washington state.

Docilla (dō-SIL-uh)
Latin— *Teachable*
Docila, Dosilla

Dodi (DŌ-dē)
Hebrew— *Beloved*
Dode, Dodie, Dody, Dora, Doris

Dolly (DOL-ē)
Greek— *Divine gift*
Famous: Dolley Madison, wife of
President James Madison.
Entertainment: Dolly Parton,
country-western singer; musical
Hello Dolly.
**Doll, Dolle, Dolley, Dollie,
Dorothy**

Dolores (duh-LOR-is)
Spanish— *Lady of sorrows*
Biblical: Santa Maria de los
Dolores, *Mary of the Sorrows*.
Famous: Delores Hope, wife of Bob
Hope.
Entertainment: Dolores Del Rio,
actress.
**Delora, Deloree, Delores,
Deloris, Deloritas, Dolorcitas,
Dolorita, Dori, Dorrie, Dorry,
Lola, Lolita**

Donna (DON-uh)
Latin, Italian— *Lady*
Entertainment: Donna Fargo,
country-western singer; Donna
Reed, actress.
Sports: Swimmer Donna
DeVerona.
**Dana, Danella, Dode, Dodi,
Dodie, Dody, Donia, Donni,
Donnie, Donny, Dora, Doralia,
Doralin, Doraline, Doralisa,
Doralyn, Doralynn, Doralynne,
Dore, Doreen, Dorelia, Dorella,
Dorelle, Dorena, Dorene, Doretta,
Dorette, Dorey, Dori, Doria,
Dorice, Dorie, Doris, Dorlisa,
Dorita, Dorothy, Dory**

Doreen (dor-ĒN) or (DOR-ēn)
Gaelic— *Sullen*
French— *Golden*
Dora, Dorecna, Dorene, Dorine

Doris (DOR-is)
Greek— *Bountiful*
Mythological: Wife of Nereus.
Entertainment: Doris Day, actress.
Dora, Dorian

DRISANA—*Daughter of the sun*

Dorothy (DOR-uh-thē)
Greek—*Gift of God*
Literature: Dorothy Sayers,
 detective fiction; Dorothy in the
 Wizard of Oz.
Entertainment: Dorothy Gish,
 actress.
Sports: Dorothy Hamill, Olympic
 gold medal figure skater.
**Dasha, Dode, Dody, Doll, Dolley,
Dolli, Dollie, Dolly, Dora,
Dorathy, Dori, Dorlisa, Doro,
Dorolice, Dorotea, Doroteya,
Dorothea, Dorothee, Dorthea,
Dorthy, Dory, Dosi, Dosya,
Dot, Dotti, Dottie**

Dove (DUV)
German—*Dark*

Drina (DRĒ-nuh)
Spanish—*Helper*
Drisa, Drise

Drisana (dri-SAN-uh)
Sanskrit—*Daughter of the sun*
Drisa

Drusilla (drōō-SIL-uh)
Greek—*Soft eyes*
**Dru, Druci, Drucie, Drucilla,
Drucy, Drus, Drusi, Drusie,
Drusus, Drusy**

Dulcia (dul-SĒ-uh)
Latin — *Sweet or delightful*
Literature: For his love, Aldonza,
Don Quixote chose the nickname
Dulcinea.
**Delcina, Delcine, Dulce, Dulcea,
Dulci, Dulciana, Dulcie,
Dulcinea, Dulcy, Dulsea**

Ea (Ē-uh)
Babylonian — *Goddess of spring*
Literature: Ea is the goddess of
spring in the Sumerian epic,
Gilgamesh.

Eartha (ER-thuh)
Old English — *Child of the earth*
Entertainment: Eartha Kitt, pop
singer.
Erda, Ertha, Heatha, Hertha

Easter (Ē-ster)
Old English — *Easter time*
Mythological: Anglo-Saxon
goddess of spring; Greek goddess
of dawn.
Biblical: Name of a child born at
Eastertide.

Echo (EK-ō)
Greek — *Repeated voice*
Mythological: Echo was a nymph
who yearned for love which was
unreturned.

Eda (Ē-duh)
Anglo-Saxon — *Happy or prosperous*
Edda, Edie

Edana (e-DAN-uh)
Celtic — *Zealous or fiery*
Feminine form of Edan.

Edeline (Ē-duh-lin) or (Ē-duh-līn)
Teutonic — *Noble and of good cheer*
Adeline

Eden (Ē-din)
Hebrew — *Delight*
Babylonian — *A plain*
Biblical: Earthly paradise where
Adam and Eve lived.
Edin

Edie (Ē-dē)
Teutonic — *Rich gift*
Entertainment: Edie Gormé,
singer; Edie Adams, actress and
singer.
**Eadie, Eadith, Eda, Ede,
Edina, Edith, Edythe**

Edina (e-DĒN-uh)
Anglo-Saxon — *Prospering, happy*
Interesting: Poetic name for the
city of Edinburgh.

Edith (Ē-dith)
Teutonic — *Rich gift*
Literature: Edith Wharton, writer.
Entertainment: Wife of Archie
Bunker, in *All in the Family.*
**Eadie, Eadith, Eda, Ede, Edi,
Edil, Edina, Edita, Editha, Edithe,
Edy, Edyth, Edythe, Eyde**

Edlyn (ED-lin)
Anglo-Saxon — *Noblewoman*
Eddie, Edie, Lyn

Edna (ED-nuh)
Hebrew — *Rejuvenation, pleasure*
Literature: Edna St. Vincent
Millay, poetess.
Eddi, Eddie, Eddy, Edie, Edny

Ednee (ED-nā)
Anglo-Saxon—*Prosperous protector*
Feminine form of Edmond.
Edmonda, Edmunda

Edolie (ED-ō-lē)
Teutonic—*Noble and of good cheer*
Dolie

Edrea (ed-RĒ-uh)
Hebrew—*Mighty*
Teutonic—*Prosperous*
**Eddi, Eddie, Eddy, Edra,
Edrena, Edrine, Edris**

Edwina (ed-WĒN-uh)
Anglo-Saxon—*Valued friend*
Feminine form of Edwin.
**Eadwina, Eadwine, Edwin,
Edwine, Edwyna, Win,
Wina, Winnie, Winny**

Effie (EF-ē)
Greek—*Of fair fame*
**Effy, Eppie, Euphemia,
Euphemie, Phemie**

Eglantine (EG-lan-tēn)
French—*Sweet-briar*
Interesting: A flower name.

Eileen (ī-LĒN)
Greek—*Light*
Literature: Ruth McKenney's *My
Sister Eileen.*
Aileen

Eirene (ī-RĒN)
Norwegian—*Peace*
Eir, Eirenea, Irene

Elaine (ē-LĀN)
Greek—*Light*
Literature: Elaine, in Tennyson's
Idylls of the King.
**Alaine, Alayne, Elana, Elane,
Elayne, Laine, Lainey, Lani**

Elata (ē-LĀ-tuh)
Latin—*Exalted or triumphant*

Elberta (el-BER-tuh)
Teutonic—*Nobly brilliant*
Feminine form of Elbert.
Interesting: Variety of peach.
Alberta, Berta, Bertia

Eldora (el-DOR-uh)
Spanish—*Golden or gilded*
Feminine form of Eldorado.
Eldoree, Eldoria

Eldrida (el-DRĒ-duh)
Anglo-Saxon—*Sage counselor*
Feminine form of Eldred.

Eleanor (EL-uh-nor)
Greek—*Light*
Famous: Eleanor Roosevelt, wife of
President Franklin D. Roosevelt.
Literature: Elinor Trent, heroine in
Old Curosity Shop, by Dickens.
**Eleanora, Eleanore, Elenore,
Eleonore, Elianore, Elinor,
Elinore, Ella, Elladine, Elle,
Ellene, Elli, Elly, Ellyn,
Elna, Elnora, Elnore, Elora,
Elyn, Helen, Leanor, Leanora,
Lena, Lenora, Lenore, Leonore,
Leora, Nell, Nellie, Nelly, Nora**

Electra (e-LEK-truh)
Greek—*Bright, shining*
Mythological: One of seven sister
stars of the Pleiades.
Lectra

Eleni (EL-uh-nē)
Greek—*Light or torch*
**Elena, Elenie, Elenitsa,
Helen, Nitsa**

Elexa (e-LEKS-uh)
See Alexandra.
Feminine form of Alfred.
Elfrida, Elfride, Freda

Elga (EL-guh)
Teutonic—*Holy*
Anglo-Saxon—*Elfin spear*

Eli (Ē-lē)
Norwegian—*Light*

Eliora (EL-ē-or-uh)
Hebrew — *The Lord is my light*
Eleora, Leora

Elisa (e-LĪ-zuh) or (e-LĒ-suh)
Spanish — *Dedicated to God*
Entertainment: Eliza Doolittle, in *My Fair Lady*.
Belita, Elisheba, Elisia, Elisis, Elissa, Elissie, Eliza, Elyse, Ysabel

Elita (e-LĒ-tuh)
French, Latin — *The chosen, selected*

Elizabeth (e-LIZ-a-beth)
Hebrew — *Consecrated to God*
Biblical: Mother of John the Baptist.
Famous: Elizabeth Barrett of Winnpole Street; Queen Elizabeth of England.
Literature: Elizabeth, heroine of Jane Austen's *Pride and Prejudice*.
Entertainment: Elizabeth Taylor, Elizabeth Montgomery, actresses.
Belita, Belle, Bess, Bessie, Bessy, Beth, Betsey, Betsy, Betta, Bette, Betti, Bettina, Bettine, Betty, Ealasaid, Elis, Elisa, Elisabet, Elisabeth, Elisabetta, Elissa, Eliza, Elizabet, Elsa, Elsbeth, Else, Elsey, Elsi, Elsie, Elspet, Elspeth, Elsy, Helsa, Isabel, Isabell, Lib, Libbey, Libbi, Libbie, Libby, Lillibeth, Lily, Lisa, Lisabeth, Lisbeth, Lise, Lisette, Lissa, Liz, Liza, Lizabeth, Lizbeth, Lizzie, Lizzy, Lusa, Ysabel, Ysabell

Ella (EL-uh)
Anglo-Saxon — *Elfin*
Entertainment: Ella Fitzgerald, singer.

Ellen (EL-un)
See Helen.
Literature: Ellen Glosgow, Pulitzer Prize-winner for *In This Our Life*.
Entertainment: Ellen Burstyn, Oscar-winning actress.
Ellene, Ellie, Elly, Ellyn

Elma (EL-muh)
Greek — *Amiable*
Turkish — *Apple*
Feminine form of Elmo.

Elmina (el-MĒN-uh)
Teutonic — *Awe-inspiring fame*
Anglo-Saxon — *Tree*
Feminine form of Elmer.

Elna (EL-nuh)
Greek — *Light*

Elnora (el-NOR-uh)
Greek — *Light*

Elodie (EL-ō-dē)
Latin — *White blossom of the water*

Eloine (EL-ō-ēn)
Latin — *Worthy to be chosen*
Biblical: St. Elloy, patron of workers in precious metals.
Eloi, Elloi, Elloy

Eloise (EL-ō-ēs)
Teutonic — *Famous in battle*
French, German — *Hale and wide*
Literature: *Hints from Heloise*, popular newspaper column.
Eloisa, Heloise

Elsa (EL-suh)
Swedish, Spanish, Greek — *Truthful*
Entertainment: Elsa Martinelli, actress; in Wagner's opera *Lohengrin*, bride for whom the wedding march is played.
Alicia, Alika, Alisa, Aliz, Alizka, Alizz, Alya, Else, Elsie, Elsy, Ilsa, Ilse

Elspeth (EL-speth)
Scottish, Hebrew — *Consecrated to God*
See Elizabeth.

ELVIRA — *Befriended by the elves*

Elva (EL-vuh)
Anglo-Saxon — *Elfin*
Feminine form of Alvin.
Elffie, Ellfia, Elvi, Elvie

Elverda (EL-ver-duh)
Latin — *Virginal*

Elvira (el-VĪ-ruh) or (EL-vir-uh)
Anglo-Saxon — *Befriended by the elves*
Feminine form of Elvin.
Entertainment: Character in
   Mozart's opera *Don Giovanni;*
   pop song *Elvira.*
Elva, Elvera, Elvie, Elvina

Elysia (e-LĒ-shuh)
Latin — *Sweetly blissful*
Mythological: Elysium was a
   dwelling place of happy souls.

Elza (EL-zuh)
Hebrew — *God is my joy*

Ema (E-muh)
Polynesian — *Beloved*
**Emalaine, Emelin, Emelina,
Emiline, Emma**

Emalia (e-MĀ-lē-uh)
Polynesian, Latin — *Flirt*

Emele (e-MĒL)
Polynesian — *Industrious*
Emilia, Emilie, Emily

Emily (EM-uh-lē)
Gothic— *Industrious*
Latin— *To flatter*
Feminine form of Emil.
Famous: Emily Post, American
  authority on etiquette.
Literature: Emily Bronte, author of
  Wuthering Heights.
**Aimil, Amalea, Amalia, Amalie,
Amelia, Amelie, Ameline,
Amelita, Amy, Eimile, Em,
Emalia, Emelda, Emelia,
Emelina, Emeline, Emelita,
Emelyne, Emera, Emilia, Emilie,
Emiline, Emlyn, Emlynn,
Emlynne, Emmaline, Emmalyn,
Emmalynn, Emmalynne,
Emmelyn, Emmey, Emmi,
Emmie, Emmy, Emmye, Milka**

Emma (EM-uh)
German— *Universal*
Interesting: Emmy awards are
  given by the National Television
  Academy of Arts and Sciences.
Famous: Script on the Statue of
  Liberty was written by Emma
  Lazarus.
Literature: Heroine of *Madame
  Bovary,* by Flaubert.
**Em, Ema, Emmaline, Emmalyn,
Emmalynn, Emmalynne, Emmi,
Emmie, Emmy, Emmye**

Emuna (e-MOON-uh)
Hebrew— *Faithful*
Emunah, Emuni, Emunie

Enid (Ē-ned)
Welsh, Latin— *Spotless purity or a
  woodlark*
Literature: Enid, heroine of the
  King Arthur legends in
  Tennyson's *Idylls of the King.*
En, Enit

Erda (ER-duh)
German— *Earth*

Erica (AIR-i-kuh)
Norwegian— *Ever powerful*
Feminine form of Eric.
Literature: Erica Jong, novelist.
Entertainment: Erica Morini,
  concert violinist.
**Enrica, Enrika, Erichci, Erika,
Erikie, Ricki, Rickie, Ricky, Rikki**

Erin (AIR-in)
Gaelic— *Peace; Ireland*
Erina, Erinna, Erlina, Erline

Erma (ER-muh)
See Irma.
Literature: Erma Bombeck, author
  and syndicated columnist.
**Ermina, Erminia, Erminie,
Hermione**

Ernesta (er-NEST-uh)
Teutonic— *Intent in purpose*
Feminine form of Ernest.
Erna, Ernaline, Ernestine

Ertha (ER-thuh)
Old English— *Child of the earth*
**Eartha, Erda, Erth, Herta,
Hertha**

Esmeralda (ez-muh-RAL-duh)
Spanish, Greek— *The emerald*
Esma, Esme, Ezmeralda

Estelle (e-STEL)
Latin, French— *A star*
Literature: Estella, heroine in
  Dickens' *Great Expectations.*
**Essie, Estel, Estele, Estell,
Estella, Esther, Estrella,
Estrellita, Hetty, Stella**

Esther (ES-ter)
Persian— *A star*
Biblical: Esther, heroine in the Old
  Testament.
**Essa, Essie, Essy, Esta, Ester,
Estra, Estrella, Etti, Ettie, Etty,
Hester, Hesther, Hetty, Hettie**

Ethel (ETH-ul)
Teutonic— *Noble*
Entertainment: Ethel Barrymore,
Ethel Merman, actresses.
**Ethelburga, Ethelda, Ethelin,
Ethelinda, Etheline, Ethelred,
Ethelyn, Ethyl, Ethyle**

Etta (ET-uh)
Teutonic— *Little*
Famous: Etta Place, Butch
Cassidy's girlfriend.
Etty, Henrietta

Eudocia (ū-DŌ-shuh)
Greek— *Esteemed or honored*
Eudosia, Eudoxia

Eudora (ū-DOR-uh)
Greek— *Honored*
Dora

Eugenia (ū-JĒN-ē-uh)
Greek— *Femine form of Eugene.*
Famous: Empress Eugénie, wife of
Napoleon III.
Eugenie, Gena, Gene, Genia

Eulalia (ū-LĀ-lē-uh)
French, Greek— *Fair of speech*
Eula, Eulalee

Eunice (Ū-nis)
Greek— *Happy victory*
Feminine form of Nicholas.
Biblical: Mother of Timothy.

Euphenia (ū-FĒN-ē-uh)
Greek— *Of fair fame*
Effie, Euphemie, Phemie

Eurydice (ū-RID-uh-sē)
Greek— *Broad separation*
Mythological: Wife of Orpheus.

Eustacia (ū-STĀ-shuh)
Latin— *Fruitful or tranquil*
**Eustaci, Stacey, Stacia, Stacie,
Stacy**

Eva (Ē-vuh)
Hebrew, Latin— *Life*
Literature: Little Eva, heroine of
the novel *Uncle Tom's Cabin.*
Entertainment: Eva-Marie Saint,
Eva Gabor, actresses.
Evangelina, Eve, Zoe

Evadne (e-VAD-nē)
Greek— *Fortunate*
Mythological: Evadne was a
water-nymph.

Evangeline (ē-VAN-juh-lēn)
Greek— *Bearer of good news*
Literature: Heroine of the poem
Evangeline, by Longfellow.
**Eva, Evangelia, Evangelina,
Evangellia, Eve**

Evania (ē-VĀN-ē-uh)
Greek— *Tranquil or untroubled*

Evanthe (Ē-vanth)
Greek— *A flower*
Evadne

Eve (ĒV)
Hebrew— *Life*
Biblical: Eve, the first mother.
Entertainment: Eve Arden, actress.
**Eba, Ebba, Eva, Evaleen,
Evelina, Eveline, Evelyn, Evey,
Evie, Evita, Evonne, Evvie,
Evvy, Evy**

Ezrela (EZ-rel-uh)
Hebrew— *God is my help*
Ezraela, Ezraele, Ezraella, Ezraelle

Fabiola (FĀB-ē-ō-luh) or
(fab-ē-Ō-luh)
Feminine form of Fabian.
Famous: *Fabiola*, a portrait by Jean
Jacques Henner; name of the
Queen of Belgium.
**Fabia, Fabian, Fabrie,
Fabriene, Fabrienne**

Faith (FĀTH)
Latin — *Trusting or faithful*
Literature: Novelist Faith Baldwin.
Fae, Fay, Faye, Fayth, Faythe

Falda (FAL-duh)
Icelandic — *Folded wings*

Fanchon (FAN-shōn)
Teutonic — *Free*
Feminine form of Francis.

Fancy (FAN-sē)
Latin, Greek — *Fantasy*
See Frances.
Literature: *To Fancy*, by John Keats.
**Fancee, Fanci, Fancie, Fania,
Fanya**

Fanny (FAN-ē)
Teutonic — *Free*
Literature: Fanny Burney and
Fannie Hurst, authors; Fanny
Browne, Keat's love.
Entertainment: Fanny Brice,
actress; musical *Fanny*, one of
Pagnol's trilogy.
Fan, Fanni, Fannie

Fanya (FAN-yuh)
See Fayina.

Farica (fa-RĒ-kuh)
Teutonic — *Peaceful ruler*
Fara, Farrah, Feriga

Farrah (FAIR-uh)
English — *Beautiful*
Entertainment: Farrah Fawcett,
actress.
Farand, Farra, Farrand, Fayre

Fatima (fa-TĒM-uh) or
(FA-ti-muh)
Arabic — *Unknown*
Famous: Fatimah, daughter of
Muhammad.
Fatimah, Fatma

Faustina (faw-STĒN-uh)
Latin — *Very lucky*
Fausta, Faustine

Fawn (FAWN)
French, Latin — *A young deer*
**Doe, Dorcas, Faunia, Fawnia,
Hinda, Sivia, Tabitha**

Fay (FĀ)
French — *Fairy*
Entertainment: Fay Bainter, Faye
Emerson, Fay Wray, Faye
Dunaway, actresses.
**Fae, Faina, Fanechka, Fanya,
Faye, Fayette, Fayina**

Fayina (fā-ĒN-uh)
Russian, Ukranian — *Free one*
Faina, Fanechka, Fanya

• **Fayola** (fā-Ō-luh)
Nigerian — *Good luck*

Fayre (FAIR)
Old English—*Comely*

Fedora (fē-DOR-uh)
Greek—*Divine gift*
Feminine form of Theodore.
Fedore, Fedoree, Fedoria, Fedorie

Felda (FEL-duh)
Teutonic—*A field*

Felicia (fuh-LĒ-shuh)
Polish, Latin—*Happy*
Feminine form of Felix.
Entertainment: Felicia Farr, actress.
**Fela, Felice, Felicidad,
Felicie, Felicity, Felise,
Felita, Feliza, Felka**

Femi (FEM-ē)
Yoruban—*Love me*

Fenella (fi-NEL-uh)
Celtic—*White-shouldered*
Fenelia, Fenelle, Fenellea

Fern (FERN)
Old English—*Fern or feather*
Ferne

Fernanda (fer-NAN-duh)
Gothic—*Adventure*
Feminine form of Ferdinand.
**Ferdinanda, Ferdinande, Fern,
Fernande, Fernandine**

Fidela (fi-DEL-uh)
Latin—*Faithful woman*
**Fidelia, Fidelity, Fidella,
Fidellia**

Fifine (fē-FĒN)
French, Hebrew—*He shall add*
Fifi, Fifin

Fionna (fē-Ō-nuh)
Celtic—*The white*
Fenella, Finella, Fiona, Fionnula

Flavia (FLĀ-vē-uh)
Latin—*Blonde or yellow-haired*

Flora (FLOR-uh)
Latin—*A flower*
Mythological: Roman goddess of
spring and flowers.
**Fiora, Fiore, Fleur, Fleurette,
Flo, Flor, Flore, Floreen,
Florella, Floria, Florie, Floris,
Florri, Florrie, Florry, Flossie**

Florence (FLOR-ens)
Latin—*Blooming*
Famous: Florence Nightingale,
nurse and philanthropist.
Entertainment: Florence
Henderson, actress.
**Flo, Flor, Flora, Florance,
Flore, Florencia, Florentia,
Florenza, Flori, Floria,
Floridia, Florie, Florinada,
Florine, Floris, Florri,
Florrie, Florry, Floss,
Flossi, Flossie, Flossy, Flouna**

Fonda (FON-duh)
Spanish, Latin—*The profound*

Fortuna (for-CHŌŌ-nuh)
Latin—*The fortunate*
Mythological: Roman goddess of
good luck.
Fortune

Frances (FRAN-ses)
Teutonic—*Free*
Feminine form of Francis.
**Fanny, Fereng, Ferike, Fran,
France, Francesca, Franci,
Francille, Francine, Francis,
Franciska, Francoise, Franke,
Frankie, Frannie, Franny**

Freda (FRĒ-duh)
Teutonic—*Peaceful*
Feminine form of Frederick.
**Frayda, Fredella, Freida,
Freidia, Frida**

FLORENCE—*Blooming*

Frederica (fred-er-Ē-kuh)
Teutonic—*Peaceful ruler*
Feminine form of Frederick.
**Farica, Fred, Freddie, Freddy,
Frederic, Fredericka,
Frederique, Fredrika, Frici,
Frida, Frieda, Friederika,
Rica, Ricki, Rickie, Ricky,
Rikki**

Freya (FRĀ-uh)
Norwegian—*Noble woman*
Literature: *Freya of the Severn Isles,*
by Joseph Conrad.
Fray, Fraya, Frayia, Frayie

Fritzi (FRITZ-ē)
Teutonic—*Peaceful ruler*
Feminine form of Fritz.
Fritz, Fritzie

Frodine (FRŌ-dēn)
Teutonic — *Wise friend*
Frodinne

Froma (FRŌ-muh)
German — *Pious*
Fromma, Frume, Frumie

Fulvia (FUL-vē-uh)
Latin — *The blonde*

Gabrielle (GĀ-brē-el) or
(GĀ-bre-el-uh)
Hebrew — *God is my strength*
Feminine form of Gabriel.
Literature: Gabriela Mistral,
  Chilean poet, winner of the
  Noble Prize for Literature.
**Gabey, Gabi, Gabie, Gabriel,
Gabriela, Gabriell, Gabriella,
Gabriellia, Gabrila, Gaby, Gavra**

Gada (GĀ-duh)
Hebrew — *Lucky*

Gafna (GAF-nuh)
Hebrew — *Vine*

Gail (GĀL)
Old English — *Gay, lively*
See Abigail.
**Gael, Gale, Gayla, Gayle,
Gayleen, Gaylene**

Gala (GĀ-luh)
Scandinavian — *Singer*

Galatea (gal-a-TĒ-uh)
Greek — *Milk white*
Mythological: Galatea was an
  ivory statue brought to life by
  Aphrodite.

Gali (GĀ-lē)
Hebrew — *A fountain*
Gal, Galice, Galit

Galina (gā-LĒN-uh)
Russian — *Light*
See Helen.
Entertainment: Galina Ulanova,
  ballet dancer; Galina
  Visnevskaya, opera singer.
**Galinka, Galya, Galye, Jelena,
Jelene, Lena, Yalena**

Galya (GĀL-yuh)
Hebrew — *God has redeemed*

Garda (GAR-duh)
Teutonic — *The protected*

Garland (GAR-land)
French — *Garland*

Garnet (GAR-net)
Teutonic — *Radiant red jewel*
Ganit, Garnette

Gauri (GOW-rē)
Hindi — *Yellow*

Gavrila (ga-VRIL-uh)
Hebrew — *Heroine*

Gay (GĀ)
English — *Lighthearted*
Gae, Gaye

Gazit (GĀZ-it)
Hebrew — *Hewn stone*

GABRIELLE—*God is my strength*

Gemini (JEM-i-nē) or (JEM-i-nī)
Greek— *Twin*
Gemina

Gemma (JEM-uh)
Latin, Italian— *Jewel*

Gene (JĒN)
See Eugenia.
Gena, Gina

Geneva (ja-NĒV-uh)
French— *The juniper tree*
Gena, Genevra, Ginevra, Janeva

Genevieve (JEN-uh-vēv)
Celtic— *White or pure*
Biblical: St. Genevieve is the patron
  saint of Paris.
Literature: Genevieve Taggard,
  American poet and critic.
Entertainment: Genevieve Bujold,
  actress.
**Gena, Geneva, Genevera,
Genevra, Gennie, Gina,
Ginny, Janeva, Jennie,
Jenny**

97

Georgia (JOR-juh)
Greek— *Husbandman*
Feminine form of George.
Entertainment: Song *Sweet Georgia
Brown.*
**George, Georgeanna, Georgeanne,
Georagena, Georgetta, Georgette,
Georgi, Georgiana, Georgianna,
Georgianne, Georgie, Georgina,
Georgine, Giorgia**

Geraldine (JER-al-dēn)
Teutonic— *Ruler with a spear*
Feminine form of Gerald.
Entertainment: Geraldine Chaplin,
actress and daughter of Charlie
Chaplin; Geraldine Farrar,
singer; Geraldine, character of
comedian Flip Wilson.
**Geralda, Gerhardine, Geri,
Gerianna, Gerianne, Gerri,
Gerrie, Gerrilee, Gerry,
Gerrylee, Giralda, Jeraldine,
Jeralee, Jere, Jeri, Jerrie,
Jerrilee, Jerry, Jerrylee**

Gerda (GER-duh)
Scandinavian— *Protection*
Garda, Gerdi

Germaine (jer-MĀN)
French— *A German*
Celtic— *The shouter*
Literature: Germaine Greer,
author.
Germain, Germana

Gertrude (GER-trōōd)
Teutonic— *Spear-maiden*
Literature: Gertrude Stein, author.
Entertainment: Gertrude
Lawrence, actress.
**Gerda, Gert, Gerta, Gerti,
Gertie, Gertrud, Gertruda,
Gertrudis, Gerty, Trude,
Trudi, Trudie, Trudy**

Gilada (gil-Ā-duh)
Hebrew— *My joy is eternal*
Entertainment: Daughter of
Rigoletto in Verdi's opera,
Rigoletto.

Gilberte (GIL-bert) or
(JIL-ber-tuh)
Teutonic— *Hostage*
Feminine form of Gilbert.
**Berta, Berte, Berti, Bertie,
Berty, Gigi, Gilberta, Gilbertina,
Gilbertine, Gill, Gilli, Gillie,
Gilly**

Gilda (GIL-duh)
Celtic— *God's servant*
Entertainment: Gilda Gray, Gilda
Radner, actresses.
Gilli

Gillian (GIL-ē-un) or (JIL-ē-un)
Latin— *Youthful*
**Gill, Gillia, Jilana, Jile,
Jillis, Jilly, Julia, Juliana**

Gimra (JIM-ruh)
Hebrew— *Ripened*

Gina (JĒN-uh)
Japanese— *Silvery*
Entertainment: Gina Lollobrigida,
actress.

Ginger (JIN-jer)
Latin— *Ginger*
Entertainment: Ginger Rogers,
actress and dancer.
Ginny, Jinger, Virginia

Giselle (juh-ZEL)
Teutonic— *A promise*
Entertainment: Giselle McKenzie,
singer.
Gisela, Gisele, Gisella, Gizela

Gittel (GIT-el)
Hebrew— *Maiden of the winepress*
Gitel, Gitle, Gittle

Gizi (JĒ-zē)
Hungarian— *Pledge*
Giselle, Gizela, Gizike, Gizus

Gladys (GLAD-is)
Latin — *Frail*
Celtic — *Princess*
Feminine form of Claude.
Entertainment: Gladys Swarthout, actress; Gladys Knight and the Pips, rock group.
Glad, Gladdie, Gladine, Gladis, Glady, Gladyce

Glenna (GLEN-nuh)
Gaelic — *From the valley*
Feminine form of Glen.
Entertainment: Glynis Johns, Glenda Jackson, actresses.
Glen, Glenda, Glenine, Glenn, Glennie, Glennis, Glyn, Glynis, Glynnis

Gloria (GLOR-ē-uh)
Latin — *The glorious*
Entertainment: Gloria Swanson, actress.
Glori, Gloriana, Gloriane, Glorianna, Glory

Goldie (GOL-dē)
Teutonic — *The golden-haired one*
Famous: Golda Meir, Prime Minister of Israel.
Entertainment: Goldie Hawn, actress.
Golda, Goldi, Goldy

Grace (GRĀS)
Latin — *The graceful*
Mythological: The three graces of mythology are beauty, joy and grace.
Famous: Princess Grace of Monaco, the former Grace Kelly.
Entertainment: Grace Slick, rock singer; Gracie Burns, actress and wife of George Burns.
Gracia, Gracie, Gracye, Grata, Gratia, Gratiana, Gray, Grayce, Grazia

Grania (GRAN-yuh)
Celtic — *Love*
Interesting: Gaelic folklore heroine.

Gratiana (grat-ē-AN-uh)
Latin — *Divine favor*
Grania, Grata, Gratia

Greer (GRĒR)
Greek — *Watchful*
Feminine form of Gregory.
Entertainment: Greer Garson, actress.

Greta (GRET-uh)
Slavic — *A pearl*
Entertainment: Greta Garbo, actress.
Gretchen, Grete, Gretel, Gretta

Griselda (gri-ZEL-duh)
Teutonic — *The heroine*
Griseldis, Grishilda, Grishilde, Grissel, Grizel, Grizelda, Selda, Zelda

Guinevere (GWEN-a-vēr)
Welsh — *Fair lady*
Literature: Wife of King Arthur in the Round Table legend.
Famous: Oona Chaplin, wife of Charlie Chaplin.
Gaynor, Gen, Genevieve, Genna, Genni, Gennie, Gennifer, Genny, Ginevra, Guenevere, Guenna, Guinna, Gwen, Gwendolen, Gwendolin, Gwendolyn, Gweneth, Gwenith, Gwenn, Gwenora, Gwenore, Gwyn, Gwynne, Jan, Janifer, Jen, Jenifer, Jennee, Jenni, Jennie, Jennifer, Jenny, Ona, Oona, Una, Winifred, Winni, Winnie, Winny

Gussie (GUS-ē)
See Augusta.

Gwendolyn (GWEN-dol-en)
Welsh — *White-browed*
Literature: Wife of Merlin in King Arthur legend.
Guendolen, Guenna, Gwen, Gwendolen, Gwenni, Gwennie, Gwenny, Gwyn, Gwyneth, Wanda, Wendie, Wendy, Wynne

Gypsy (JIP-sē)
Old English — *Wander*
Gipsy

Habibah (ha-BĒ-buh)
Arabic — *Beloved*
Feminine form of Habib.
Haviva

Hadassah (huh-DOS-uh)
Hebrew — *Myrtle*
Esther

Hadiya (ha-DĒ-yuh) or
(HĀ-dē-yuh)
Swahili — *Gift*

Hagar (HĀ-gar)
Hebrew — *One who flees*
Biblical: Mother of Ishmael.
Haggar, Hagit

Haidee (HĀ-dē)
Greek — *Respectful*
Entertainment: Haidee Wright,
actress.

Haila (HĀ-luh)
German — *Healthy, strong*
Entertainment: Haila Stoddard,
actress.

Haldis (HAL-dis)
Teutonic — *Stone spirit*

Hali (HĀ-lē)
Greek — *Sea*
Feminine form of Henry.
Entertainment: Hayley Mills,
actress.
**Halette, Halimeda, Hallie,
Hally, Hayley**

Hallie (HAL-ē)
Greek — *Thinking of the sea*
Hanrieta, Harriet

Halona (ha-LŌ-nuh)
American Indian — *Of happy fortune*

Hama (HA-muh)
Japanese — *Shore*
Hamako

Hana (HA-nuh)
Japanese — *Flower*
Hanae, Hanako, Hauna, Haunah

Haniya (ha-NĒ-yuh) or
(HĀ-ne-yuh)
Hebrew — *Resting place*
Hania, Hanice, Hanit

Hannah (HAN-nuh)
Hebrew — *Grace, mercy or prayer*
Biblical: Mother of the prophet
Samuel.
**Hana, Hanna, Hanni, Hannie,
Hanny**

Hannele (ha-NĒL)
German, Hebrew — *Merciful*
Hanna, Hannah, Hanne, Hanni

Happy (HA-pē)
English — *Happy child*

Hara (HAR-uh)
Sanskrit — *Seizer*
Mythological: Another name for
the god Shiva.

Harmony (HAR-mō-nē)
Latin — *Harmony*
Harmonia, Harmonic

Harriet (HAR-ē-et)
French — *Ruler of the home*
Feminine form of Henry.
Literature: Harriet Beecher Stowe,
  author of *Uncle Tom's Cabin*.
**Harri, Harrie, Harrietta,
Harriette, Harriot, Harriott,
Hatti, Hattie, Hatty**

Hasina (ha-SĒ-nuh)
Swahili — *Good*
Hebrew — *Strong*

Hattie (HA-tē)
Teutonic — *Mistress of the home*
Harriet, Hatti, Hatty, Henrietta

Hazel (HĀ-zel)
Old English — *Authority or
  commander*

Heather (HETH-er)
Anglo-Saxon — *A flower*
Entertainment: Heather Angel,
  actress.
Heath

Hebe (HĒ-bē)
Greek — *Youth*
Mythological: Cupbearer of the
  Gods.

Hedda (HED-uh)
Teutonic — *War*
Literature: Hedda Gabler, heroine
  of one of Ibsen's plays.
Entertainment: Hedda Hopper,
  Hollywood columnist; Hedy
  Lamar, actress.
**Heda, Heddi, Heddie, Heddy,
Hedvige, Hedwig, Hedwiga,
Hedy**

Hedia (HE-dē-yuh)
Hebrew — *The voice of God*
Hedya

Hedva (HED-vuh)
Hebrew — *Joy*

Hedwig (HED-wig)
German — *Strife*
**Edvig, Edwig, Hedda, Hedi,
Hedvig, Hedy**

Heidi (HĪ-dē)
German — *Battle-maiden*
Literature: *Heidi,* children's classic
  by Johanna Spuri.
Heidie, Hilda

Helen (HEL-un)
Greek — *Light*
Famous: Helen of Troy.
Literature: Helen Keller, author.
Entertainment: Helen Hayes,
  actress; Helen Reddy, singer.
**Aila, Aileen, Ailene, Aleen,
Eileen, Elaine, Elana, Elane,
Elayne, Eleanor, Eleanore, Eleen,
Elena, Elene, Eleni, Elenitsa,
Elenore, Eleonora, Eleonore,
Elianora, Elinor, Elinore, Ella,
Elladine, Elle, Ellen, Ellene,
Ellette, Elli, Ellie, Estonian,
Galina, Helena, Helene,
Helenka, Hellene, Helli, Ileana,
Ileane, Ilene, Ilona, Ilonka,
Jelena, Lana, Leanor, Leanore,
Leen, Lena, Lenka, Lenora,
Lenore, Leonora, Leonore,
Leora, Lina, Lora, Nell, Nelli,
Nellie, Nelly, Nora, Norah**

Helga (HEL-guh)
Teutonic — *Holy*
Olga

Helma (HEL-muh)
German — *Helmet*
Feminine form of William.
**Helmine, Mina, Minchen,
Mine, Minna**

Heloise (HEL-ō-ēs)
French — *Famous in battle*
Literature: *Hints from Heloise*
  newspaper column.

Helsa (HEL-suh)
Hebrew — *Given to God*

HESTER—*A star*

Henrietta (hen-rē-ET-uh)
French — *Mistress of the home*
Feminine form of Henry.
Famous: Henrietta Szold,
  American Zionist leader.
Literature: Henriette, a heroine in
  Moliere's *Les Femmes Savantes*.
**Enrichetta, Enriqueta, Etta,
Etti, Ettie, Etty, Hatti, Hattie,
Hatty, Hendrika, Henka, Henrie,
Henrieta, Henriette, Henryetta,
Hetti, Hettie, Hetty, Yetta,
Yettie, Yetty**

Hephzibah (HEP-si-buh)
Hebrew — *My delight is in her*
Biblical: Wife of King Hezekiah.
Literature: Heroine of
  Hawthorne's *House of Seven
  Gables*.
**Hephziba, Hepsiba, Hepsibah,
Hepsibetha, Hepzibeth**

Hera (HAIR-uh)
Greek — *Queen of the Gods*

Hermione (her-MĪ-ō-nē)
Greek— *Of the earth*
Feminine form of Herman.
Mythological: Daughter of Helen
   of Troy.
Literature: Queen in Shakespeare's
   The Winter's Tale.
Entertainment: Hermione
   Gingold, actress.
**Erma, Harmione, Hermia,
Hermina, Hermine, Herminia,
Hermionia**

Hermosa (her-MŌ-suh)
Spanish— *Beautiful*

Hertha (HERTH-uh)
Teutonic— *Mother earth*
Mythological: Earth goddess;
   goddess of fertility and peace.
Entertainment: Eartha Kitt, singer.
Eartha, Erda, Erta

Hesper (HES-per)
Greek— *The evening star*

Hester (HES-ter)
Greek— *A star*
Literature: Hester Prynne, heroine
   of Hawthorne's *The Scarlet Letter.*
Hestia, Hettie, Hey

Hestia (HES-tē-uh)
Persian— *A star*
Mythological: Goddess of the
   home.

Hetty (HET-ē)
Persian— *A star*
Esther, Hester

Hilary (HIL-uh-rē)
Greek— *Cheerful or merry*
Hillary

Hilda (HIL-duh)
Teutonic— *Woman warrior*
Literature: Hilda Doolittle, poet.
Hilde, Hildy

Hildegarde (HIL-duh-gard)
Teutonic— *Fortress*
**Hilda, Hildagard, Hildagarde,
Hilde, Hildegaard**

Hinda (HIN-duh)
Anglo-Saxon— *Female deer*
Hynda

Hoa (HŌ-uh)
Vietnamese— *Flower*

Holly (HAWL-ē)
Old English— *Holly tree*
Literature: *Hollie Hobby,* heroine of
   children's books and greeting
   cards.
Holley, Holli, Hollie

Honey (HUN-ē)
German— *Sweet*
Honora, Honoria

Honora (on-OR-uh)
Latin— *Honorable*
**Honey, Honor, Honoria,
Honorine, Nora, Norah,
Norri, Norrie, Norry**

Hope (HŌP)
Anglo-Saxon— *Optimistic and
   cheerful*
Entertainment: Hope Lang, actress.

Hortense (HOR-tens)
Latin— *Gardener*
Hortensie, Ortensia

Hoshi (HŌ-shē)
Japanese— *A star*

Huberta (Ū-ber-tuh)
Teutonic— *Bright-minded*
Feminine form of Hubert.

Huette (Ū-et)
Teutonic— *Small, intelligent girl*
Feminine form of Hugh.
Hugette, Huguette

Hulda (HUL-duh)
Austrian— *Gracious*
Hebrew— *Weasel*
Huldah

Huyana (hī-AN-uh)
Miwok Indian— *Rain falling*

Hyacinth (HĪ-uh-sinth)
Greek — *Hyacinth flower*
**Giacinta, Huacintha, Hyacinthe,
Hyacinthia, Hyacinthie, Jacenta,
Jacinda, Jacinta, Jacintha,
Jacinthe, Jacynth**

Hypatia (hī-PA-tē-uh)
Greek — *Surpassing*

Ianthe (Ē-anth)
Greek — *Purple flower*
Ian

Ida (I-duh)
Old English — *Prosperous*
German — *Hard-working*
Literature: Heroine of *The Princess*,
a poem by Tennyson.
Entertainment: Ida Lupino, actress.
**Idalia, Idalina, Idaline, Idelle,
Idette**

Idelia (ī-duh-LĒ-uh)
Teutonic — *Noble*

Idona (Ī-DŌ-nuh)
Teutonic — *Industrious*

Ignacia (ig-NĀ-sē-uh)
Latin — *Ardent or fiery*
Ignatia, Ignatzia

Ilana (i-LA-nuh)
Hebrew — *Big tree*

Ilene (ī-LĒN)
See Aileen or Eileen.
Iline, Illene, Illona

Ilka (IL-kuh)
Slavic — *Hard-worker*
Literature: Ilka Chase.
Ilke, Milka

Ilona (IL-ō-nuh)
Hungarian — *Beautiful*
**Ica, Ila, Ilka, Ilonka, Ilu,
Iluska, Lenci**

Imala (IM-al-uh) or (i-MĀ-luh)
North American
Indian — *Disciplinarian*

Imogene (IM-ō-jēn)
Latin — *An image*
Literature: Heroine in *Cymbeline*,
by Shakespeare.
Entertainment: Imogene Coca,
comedienne.
Emogene, Imogen, Imojean

Ina (Ī-nuh)
See Katherine.
Famous: Ina Coolbrith,
stateswoman and poetess.
Entertainment: Ina Claire,
comedienne.

Ines (ī-NEZ)
Greek — *Chaste*
Literature: Mother of Don Juan in
Byron's poem.
Inesita, Inez, Ynes, Ynez

Ingrid (ING-rid)
Swedish — *Hero's daughter*
Entertainment: Inga Swenson,
Inger Stevens, Ingrid Bergman,
actresses; Inge Borkh, singer.
Inga, Inge, Inger

Iona (ī-Ō-nuh)
Greek — *A violet*
Literature: Heroine of *The Last
Days of Pompeii*, by Sir Edward
Bulwer-Lytton.

IRIS—*The rainbow*

Iphigenia (if-uh-juh-NĒ-uh)
Greek—*Sacrifice*
Mythological: Maiden to be
sacrificed, but rescued by Artemis.

Irene (ī-RĒN)
Greek—*Peace*
Famous: Scientists Irene and
Frederic Joliot Curie, winners of
Noble Prize in medicine.
Entertainment: Irene Dunn,
actress.

Iris (Ī-ris)
Greek—*The rainbow*
Literature: Iris Murdoch, novelist.
Irisa, Irita

Irma (ER-muh)
German—*Power*
**Erma, Erme, Irme,
Irmina, Irmine**

105

Isabel (IZ-uh-bel)
Spanish— *Consecrated to God*
Historical: Queen Isabella sent
  Christopher Columbus on his
  voyage to the new world.
Literature: Poem *Isabella* or *The Pot
  of Basil.*
**Belia, Belicia, Belita, Bell,
Bella, Belle, Ibbie, Ibby, Isa,
Isabeau, Isabelita, Isabella,
Isabelle, Iseabal, Issi, Issie,
Issy, Izabel, Ysabel**

Isadora (iz-uh-DOR-uh)
Greek— *Gift of the moon*
Entertainment: Isadora Duncan,
  dancer.
**Dora, Dori, Dory, Isidora,
Issy, Izzy**

Isis (Ī-sis)
Egyptian— *Supreme goddess*
Interesting: Egyptian goddess of
  the beginning of time and
  mother of all things.

Isolda (iz-ŌL-duh)
Celtic— *The fair*
Literature: *Tristan and Isolde,* by
  Gottfried Von Strassburg.
Isolde, Isolt, Yseult

Ivana (i-VA-nuh)
Hebrew— *God is gracious gift*
Feminine form of Ivan.
Ivane

Ivilla (i-VIL-uh)
Afro-American— *I will arise again*

Ivy (Ī-vē)
Greek, German— *Ivy tree*
Literature: Ivy Compton-Burnett,
  British novelist.
Ivie, Ivi

Izusa (i-ZOO-zuh)
North American Indian— *White
  snow*

Jacinda (ha-SIN-duh)
Greek— *Beautiful, comely*
Jacenta, Jacinta, Jacynth

Jacoba (JĀ-kō-buh) or
  (YAK-uh-buh)
Hebrew— *Supplanter*
Feminine form of Jacob.
**Jacki, Jackie, Jacky,
Jacobina, Jacobine**

Jacqueline (JAK-wil-in)
Hebrew— *Supplanter*
French— *Little Jacques*
Famous: Jacqueline Kennedy,
  former First Lady.
Entertainment: Jaclyn Smith,
  Jacqueline Bisset, actresses.
**Jackelyn, Jacki, Jackie, Jacklin,
Jackquelin, Jackqueline, Jacky,
Jaclin, Jaclyn, Jacque,
Jacquelyn, Jacquetta,
Jacquette, Jacquie,
Jaquenetta, Jaquenette, Jaquith**

Jade (JĀD)
Hebrew— *Wise*
Jadah, Jadda

Jael (JĀ-el)
Hebrew— *Mountain goat*

Jafit (JAF-it)
Hebrew— *Lovely*

Jaimie (JĀ-mē)
French — *I love*
Jaime

Jambu (JAM-boo)
Hindi — *Rose apple tree*

Jamie (JĀ-mē)
Feminine form of James.
Jamee, Jamesina, Jami, Jayme, Jaymee

Jamila (juh-MĒL-uh)
Muslim — *Beautiful*

Jane (JĀN)
Hebrew — *God's gracious gift*
Feminine form of John.
Famous: *Jane Eyre*, novel by
Charlotte Bronte; *Pride and Prejudice*, by Jane Austen; Jane, mate of Tarzan, in novel by Edgar Rice Burroughs.
Entertainment: Jane Pauley, newscaster; Jane Wyman, Jane Fonda, Jane Alexander, actresses; Janis Joplin, singer and songwriter.
Gene, Gianina, Giovanna, Jan, Jana, Janeczka, Janel, Janela, Janella, Janelle, Janet, Janetta, Janette, Janey, Jania, Janice, Janie, Janina, Janine, Janis, Janith, Janka, Janna, Jannel, Janyte, Jasisa, Jayne, Jean, Jeanette, Jeannine, Jenda, Jenica, Jeniece, Jenni, Jennie, Jenny, Jess, Jessie, Jinny, Jo-Ann, JoAnn, Joan, Joane, Joanna, Joanne, Joanta, Joasia, Joeann, Johanna, Joni, Jonie, Juana, Juanita, Sheena, Shena, Sine, Vania, Vanya, Zanela, Zanna

Janet (JAN-it)
See Jane.
Entertainment: Janet Blair, Janet Leigh, actresses; Janis Ian, singer.
Janice, Janis, Janot, Jessie

Jardena (jar-DĒ-nuh)
Hebrew — *To flow downward*
Feminine form of Jordan.

Jasmine (JAZ-min)
Persian — *Fragrant flower*
Jamina, Jasmin, Jasmina, Jemi, Jemie, Jemmy, Jessamine, Jessamyn, Yasmin

Jay (JĀ)
Latin — *Jaybird*
Jae, Jaie, Jaye

Jayne (JĀN)
Hindi — *Victorious*
Entertainment: Jayne Mansfield, actress.

Jean (JĒN)
See Jane.
Famous: Jeane Dixon, ESP-user and fortuneteller.
Entertainment: Jean Arthur, Jean Stapleton, Jeanette Nolan, actresses.
Gene, Jeane, Jeanette, Jeanie, Jeanne, Jeannette, Jeannine, Joan, Nina, Ninon

Jemima (juh-MĪ-muh)
Hebrew — *A dove*
Jamima, Jemie, Jemimah, Jemmie, Jemmy

Jennifer (JEN-i-fer)
Welsh — *White, fair*
Entertainment: Jennifer O'Neill, actress.
Genna, Genni, Gennie, Gennifer, Genny, Jen, Jennee, Jenni, Jennie, Jenny

Jenny (JE-nē)
See Jane.
Entertainment: Jenny Lind, opera singer.
Janey, Jen, Jennie, Jinny

Jensine (jen-SĒN)
Danish, Hebrew — *God is gracious*

Jerri (JER-ē)
See Geraldine.
Jeraldine, Jerrie, Jerry, Jeryl, Jerylin

Jessica (JES-i-kuh)
Hebrew — *Wealthy*
Feminine form of Jesse.
Entertainment: Jessica Savitch, newscaster; Jessica Dragonette, singer; Jessica Tandy, heroine of Tennesee Williams' *A Streetcar Named Desire.*
Jess, Jessalin, Jessalyn, Jesse, Jessi, Jessie, Jessy

Jewel (JOO-ul)
Latin — *Precious stone*
Jewell, Jewelle

Jill (JIL)
See Julia.
Famous: Queen Juliana of the Netherlands.
Literature: Nursery rhyme, *Jack and Jill.*
Entertainment: Jill Ireland, Jill St. John, Jill Clayburgh, actresses.
Jillana, Jillen, Jilleun, Juliana

Jinny (JI-nē)
See Virginia.
Jenni, Jennie, Jenny, Jin, Jinnie

Joan (JŌN)
Hebrew — *God's gracious joy*
Famous: Joan of Arc.
Literature: *St. Joan,* play by George Bernard Shaw; Jo, heroine of Louisa May Alcott's *Little Women.*
Entertainment: Joanne Woodward, Joan Crawford, actresses; Joan Rivers, comedienne.
Jo, Joana, Joanna, Joanne, Jodi, Jodie, Jody, Joeann, Johanna

Jobina (jō-BĒ-nuh)
American — *Persecuted*
Feminine form of Job.
Jobey, Jobi, Jobie, Joby, Jobye, Jobyna

Jocelyn (JOS-len)
Latin — *Merry*
Old English — *Just*
Jocelin, Joceline, Josselyan, Josselyn, Joyce, Joycelin, Lyn, Lynn

Jody (JŌ-dē)
See Joan.
Entertainment: Jodie Foster, actress; Joni Mitchell, singer.
Jodee, Jodi, Jodie, Joni, Judith

Joella (jō-EL-uh)
Hebrew — *The Lord is willing*
Feminine form of Joel.
Joela, Joelle, Joellen, Jola, Jolanka, Jolanta, Joli, Yolanda

Jolan (JŌ-lan)
Greek — *Violet blossom*

Jolie (JŌ-lē)
French — *Pretty*
Jolan, Joli, Joly

Joline (JŌ-lēn)
English — *He will increase*
Feminine form of Joseph.

Jonine (jō-NĒN)
Hebrew — *Dove*
Jonati, Jonina, Jonit, Yonina, Yonit, Yonita

Jora (JOR-uh)
Hebrew — *Autumn rain*
Jorah

Josephine (JŌ-sa-fēn)
Hebrew — *He shall increase*
Feminine form of Joseph.
Famous: Napoleon's wife, Empress Josephine.
Fifi, Fifine, Fina, Jo, Joette, Joey, Joline, Josefa, Josefina, Josepha, Josephina, Josi, Josie, Josy

Joy (JOI)
Latin — *Merry*
Joya

JORA — *Autumn rain*

Joyce (JOIS)
Latin — *Rejoicing*
Famous: Dr. Joyce Brothers,
   psychologist.
Literature: Joyce Carol Oates,
   author.
Jocelyn, Joice, Joyous

Juanita (wa-NĒ-tuh)
See Jane.
Entertainment: Song *Juanita*.

Judith (JOO-dith)
Hebrew — *Admired*
Entertainment: Dame Judith
   Anderson, actress.
**Guiditta, Jodi, Jodie, Jody,
Judi, Judie, Juditha, Judy, Judye**

109

Judy (JŌŌ-dē)
See Judith.
Literature: Judy Blume, children's author.
Entertainment: Judy Garland, Judy Holiday, actresses.

Julia (JŌŌ-lē-uh)
Latin— *Youthful*
Feminine form of Julius.
Famous: Julia Child, gourmet cook and author.
Literature: Julia Peterkin, author.
Entertainment: Julia Marlowe, actress.
Giulia, Giulietta, Joletta, Julee, Juli, Juliana, Juliane, Juliann, Julianne, Julie, Julienne, Juliet, Julieta, Julietta, Juliette, Julina, Juline, Julita, Julius

Julie (JŌŌ-lē)
See Julia.
Entertainment: Julie Christie, Julie Harris, Julie Andrews, Julie Newmar, actresses.
Juliene, Julienne

Juliet (jōō-lē-ET)
See Julia.
Literature: Heroine of Shakespeare's *Romeo and Juliet*.
Entertainment: Juliet Prowse, modern dancer.
Julietta, Juliette, Julita

June (JŌŌN)
Latin— *Youthful*
Entertainment: June Lockhart, actress.
Junetta, Junette, Junia, Junieta, Junina, Junis

Juno (JŌŌ-nō)
Latin— *Queen of the gods*
Mythological: Goddess of heaven, wife of Jupiter. Also a special guard of women.

Justine (just-ĒN)
Latin— *Just*
Feminine form of Justin.
Giustina, Justina, Justinn, Tina

Jyotis (JĪ-ō-tis)
East Indian— *Sun's light*
Jiotis

Kachina (ka-CHĒ-nuh)
North American Indian— *Sacred dancer*

Kagami (ka-GAM-ē)
Japanese— *Mirror*

Kaimi (ka-Ē-mē)
Polynesian— *The seeker*

Kala (KAL-uh)
Hindi— *Black or time*

Kalama (ka-LAM-uh)
Polynesian— *The flaming torch*

Kalanit (ka-LAN-it)
Hebrew— *Flower*

Kali (KĀL-ē)
Sanskrit— *Energy*
Hindi— *The black goddess*
Interesting: Hindi mother goddess.

Kalila (kuh-LĪ-luh)
Arabic — *Girlfriend or sweetheart*

Kalinda (ka-LIN-duh)
Hindi — *The sun*
Kalindi

Kalyca (ka-LĒ-kuh)
Greek — *Rosebud*
Kali, Kalica, Kalika, Kaly

Kama (KAM-uh)
Hindi — *Love*
Mythological: This goddess rode a
parrot and shot flower-tipped
love arrows from a bow.

Kamaria (ka-MAR-ē-uh)
Swahili — *Like the moon*

Kameko (ka-MĒ-kō)
Japanese — *Child of the tortoise*
Mythological: The tortoise
symbolizes longevity.

Kanani (ka-NA-nē)
Polynesian — *The beauty*

Kanene (ka-NĒN)
African — *A little thing in the eye is
big*

Kanoa (ka-NŌ-uh)
Polynesian — *The free one*

Kanya (KON-yuh)
Hindi — *Virgin*

Kapua (ka-POO-uh)
Polynesian — *Blossom*

Kapule (ka-POOL)
Polynesian — *A prayer*

Kara (KAIR-uh)
Greek — *Pure*
Karena, Katharine

Karen (KAIR-en)
Greek, Danish — *Pure*
Famous: Karen Horney,
psychiatrist.
Entertainment: Karen Black,
actress; Karen Carpenter, singer
and songwriter.
**Caren, Carin, Karena, Kari,
Karin, Karna**

Kasia (KĀZ-yuh)
Polish, Greek — *Pure*
Kassia

Kate (KĀT)
Greek — *Pure*
Entertainment: Kate Smith, singer;
Kate Jackson, actress.
Katee, Kati, Katie

Katherine (KATH-er-in)
Greek — *Pure*
Historical: Queen Catherine the
Great, of Russia.
Entertainment: Katherine
Hepburn, Katherine Cornell,
Katherine Ross, Kitty Carlisle,
actresses; Katerina Valenti,
singer.
**Caisie, Caitlin, Caitrin, Caren,
Carin, Caron, Caryn, Cass,
Cassy, Cataina, Catarina, Cate,
Catee, Caterina, Catha, Catharina,
Catharine, Cathe, Cathee,
Catherina, Catherine, Cathi,
Cathie, Cathleen, Cathlene,
Cathrine, Cathryn, Cathy,
Cathyleen, Cati, Catriona,
Caty, Caye, Ekaterina,
Ekaterine, Karen, Karena,
Kari, Karin, Karna, Kass,
Kassi, Kassia, Kassie, Kata,
Katalin, Katalina, Kate,
Katerina, Katerine, Katey,
Katha, Katharine, Kathe,
Kathi, Kathie, Kathleen,
Kathryn, Kathy, Kathye,
Katie, Katina, Katinka,
Katrinka, Katrinkie, Katti,
Katuscha, Katushka, Katya,
Kay, Kaye, Ketti, Kettie,
Ketty, Kit, Kitti, Kittie, Kitty**

KAMEKO — *Child of the tortoise*

Kathleen (kath-LĒN)
  See Katherine.
  Entertainment: Song *I'll Take You Home Again, Kathleen.*

Kathy (KATH-ē)
  See Katherine.
  Kathleen

Kaula (ka-OO-luh)
  Polynesian — *Prophet*

Kavindra (ka-VIN-druh)
  Hindi — *Mighty poet*

Kay (KĀ)
  See Katherine.
  Literature: Kay Boyle, novelist and short-story writer.

Kei (KĒ-uh)
  Japanese — *Rapture*
  Keiko

Kelly (KEL-ē)
  Gaelic — *Warrior woman*
  Keelia, Keely, Kelley, Kelli, Kellia, Kellie

Kelsey (KEL-sē)
Norwegian— *From the ship island*
Kelci, Kelcie, Kelcy, Kelda, Kelsi, Kelsy

Kendra (KEN-druh)
Anglo-Saxon— *The knowing woman*

Kim (KIM)
Old English— *Chief, ruler*
Entertainment: Kim Novak, Kim Hunter, actresses.

Kimama (ki-MAW-muh)
Shoshone Indian— *Butterfly*

Kimberly (KIM-ber-lē)
Old English— *From the royal fortress meadow*
Cimberly, Cymbre, Kim, Kimbra, Kimbre, Kimmie

Kira (KĒR-uh)
Persian— *Sun*

Kirby (KIR-bē)
Anglo-Saxon— *From the church town*
Kirbee, Kirbie

Kirima (ka-RĒ-muh)
Eskimo— *A hill*
Kirimia

Kirsten (KER-sten)
Scandinavian— *The anointed one*
Kirsti, Kirstin, Kristie

Kisa (KĒ-suh)
Russian— *Kitty*

Kitty (KI-tē)
See Katherine.
Literature: *Kitty Foyle,* novel by Christopher Morley.
Entertainment: Miss Kitty, heroine of TV series *Gunsmoke.*

Kiva (KĒ-vuh)
Russian, Hebrew— *Hope*

Klarika (kla-RĒ-kuh)
Hungarian— *Brilliant*
Klara, Klarissa, Klarysa

Kolina (kō-LĒN-uh)
Swedish, Greek— *Pure*
Katina, Kola

Koma (KŌ-muh)
Japanese— *Filly*
Komako

Kora (KOR-uh)
Greek— *Maiden*
Cora, Corabel, Corabella, Corabelle, Corella, Corena, Corene, Coretta, Corette, Corey, Cori, Corie, Corina, Corinna, Corinne, Coriss, Corissa, Corrina, Corrine, Corry, Kore, Koren, Kori, Korie

Kristen (KRIS-ten)
See Christine.
Entertainment: Kristy McNichols, actress.
Krista, Kristel, Kristi, Kristian, Kristiana, Kristin, Kristine, Kristy, Krysta, Krytyna

Kyle (KĪL)
Gaelic— *Comely*
Entertainment: Kyle MacDonnell, actress.

Lahela (la-HĒ-luh)
Polynesian, Hebrew — *Ewe*
Rachel, Rahela

Lala (LĀ-luh)
Slavak — *Tulip*

Lalage (la-LAWJ)
Greek — *Free of speech*

Lalasa (la-LAW-suh)
Hindi — *Love*

Lana (LA-nuh)
Polynesian — *To float*
Entertainment: Lana Turner,
actress.
**Lane, Lanna, Lanny,
Linette, Linnette**

Lane (LĀN)
English — *From the narrow road*
Entertainment: Lanie Kazan,
actress.
Laney, Lanie, Lanni, Lanny

Lani (LA-nē)
Polynesian — *Sky*

Lara (LAR-uh)
Latin — *Well-known*
Mythological: Nymph punished
for her talkativeness.
Literature: Lara, heroine in the
novel *Dr. Zhivago*.
Laraine, Laura, Lorriane

Laraine (luh-RĀN)
Latin — *Sea-bird*
Entertainment: Lorraine Day,
Laraine Newman, actresses.
**Lara, Larina, Larine, Laura,
Lorraine**

Lari (lar-Ē)
English — *Crowned with laurel*

Larissa (lar-RĒ-suh) or (la-RIS-uh)
Russian, Greek — *Cheerful one*
Lacey, Lara, Larochka, Lissa

Lark (LARK)
English — *Skylark*

Laura (LOR-uh)
Latin — *Crown of laurel*
Entertainment: Lauren Bacall,
actress.
**Lari, Laure, Laureen, Laurel,
Laurella, Lauren, Laurena,
Laurene, Lauretta, Laurette,
Laurice, Laurie, Lora, Loralie,
Loree, Loreen, Lorelie, Loren,
Lorena, Lorene, Lorenza,
Loretta, Lorette, Lori, Lorie,
Lorinda, Lorine, Lorita, Lorna,
Lorne, Lorri, Lorrie, Lorry**

Laurel (LOR-ul)
Greek — *To gain the laurels*
Interesting: In England, the official
court poet is called Poet Laureate.
Entertainment: Laurette Taylor,
Lauren Hutton, actresses; Laurel
Hurley, Metropolitan Opera
singer.
Laurell, Lauren, Laurette

Laverne (luh-VERN)
French — *Springlike*
Mythological: Goddess of profit or
gain.
Literature: Wife of Aeneas in
Virgil's *Aeneid*.
Entertainment: Main character in
show, *Laverne and Shirley*.
**LaVerne, Laverna, Lavina,
Lavinia**

114

Leah (LĒ-uh)
Hebrew— *Weary*
Biblical: Wife of Jacob.
Entertainment: Leigh
  Taylor-Young, actress.
**Lea, Leda, Lee, Leigh,
Lia, Lida**

Leandra (lē-AN-druh)
Latin— *Like a lioness*
**Leodora, Leoine, Leoline,
Leona, Leonanie, Leonelle**

Leanne (lē-AN)
Combination of the names Lee and
Ann.
Liana, Lianne

Leda (LĒ-duh)
Greek— *Lady*
Mythological: Leda and the Swan.
Alida, Leah, Leta, Lettitia

Lee (LĒ)
Gaelic— *Poetic*
Old English— *From the pasture
  meadow*
Entertainment: Lee Grant, Lee
  Remick, actresses.
Leann, Leanna, LeeAnn, Leigh

Leila (LĀ-luh)
Arabic— *Black*
Literature: Slave girl in Byron's
  narrative poem, *The Giaour.*
**Deliah, Layla, Leela, Leilah,
Lela, Lelah, Leland, Lelia,
Lilla, Lillian**

Leilani (lā-LON-ē)
Polynesian— *Heavenly child*

Lemuela (LEM-ūl-uh)
Hebrew— *Dedicated to God*

Lena (LĒ-nuh)
Latin— *Temptress*
Hebrew— *Dwelling*
Entertainment: Lena Horne, singer
  and actress.
Lenette, Lina

Lenita (le-NĒ-tuh)
Latin— *Gentle or mild*
Leneta, Lenetta

Lenore (le-NOR)
See Helen.
Entertainment: Lenore Ulric,
  actress.
**Lenore, Leonora, Leonore,
Nora, Norah**

Leona (lē-Ō-nuh)
Latin— *Lion*
Entertainment: Leonie Rysanek,
  Metropolitan Opera singer.
**Leoine, Leola, Leone,
Leonelle, Leonie**

Leonora (lē-uh-NOR-uh)
See Helen.
Literature: Leonora Speyer,
  Pulitzer Prize winner in poetry.
Leonore, Nora, Norah

Leontine (LĒ-on-tīn)
Latin— *Brave as a lion*
Feminine form of Leo.
Entertainment: Leontyne Price,
  Metropolitan Opera singer.
Leontyne

Leora (lē-OR-uh)
Greek— *Light*

Leota (lē-Ō-tuh)
Teutonic— *Women of the people*
Leoda

Leotie (lē-Ō-tē)
North American Indian— *Prairie
  flower*

Leslie (LEZ-lē)
Scottish, Gaelic— *From the gray fort*
Entertainment: Leslie Caron,
  actress.
**Les, Lesley, Lesli, Lesly,
Lez, Lezlie**

LEILANI—*Heavenly child*

Leticia (luh-TI-shuh)
Spanish, Latin—*Gladness*
Literature: Heroine of Mary
  Robert Rinehart's *Tish* series.
**Leta, Letitia, Lettie, Letty,
Tish**

Levana (le-VAN-nuh)
Latin—*Rising sun*

Levia (la-VĒ-uh)
Hebrew—*To join*

Levina (la-VĒN-uh)
Latin—*Flash, lightning*

Lexine (leks-ĒN)
Greek—*Helper of mankind*
Lex, Lexie, Lexy

Leya (LĀ-uh)
Spanish—*Loyalty to the law*

Lian (LĪ-an)
Chinese—*The graceful willow*

Libby (LIB-ē)
Hebrew — *Consecrated to God*
Entertainment: Libby Holman,
actress.
Lib, Libbey, Libbie

Lida (LĪ-duh)
Slavic — *Beloved of people*
Lidiya, Lyda, Lydia

Lila (LĪ-luh)
Hindi — *Free will of God*
Leopoldine

Lilian (LIL-ē-un)
Greek — *A lily*
Interesting: In Egypt, the lily is
considered a symbol of life and
resurrection.
Entertainment: Lillian Gish,
actress; Lillian Hellman,
playwright.
**Lib, Lila, Lilac, Lilas, Lili,
Lilia, Liliane, Lilias, Lilis,
Lilith, Lilli, Lillie, Lilly,
Lily, Lilyan, Luika**

Lilka (LIL-kuh)
Polish — *Famous warrior-maiden*
**Liza, Lodoiska, Ludisa,
Ludka, Ludwika, Luisa**

Lily (LIL-ē)
Latin — *Lily flower*
Entertainment: Lily Pons,
Metropolitan Opera singer; Lilli
Palmer, Lily Tomlin, actresses.
**Lil, Lili, Lilith, Lilli,
Lillian, Lillie, Lilly**

Linda (LIN-duh)
Latin — *Beautiful*
Entertainment: Lynda Carter,
Linda Darnell, Linda Blair,
actresses; Linda Ronstadt, singer.
**Lind, Lindi, Lindie, Lindy,
Lynda, Lynde, Lyndy**

Lindsay (LIND-zē)
Old English — *From the linden-tree
island*
Entertainment: Lindsay Wagner,
actress.

Linette (lin-ET)
Celtic — *Graceful*
French — *Linnet bird*
**Linet, Linnet, Linnett,
Lynette, Lynnet, Lynnette**

Linnea (lin-NĀ-yuh)
Norwegian — *Lime tree*
Lynnea

Lisa (LĒ-suh)
Hebrew — *Consecrated to God*
Interesting: Tin Lizzie, nickname
for an early motor car.
Entertainment: Liza Minnelli,
singer and actress.
**Leesa, Lise, Lisetta, Lisette,
Liza, Lizetta, Lizette, Lizzie**

Lissa (LIS-uh)
English — *Honey*

Lissilma (lis-SIL-muh)
North American Indian — *Butterfly*

Livia (LIV-ē-uh)
Latin — *The olive*
Historical: Wife of Augustus.
Levvie, Livius

Lois (LŌ-is)
Greek — *Battle-maiden*
Entertainment: Lois Lane,
character in *Superman* series.

Lokelani (lō-kuh-LAN-ē)
Polynesian — *Heavenly rose*

Lola (LŌ-luh)
Spanish — *Strong woman*
Literature: *Lolita*, novel by
Vladimir Nabokov.
Entertainment: Lola Falana,
actress.
Loleta, Lolita, Lolite, Lulita

Lolly (LOL-ē)
See Laura.

Lolotea (LŌ-lō-tē-uh)
Zuni Indian — *Gift from God*

Lomasi (lō-MAS-ē)
North American Indian — *Pretty
flower*

Lona (LŌ-nuh)
English—*Single or alone*
Entertainment: Loni Anderson, actress.
Lonee, Loni, Lonni, Lonnie

Lora (LOR-uh)
See Laura.
Laura, Lorella, Lorelle, Lori

Lorelei (LOR-uh-li)
German—*Alluring*
Interesting: In German folklore, Lorelei was a siren of the Rhine.
Literature: Lorelei, heroine of Anita Loos's novel *Gentlemen Prefer Blondes*.
Lorilee, Lura, Lurette, Lurleen, Lurlene, Lurline

Lorelle (LOR-el)
Latin, Teutonic—*Little*

Lorena (lor-Ē-nuh)
Latin—*The laurel*
Feminine form of Lawrence.
Laura, Lurena

Loretta (lor-ET-uh)
See Laura.
Entertainment: Loretta Young, actress; Loretta Lynn, singer.
Lori, Lorie, Lorrie

Lorna (LOR-nuh)
Latin—*The laurel*
Literature: *Lorna Doone,* by Richard D. Blackmore.

Lorraine (lor-ĀN)
French, Teutonic—*Famous in battle*
Entertainment: Lorraine Day, actress.
Laraine, Lorain, Loraine, Lori, Lorrayne

Lottie (LOT-ē)
See Charlotte.
Entertainment: Lotte Lehmann, opera singer.
Lotta, Lotte, Lotti, Lotty

Lotus (LŌ-tus)
Egyptian, Greek—*Lotus flower*

Louella (loo-EL-uh)
See Louise.
Lou, Louela, Luella

Louise (loo-ĒS)
Teutonic—*Battle-maiden*
Feminine form of Louis.
Literature: Louisa May Alcott, author of *Little Women*.
Entertainment: Louise Lasser, actress.
Alison, Allison, Aloise, Aloisea, Aloysia, Eloisa, Eloise, Heloise, Lisette, Lois, Loise, Lola, Lotita, Lou, Louisa, Louisette, Loyce, Lu, Ludovika, Luisa, Luise, Lulita, Lulu

Love (LUV)
English—*Love*

Luana (loo-A-nuh)
German, Hebrew—*Graceful woman warrior*
Lawana, Lewanna, Louanna, Louanne, Luane, Luanni, Luwana

Luba (LOO-buh)
Slavic—*Love*
Lubba

Lucasta (loo-CAS-tuh)
Latin—*Light, chaste*
Literature: Name invented by Richard Lovelace for Lucy Sacheverell.
Lucastia, Lukasta, Lukastia

Lucerne (loo-SERN)
Latin—*Life*

Lucia (LOO-chē-uh) or (loo-SĒ-uh)
Latin—*Light*
Entertainment: Donizetti's opera *Lucia di Lammermoor,* by Sir Walter Scott.
Lucie, Lucine, Lucius

Lucille (loo-SĒL)
See Lucy.
Entertainment: Lucille Ball, actress.
Lucilla, Lucillia

Lucinda (lōō-SIN-duh)
See Lucy.
Cindy, Lucindia, Lucky

Lucretia (lōō-KRĒ-shuh)
Latin—*Rich rewards*
Interesting: In Roman legend,
   Lucretia was known for wifely
   virtues.
Entertainment: Lucrezia Bori,
   opera singer.
Lucrece, Lucrezia, Lukretia

Lucy (LŌŌ-sē)
Latin—*Light bringer*
Feminine form of Luke.
Literature: Lucie Manette, heroine
   of Dickens' *A Tale of Two Cities.*
Entertainment: Luci Arnaz, actress.
**Lu, Luce, Luci, Lucia, Luciana,
Lucie, Lucienne, Lucilla, Lucille,
Lucina, Lucinda, Lucine, Lucita,
Lucius, Luz**

Ludmilla (lōōd-MIL-uh)
Old Slavic—*Dear to the people*
Ludie, Ludovika, Mila

Luella (lōō-EL-uh)
Old English—*Elf*
Entertainment: Louella Parsons,
   Hollywood columnist.
**Loella, Lou, Louella, Lu,
Luelle, Lula, Lulu**

Lukina (lōō-KĒ-nuh)
Ukrainian—*Graceful and bright*
Luciana, Lukyna

Lulani (lōō-LA-nē)
Polynesian—*Highest point in heaven*
Luanna, Luannie

Lulu (LŌŌ-lōō)
North American Indian—*Rabbit*
Luella, Lulie

Luna (LŌŌ-nuh)
Latin—*Of the moonlight*
Mythological: Roman goddess of
   the moon.
**Lunetta, Lunette, Lunneta,
Lunnete**

Lurleen (lur-LĒN)
See Lorelei.
Famous: Lurleen Wallace,
   governor of Alabama.
Lura, Lurette, Lurlene, Lurline

Lydia (LID-ē-uh)
Latin—*A woman of Lydia*
Lidia, Lydie

Lynn (LIN)
Anglo-Saxon—*A cascade*
Entertainment: Lynn Redgrave,
   actress.
**Lyn, Lynette, Lynna, Lynne,
Lynnet**

Lyris (LIR-is)
Greek—*Lyrical*
Liris

Mabel (MĀ-bul)
Latin—*Loveable*
Literature: Mable Hoffman,
   cookbook author.
Entertainment: Mabel Normand,
   actress in silent movies;
   Maybelle Carter, singer and
   mother of June Carter.
**Amabel, Mab, Mabelle, Mable,
Mae, Maible, Maybelle**

Macha (MA-cha)
North American Indian— *The aurora*

Machi (MA-chē)
Japanese— *Ten thousand*

Madeline (MAD-uh-lin)
Hebrew— *Woman from Magdala*
Literature: Heroine of *Eve of St. Agnes,* by John Keats.
Entertainment: Madeline Kahn, actress.
Dalenna, Lena, Lenna, Lina, Linn, Lynn, Lynne, Madalena, Madalyn, Maddalena, Maddi, Maddie, Maddy, Made, Madel, Madelaine, Madeleine, Madelena, Madelene, Madelina, Madella, Madelle, Madelon, Madge, Madid, Madlen, Madlin, Mady, Magda, Magdala, Magdalena, Magdalene, Maidel, Maighdlin, Mala, Malena, Malina, Marleah, Marleen, Marlena, Marlene, Marline, Maud, Maude

Madge (MADJ)
Greek— *A pearl*

Madra (MAW-druh)
Italian— *Mother*

Mae (MĀ)
See May.
Entertainment: Mae West, actress.

Magda (MAG-duh)
Hebrew— *A high tower*
Literature: Heroine in *The Sunken Bell,* a play by Hauptmann.
Madalena, Magdala, Magdalena, Magdalina, Magdaline, Magdelene

Magena (muh-JĒN-uh)
North American Indian— *The coming moon*

Maggie (MAG-ē)
Greek— *A pearl*
Literature: Maggie Wylie, heroine of Barrie's *What Every Woman Knows;* Maggie Tulliver, heroine of *Mill on the Floss,* by George Eliot.
Mag, Maggee, Maggy

Mahala (muh-HĀ-luh)
North American Indian— *Woman*
Mahalia, Mahela, Mahila

Mahalia (muh-HĀL-yuh)
Hebrew— *Affection*
Entertainment: Mahalia Jackson, singer of spirituals.
Mahala

Mahesa (muh-HĒ-suh)
Hindi— *Great Lord*

Mahina (muh-HĒ-nuh)
Polynesian— *Moon*

Mahira (muh-HIR-uh)
Hebrew— *Quick*
Mehira

Maia (MĪ-yuh)
Greek— *Nurse or mother*
Mythological: Daughter of Atlas and Pleione; Goddess of springtime.

Maida (MĀ-duh)
Anglo-Saxon— *A maiden*
Maddie, Maddy, Mady, Magda, Maidel, Maidie, Mayda

Maisie (MĀ-sē)
Greek— *A pearl*

Malka (MAL-kuh)
Hebrew— *Queen*

Malva (MAL-vuh)
Greek— *Soft*
Famous: Malvina Hoffman, sculptor and author.
Malve, Malvina

MADRA—*Mother*

Mamie (MĀ-mē)
See Mary.
Famous: Mamie Eisenhower, wife
of President Dwight Eisenhower.

Mana (MAN-uh)
Polynesian—*Supernatural power*

Manda (MAN-duh)
Spanish—*Battle-maiden*
Armanda

Mandisa (man-DĒ-suh)
South African—*Sweet*

Mandy (MAN-dē)
English—*Worthy of love*
Mandi, Mandie

Mangena (man-JĒN-uh)
Hebrew—*Song*
Mangina

Manidatta (man-i-DAT-uh)
East Indian—*Pearl given*
Interesting: The pearl is believed to
ward off evil.

Mansi (MAN-sē)
Hopi Indian—*Plucked flower*
Mancy, Mansy

Manuela (man-WEL-uh)
Hebrew—*God with us*
Feminine form of Manuel.

Mapela (ma-PĀ-luh)
Polynesian—*Loveable*
Mabel

Mara (MAR-uh)
Hebrew—*Bigger*
Damara, Mamie, Manechka, Manette, Manya, Maralina, Maraline, Marcsa, Maretta, Marette, Mari, Maria, Marica, Marie, Marija, Marika, Marilla, Marilyn, Maring, Mariquilla, Mariquita, Marishka, Mariska, Marita, Maritsa, Mariya, Marja, Marla, Marusya, Marya, Masha, Mashenka, May, Mica, Mickam, Mimi, Miriam, Mollie, Mura, Muriel

Marcella (mar-SEL-uh)
Latin—*Warlike*
Feminine form of Mark.
Marcela, Marcelle, Marcellina, Marcelline, Marcile, Marcille, Marcy, Marquita

Marcia (MAR-shuh) or (MAR-sē-uh)
Latin—*Warlike*
Feminine form of Mark.
Entertainment: Marsha Mason, actress.
Marcelia, Marcie, Marcile, Marcille, Marcy, Marquita, Marsha

Margaret (MAR-gret)
Greek—*A pearl*
Famous: Margaret Thatcher, Prime Minister of Great Britain; Margaret Mead, anthropologist.
Literature: Margaret Mitchell, author of *Gone With The Wind*.
Entertainment: Margaret Leighton, Maggie Smith, actresses.
Greta, Gretal, Gretchen, Gretel, Grethel, Gretta, Madge, Mag, Maggi, Maggie, Maggym, Maiga, Maisie, Margalo, Margareta, Margarete, Margaretha, Margarethe, Margaretta, Margarette, Margarita, Marge, Margery, Marget, Margette, Margie, Margit, Margo, Margot, Marguerita, Marguerite, Margy, Marji, Marjie, Marjorie, Marjory, Marketa, Meg, Megan, Meggi, Meggie, Meggy, Meghan, Meta, Peg, Pegeen, Peggi, Peggie, Peggy, Rita

Margery (MAR-jer-ē)
See Margaret.
Famous: Margaux Hemingway, model, actress and granddaughter of Ernest Hemingway.
Entertainment: Marjorie Mane, actress who played the character Ma Kettle.
Margaux, Marge, Margi, Margie, Margy, Marje, Marjie, Marjorie, Marjy

Margo (MAR-gō)
See Margaret.
Entertainment: Dame Margot Fonteyn, ballet dancer; Margot Kidder, actress.
Margot, Margott

MARIS—*Of the sea*

Maria (ma-RĒ-uh)
See Mary.
Entertainment: Marie Osmond,
  singer and performer; Maria
  Tallchief, ballet dancer; Maria,
  heroine in *Sound of Music*.
Marie

Marian (MAIR-ē-un)
See Mary.
Literature: Marianne Moore,
  American poetess; Maid Marian,
  sweetheart of Robin Hood.
**Mariam, Mariana, Marianna,
Marianne, Marion, Maryann,
Maryanne**

Mariana (mair-ē-AN-uh)
See Mary.
Literature: Wife of Angelo in
  Shakespeare's *Measure for
  Measure*.

Marilyn (MAIR-uh-lin)
See Mary.
Entertainment: Marilyn Miller,
  star of the Ziegfeld Follies;
  Marilyn Monroe, actress.
**Marilee, Marilin, Marylee,
Marylin, Merrile, Merrili**

Marina (muh-RĒ-nuh)
Latin—*From the sea*
Marna, Marne, Marni, Marnie

Maris (MAR-is)
Latin — *Of the sea*
Entertainment: Marissa Berenson, actress and model.
Marisa, Marissa, Marris, Marys, Meris

Marjorie (MAR-jor-ē)
See Margery.
Literature: Marjorie Kinnan Rawlings, Pulitzer Prize winner; *Marjorie Morningstar,* novel by Herman Wouk.

Marlene (mar-LĒN)
See Marilyn.
Entertainment: Marlene Dietrich, who popularized *Lili Marlene.*
Marla, Marleen, Marlena, Marlyn, Marna

Marnie (MAR-nē)
See Marian.
Marna, Marne, Marni

Marta (MAR-tuh)
Swedish, Russian — *Mistress*

Martha (MAR-thuh)
Arabic — *A lady*
Biblical: Sister of Mary Magdalen and Lazarus.
Famous: Martha Washington, wife of President George Washington.
Entertainment: Martha Graham, pioneer of modern dance; Martha Rae, comedienne.

Mary (MAIR-ē)
Hebrew — *Bitter*
Biblical: Mother of Christ.
Entertainment: Mary, of the singing group Peter, Paul and Mary; Mary Pickford, Marlo Thomas, Mary Tyler Moore, actresses.
Mair, Maire, Mairlee, Malia, Mame, Mami, Mamie, Manon, Manya, Mara, Marabel, Maren, Maria, Mariam, Marian, Marianna, Marianne, Marice, Maridel, Marie, Mariel, Marietta, Marilee, Marilin, Marilyn, Marin, Marion, Mariquilla, Mariska, Marita, Maritsa, Marja, Marje, Marla, Marlo, Marnia, Marya, Maryann, Maryanne, Maryellen, Marylin, Marylou, Marysa, Masha, Maura, Maure, Maureen, Maurene, Maurine, Maurise, Maurizia, Mavra, Meridel, Meriel, Merrili, Mimi, Minette, Minnie, Minny, Miriam, Mitzi, Mitzie, Moira, Moll, Mollie, Molly, Muire, Murial, Muriel, Murielle, Muriellie, Murita, Polly

Matilda (muh-TIL-duh)
Teutonic — *Powerful in battle*
Famous: Wife of William the Conqueror.
Entertainment: Australian song, *Waltzing Matilda.*
Maitilde, Matelda, Mathilda, Mathilde, Matii, Matilde, Mattie, Matty, Maud, Maude, Tilda, Tilly

Matrika (muh-TRĒ-kuh)
Hindi — *Mother*
Matrica

Maude (MAWD)
See Matilda.
Literature: *Maud,* by Tennyson; Maud Gonne, heroine in *When You Are Old,* by William Butler Yeats.
Entertainment: Character in TV program, *Maude;* Maude Adams, actress.
Maudie

Maureen (mor-ĒN)
French — *Dark-skinned*
Celtic — *Great*
Entertainment: Maureen O'Hara, Maureen Stapleton, actresses.
Maura, Maurene, Maurine, Maurise, Maurita, Maurizia, Moira, Mora, Moreen, Morena, Morene, Moria

Mavis (MĀ-vis)
French — *Strong thrush*

Maxine (maks-ĒN)
Latin — *Greatest*
Feminine form of Max.
Entertainment: Maxine Elliott, actress.
Max, Maxi, Maxie, Maxime

May (MĀ)
Latin — *Great one*
Mae, Maia, Maye

Mead (MĒD)
Greek — *Honey-wine*
Meade, Meadie

Meda (MĒ-duh)
North American Indian — *Priestess*
Meeda

Medea (me-DĒ-uh)
Greek — *Part goddess; sorceress*

Mega (MĀ-guh)
Spanish — *Gentle*

Megan (MĀ-gan)
Anglo-Saxon — *Great*
Literature: Heroine in *The Apple Tree,* by Galsworthy.
Meg, Meggi, Meggie, Meggy, Meghan

Mehetabel (muh-HET-uh-bel)
Hebrew — *One of God's favored*
Mehitable, Metabel

Mel (MEL)
Portuguese — *Honey*

Melanie (MEL-uh-nē)
Greek — *Dark-clothed*
Entertainment: Melanie, pop singer.
Malan, Mel, Mela, Melan, Melania, Melany, Melina, Melli, Mellie, Melloney, Melly, Milena

Melantha (me-LAN-thuh)
Greek — *Dark flower*

Melba (MEL-buh)
Greek — *Soft*
Latin — *Mallow flower*
Feminine form of Melvin.
Entertainment: Melba Moore, singer.
Malva, Melva

Melcia (MEL-sē-uh)
Polish — *Ambitious*
Amalie

Meli (MEL-ē)
Greek — *Honey*
Mere

Melina (muh-LĒ-nuh)
Latin — *Canary-yellow color*
Entertainment: Melina Mercouri, actress.
Malina, Melanie

Melinda (muh-LIN-duh)
Greek — *Dark, gentle*
Linda, Lindy, Lynda, Malina, Malinda, Malinde, Mandy, Melinde

Melisenda (mel-i-SEN-duh)
Spanish, German—*Honest*
Millicent

Melissa (muh-LIS-uh)
Greek—*Honey bee*
Mythological: Nymph who taught
man to use honey.
Entertainment: Melissa Hayden,
ballet dancer; Melissa
Manchester, pop singer.
**Lisa, Lissa, Malissa, Mel,
Melesa, Melessa, Melicent,
Melisa, Melisande, Melise,
Melisenda, Melisent, Melisse,
Melita, Melitta, Melleta,
Mellicent, Mellie, Melly,
Melosa, Melose, Mili,
Milicent, Milissent,
Millicent, Millie,
Millisent, Milly,
Misha, Missie, Missy**

Melody (MEL-ō-dē)
Greek—*Song*
Lodie, Melodee, Melodie

Melvina (mel-VĒN-uh)
Celtic—*Chieftainess*
Feminine form of Melvin.
Malvina, Melba, Melva

Mercedes (MER-se-dēs) or
(mer-SĀ-dēs)
Spanish—*Merciful*
Biblical: Maria de Mercedes (Mary
of Mercies).
Literature: Sweetheart of Edmond
Dante's *Count of Monte Cristo.*
Entertainment: Mercedes
McCambridge, actress.
Merci, Mercy

Mercy (MER-sē)
English—*Compassion, mercy*

Meredith (MAIR-uh-dith)
Old Welsh—*Guardian from the sea*
Entertainment: Meredith Baxter
Birney, actress.
Meridith, Merridie, Merry

Meris (MAR-is)
Latin—*Of the sea*
Mari, Maris

Merle (MERL)
Latin—*Blackbird*
Entertainment: Merle Oberon,
actress.
**Merl, Merla, Merlina,
Merline, Merola, Meryl,
Myrle, Myrlene**

Merrie (MAIR-ē)
Anglo-Saxon—*Pleasant*
**Marrille, Meri, Merilee,
Merrielle, Merrili, Merry**

Merritt (MAIR-it)
Anglo-Saxon—*Of merit*

Meta (ME-tuh)
German—*A pearl*
**Greta, Meda, Mehetabel
Mettabel**

Mia (MĒ-uh)
Latin—*Mine*
Entertainment: Mia Farrow,
actress.

Michaela (mi-KĀ-luh)
Hebrew—*Who is like the Lord*
Feminine form of Michael.
**Mia, Micaela, Michaelina,
Michaeline, Michel, Michelina,
Micheline, Michelle, Micki,
Mickie, Micky, Midge, Miguela,
Miguelita, Mikaela, Miquela,
Miquelie**

Michelle (mi-SHEL)
See Michaela.
Entertainment: Michelle Morgan,
Michelle Lee, actresses; *Michelle*,
song by the Beatles.

Michi (MĒ-chē)
Japanese—*The righteous*

Micka (MI-kuh)
Slavic—*Bitter*
Mara, Mica

Migdala (mig-DAW-luh)
Hebrew— *Fortress*
Migdela, Migdele, Migdelia

Migina (mi-JĒ-nuh)
Omaha Indian— *Moon returning*
Mihuca, Mitexi

Mignon (MIN-yon)
French— *Dainty, delicate*
Literature: Mignon Eberhart,
    author of detective fiction.
Entertainment: Heroine of the
    opera *Mignon,* by Ambroise
    Thomas.
Mignonette, Mignonettie

Mildred (MIL-dred)
German— *Mild power*
**Madge, Midge, Mil, Milli,
Millie, Milly**

Millicent (MIL-i-sent)
Teutonic— *Industrious*
**Lissa, Mel, Melicent,
Melisande, Melisenda, Mellisent,
Melly, Milicent, Milissent,
Milli, Millie, Millisent,
Milly, Milzie, Missie, Missy**

Milly (MIL-ē)
See Mildred.
Entertainment: Movie, *Thoroughly
    Modern Milly.*
Millie

Mimi (MĒ-mē)
Teutonic— *Unwavering protector*
Entertainment: Mimi, heroine of
    Puccini's opera *La Boheme.*
Mimee

Mina (MĪN-uh)
See Wilhelmina.
Minette, Minnie, Myna

Minal (min-AL)
North American Indian— *Fruit*

Minda (MIN-duh)
Indian— *Knowledge*

Mindy (MIN-dē)
English— *Love*
Minna

Minerva (mi-NER-vuh)
Greek— *Wisdom*
Mythological: Roman goddess of
    wisdom.

Minette (mi-NET)
French, German— *Unwavering
    protector*
**Guilette, Guillaumette,
Guillelmine, Mimi, Wilhelmine**

Minna (MIN-uh)
German— *Memory*
**Mina, Minda, Mindy, Minetta,
Minette, Minne, Minnie, Minny**

Miquela (mi-KĀ-luh)
Zuni Indian— *Who is like God*
Micaela, Miquel

Mira (MIR-uh)
Latin— *Wonderful*
**Mireille, Mirella, Mirelle,
Miri, Miriam, Mirilla, Myra,
Myrilla**

Mirabel (MIR-uh-bel)
Latin— *Of extraordinary beauty*
Mira, Mirabella, Mirabelle

Miranda (mir-AN-duh)
Latin— *Admirable*
Literature: Heroine of *The Tempest,*
    by Shakespeare.
**Mira, Miran, Myra, Randa,
Randie, Randy**

Miriam (MIR-ē-um)
Hebrew— *Bitter*
Literature: Hero's first love in *Sons
    and Lovers,* by D.H. Lawrence.
Mimi, Mirjan, Mitzi, Mitzie

Mirth (MIRTH)
Anglo-Saxon— *Joy, pleasure*

Missie (MIS-sē)
English— *Young girl*
Missy

MYRA — *Quiet song*

Moanna (mō-AW-nuh)
Polynesian — *Ocean*

Modesty (MOD-est-ē)
Latin — *Modest*
Modesta, Modestia, Modestine

Moina (mō-Ē-nuh)
Celtic — *Gentle and soft*
Moyna

Moira (MOI-ruh)
Gaelic — *Great*
Entertainment: Moira Shearer,
  actress.
Maura, Maureen

Molly (MOL-ē)
See Mary.
Historical: Molly Pitcher,
Revolutionary War heroine.
Mollee, Molli, Mollie

Mona (MŌ-nuh)
Teutonic, Latin — *Single or solitary*
Famous: *Mona Lisa,* painting by
Leonardo da Vinci.
Moina, Monia, Moyna

Monica (MON-i-kuh)
Latin — *Adviser*
Biblical: Mother of St.
Augustine.
Mona, Monique

Morasha (mor-A-shuh)
Hebrew — *Inheritance*

Morgana (mor-GA-nuh)
Welsh — *Edge of the sea*
Feminine form of Morgan.
Literature: Morgan LeFay, sister of
King Arthur.
Morgan, Morgania

Moriah (mo-RĪ-uh)
Hebrew — *God is my teacher*
Morice, Moriel, Morit

Morla (MOR-luh)
Hebrew — *Chosen by the Lord*
Morlia

Morna (MOR-nuh)
Gaelic — *Beloved*
Myrna

Moselle (mō-ZEL)
Hebrew — *Child rescued from the
water*
Mosellie, Mozelle, Mozellie

Moya (MOI-uh)
Celtic — *The great*
Moira

Mura (MŪR-uh)
Japanese — *Village*

Muriel (MŪR-ē-el)
Arabic — *Myrrh*
Gaelic — *Sea bright*
Literature: Muriel Sparks, author.
Meriel, Murial, Murielle

Musa (MOO-suh)
Latin — *A muse*
Musetta, Musette

Myra (MĪ-ruh)
French — *Quiet song*
Literature: Myra Kelly, author;
Myra Breckenridge, novel by Gore
Vidal.
Entertainment: Dame Myra Hess,
pianist; Myrna Loy, actress.
**Merna, Mira, Miranda, Mirna,
Moina, Morna, Moyna, Myrna**

Myrtle (MIR-tel)
Greek — *Myrtle*
Myrta, Myrtia, Myrtice, Myrtie

Nada (NĀ-duh)
Slavic — *Hope*

Nadine (nā-DĒN)
French, Slavic — *Hope*
Feminine form of Nathan.
Sports: Nadia Comaneci, gymnast.
**Dusya, Nada, Nadenka, Nadia,
Nadiya, Nady, Nadya, Nadyusha,
Nadzia, Nathka**

NATA — *Rope dancer*

Nagida (na-GĒ-duh)
Hebrew — *Wealth*

Nan (NAN)
See Ann.
Entertainment: Nanette Fabray, actress.
Nana, Nance, Nancee, Nanci, Nancie, Nancy, Nanelia, Nanelle, Nanette, Nanice, Nanine, Nanna, Nannie, Nanny, Nanon, Nette, Nettie, Netty, Ninon

Nancy (NAN-sē)
See Ann.
Famous: Nancy Reagan, wife of President Ronald Reagan.
Literature: Nancy Drew, stories for girls.
Entertainment: Nancy Sinatra, pop singer; Nancy Walker, actress.
Nance, Nancee, Nancey, Nanci, Nancie, Nanice, Nannie, Nanny

Nani (NA-nē)
Polynesian — *Beautiful*

Naomi (nā-Ō-mē)
Hebrew — *Pleasant*
Biblical: Mother-in-law of Ruth.
Literature: Naomi Mitchison,
  English author.
Naoma, Noami, Noemi, Nomi

Nara (NAIR-uh)
North American Indian,
  Japanese — *Oak*

Nari (NAR-ē)
Japanese — *Thunderpeal*
Nariko

Narilla (na-RIL-uh)
English — *Obscure*
Narilia, Narilie, Narrila,
Narrilia, Narrilla

Nashira (na-SHIR-uh)
Zodiac — *Star*

Nasnan (NAZ-nan)
Carrier Indian — *Surrounded by a
  song*

Nasya (NAZ-yuh)
Hebrew — *Miracle of God*
Nasia

Nata (NA-tuh)
North American Indian — *Speaker*
Hindi — *Rope dancer*
Polish — *Hope*
Natia

Natalie (NA-tuh-lē)
Latin — *Christmas-born*
Entertainment: Natalie Wood,
  actress; Natalie Cole, singer.
Nat, Nata, Natala, Natalina,
Nataline, Natasha, Nathalia,
Nathalie, Natividad, Natty,
Netti, Nettie, Netty, Noel

Natane (na-TAW-nē)
Arapaho Indian — *Daughter*

Natasha (na-TA-shuh)
Slavic — *Born on Christmas*
Natalie, Natascha, Nathalia,
Natica

Navit (nuh-VET)
Hebrew — *Pleasant*
Naava, Nava

Neala (NE-luh)
Celtic — *Chieftainess*
Feminine form of Neal.

Neci (NA-sē)
Hungarian, Latin — *Intense and fiery*

Neda (NE-duh)
Slavic — *Sunday's child*
Feminine form of Edward.
Nedda, Nedi, Nedra

Nediva (ne-DE-vuh)
Hebrew — *Noble and generous*

Nelda (NEL-duh)
Old English — *Of the elder tree*

Nelia (NEL-ē-yuh)
Spanish — *Yellow*
Melia

Nell (NEL)
See Allen.
Entertainment: Nell Gwyn,
  actress; songs *Nelly Bly* and *Nelly
  Was A Lady*.
Nella, Nellie, Nellis, Nelly,
Nelma

Neona (nē-Ō-nuh)
Greek — *New moon*

Nerine (na-REN)
Greek — *Sea nymph*

Nerissa (ner-IS-uh)
Greek — *Of the sea*
Literature: Confidante of Portia in
  Merchant of Venice, by
  Shakespeare.
Nerita

Nessa (NES-uh)
Greek — *Pure*
Agnes, Nessia, Nesta,
Netty, Neysa

Netia (NĒ-shuh) or (ne-TĒ-uh)
Hebrew— *Plant*
Neta, Netta

Netis (NE-tis)
North American Indian— *Trusted friend*

Neva (NĒ-vuh)
Spanish— *Snowy*
Nevada

Niabi (nē-AW-bē)
North American Indian— *A fawn*

Nicole (ni-KŌL)
Greek— *Victory of the people*
Feminine form of Nicholas.
Literature: Heroine of *Aucassin and Nicolette,* by F. W. Bourdillon.
Nicolette, Nicoli, Nicolina, Nicoline, Nika, Niki, Nikki

Nika (NĒK-uh)
Greek— *Victory*
Russian— *Belonging to God*
Domka, Mika

Niki (NI-kē)
Greek— *Victorious army*
Nikoleta, Nikolia

Nina (NĒ-nuh)
North American Indian— *Mighty*
Spanish— *Little girl*
Nanon, Ninetta, Ninette, Ninnetta, Ninnette, Ninon

Nishi (NĒ-shē)
Japanese— *West*

Nissa (NIS-uh)
Scandinavian— *Friendly elf*

Nita (NĒ-tuh)
Choctaw Indian— *Bear*

Nitara (ni-TAR-uh)
Hindi— *Deeply rooted*

Nitsa (NĒT-suh)
Greek— *Light*

Nizana (ni-ZA-nuh)
Hebrew— *Bud*
Nitana, Nizan

Noel (nō-EL)
Latin, French— *Christmas-born*
Noella, Noelle, Noellyn, Noelyn, Novelia

Nola (NŌ-luh)
Latin— *A small bell*

Noleta (nō-LĒ-tuh)
Latin— *The unwilling*

Nona (NŌ-nuh)
Latin— *Ninth*
Interesting: Name sometimes given to the ninth child.

Nora (NOR-uh)
Latin— *Honor*
Greek— *Light*
Literature: Nora Helmer, heroine of *A Doll's House,* by Ibsen.
Norah, Norina, Norine

Norma (NOR-muh)
Latin— *Ruler or pattern*
Entertainment: *Norma,* opera by Bellini; Norma Talmadge, Norma Shearer, actresses.
Noreen, Normia

Noura (NOOR-uh)
Arabic— *Light*

Nova (NŌ-vuh)
Hopi Indian— *Chasing*

Nurit (NŪR-et)
Hebrew— *Little yellow flower*
Nurice, Nurita

Nusa (NOO-suh)
Hungarian, Hebrew— *Graceful*
Anci, Aniko, Annuska, Nina, Ninacska

Oba (Ō-buh)
Yoruban—*River goddess*

Octavia (ok-TĀ-ve-uh)
Latin—*The eighth*
Feminine form of Octavius.
Ottavia, Tavi, Tavia

Odelet (Ō-de-let)
French, Greek—*Little song*
**Odel, Odele, Odelette,
Odellett, Odellette**

Odelia (ō-DĒ-le-uh)
Teutonic—*Wealthy or prosperous*
Hebrew—*I will praise God*
Feminine form of Odell.
**Odelinda, Odella, Odetta,
Odette, Odilia, Otha, Othelia,
Othilia, Ottilie, Uta**

Odera (ō-DAIR-uh)
Hebrew—*Plough*

Ogin (Ō-jin)
North American Indian—*Wild rose*

Ola (Ō-luh)
Norwegian—*Descendant or
reminder of his ancestor*

Olathe (Ō-lath)
North American Indian—*Beautiful*

Olayinka (ō-LĀ-in-kuh)
Yoruban—*Honors surround me*

Olethea (ō-LĒ-the-uh)
Latin—*Truth*
Alethea

Olga (ŌL-guh)
Teutonic, Russian—*Holy*
**Elga, Helga, Oldnka, Olechka,
Olia, Olive, Olivia, Olva**

Oliana (ō-LĒ-an-uh)
Polynesian—*Oleander*

Olisa (ō-LĒ-suh)
African—*God*

Olivia (ō-LIV-e-uh)
Latin—*Olive tree*
Interesting: The olive tree is a
symbol of peace.
Literature: Countess in *Twelfth
Night*, by Shakespeare.
Entertainment: Olivia de
Havilland, actress; Olivia
Newton-John, pop singer.
**Liva, Livi, Livia, Livvi,
Livvie, Livvy, Nola, Nolana,
Nolita, Noll, Nollie, Olga,
Olia, Olive, Olivette, Olli,
Ollie, Olly, Olva**

Olympia (ō-LIM-pe-uh)
Greek—*Heavenly*
Entertainment: Olympia, heroine
in *Tales of Hoffman*, by Offenbach.
Olimpia, Olympe, Olympie

Oma (Ō-muh)
Arabic—*Commander*
Feminine form of Omar.

Omena (ō-MĒN-uh)
Finnish—*Apple*

Ona (Ō-nuh)
Hebrew—*Graceful*
**Ane, Anikke, Annze, Onele,
Onute, Oona, Una**

Ondine (ON-dēn)
Latin—*Of water*
Undine

Onella (ō-NEL-uh)
Hungarian, English—*Light*

Opal (Ō-pel)
Sanskrit— *Precious stone*
Opalina, Opaline

Ophelia (ō-FĒL-ē-uh)
Greek— *Serpent*
Literature: Heroine in
  Shakespeare's *Hamlet.*
Ofelia, Ofilia, Ophelie, Phelia

Oralie (OR-uh-lē)
Latin— *Golden*
**Aurelia, Ora, Oralia,
Orel, Oriana, Orlene**

Oribel (OR-i-bel)
Latin— *Golden beauty*
Orlena, Orlene

Orino (or-Ē-nō)
Japanese— *Weaver's field*
Ori

Oriole (OR-ē-ōl)
Latin— *Fair-haired*
Oriel

Orlantha (or-LAN-thuh)
Teutonic— *Fame of the land*

Orlenda (or-LEN-duh)
English, Russian— *Female eagle*
Orlitza

Ornice (OR-nēs)
Hebrew— *Cedar tree*
Oenit, Orna

Ortrude (OR-trood)
Teutonic— *Serpent-maid*
Ortrud

Orva (OR-vuh)
French— *Of golden worth*

Ottilie (Ō-til-ē)
Teutonic— *Fortunate battle-maid*
German— *Fatherland*
**Odette, Odille, Ottilia, Ottillia,
Uta**

Page (PĀJ)
French— *Useful assistant*
Anglo-Saxon— *Child*
Interesting: Name was sometimes
  used in knighthood.
Paige

Paka (PA-kuh)
Swahili— *Pussycat*

Palila (puh-LĒ-luh)
Polynesian— *Bird*

Paloma (puh-LŌ-muh)
Spanish— *Dove*

Pamela (PAM-el-uh)
Greek— *All honey*
Literature: Heroine in *Arcadia,* by
  Sir Phillip Sidney; Samuel
  Richardson's novel, *Pamela, or
  Virtue Rewarded.*
Entertainment: Pamela Brown,
  Pamela Tiffin, actresses.
**Pam, Pamelina, Pamella,
Pammi, Pammie, Pammy**

Pandita (pan-DĒ-tuh)
Hindi— *Scholar*

Pandora (pan-DOR-uh)
Greek— *Talented, gifted*
Mythological: Pandora was the
first woman. She opened a sealed
box containing all the gifts of the
gods to mankind including the
ills of the world.
Doria

Pansy (PAN-sē)
Greek— *Fragrant*
Pansie

Panthea (PAN-thē-uh)
Greek— *Of all the gods*

Patia (PAT-ē-uh)
Spanish— *Leaf*

Patience (PĀ-shens)
French— *Enduring expectation*
Entertainment: Heroine of Gilbert
and Sullivan's opera, *Patience.*

Patricia (puh-TRI-shuh)
Latin— *Of the nobility*
Feminine form of Patrick.
Famous: Patricia Nixon, wife of
President Richard Nixon.
Entertainment: Patty Duke-Astin,
actress; Patsy Cline,
country-western singer; Patti
Page, pop singer; Patrice Munsel,
opera singer.
**Pat, Patrica, Patrice,
Patrizia, Patsy, Patti,
Patty, Tricia, Trish**

Paula (PAWL-uh)
Latin— *Small*
Feminine form of Paul.
Literature: Heroine of *The Second
Mrs. Tanqueray,* by Pinero; *Perils
of Pauline,* by Style and Wilcox.
Entertainment: Paulette Goddard,
Paula Prentiss, actresses.
**Paole, Paolina, Paule,
Pauletta, Paulette, Pauli,
Paulie, Paulina, Pauline,
Paulita, Pauly, Pavla, Polly**

Pavla (PAV-luh)
Latin— *Little*
Pavlina

Pazia (PĀ-zyuh)
Hebrew— *Golden*
Paz, Paza, Pazice, Pazit

Peace (PĒS)
English— *The peaceful*

Pearl (PERL)
Latin, French— *Pearl*
Literature: Pearl Buck, Pulitzer
Prize winner.
Entertainment: Pearl Bailey,
singer; Pearl Primus, dancer.
**Pearla, Pearle, Pearlie,
Pearline, Perl, Perla,
Perle, Perry**

Peg (PEG)
Greek— *Pearl*
**Margaret, Meg, Peggi,
Peggie, Peggy**

Pegeen (pe-GĒN)
Celtic— *Pearl*

Pelagie (pe-LAW-gē)
Greek— *Pertaining to the sea*
Pelagrie

Penelope (pe-NEL-ō-pē)
Greek— *Weaver*
Literature: Faithful wife in
Homer's *Odyssey.*
**Pela, Pelcia, Pen,
Penelopa, Pennie, Penny**

Penthea (pen-THĒ-uh)
Greek— *The fifth*

Peony (PĒ-ō-nē)
Greek— *Flower*
Peonie

Pepita (pe-PĒ-tuh)
Spanish— *She shall add*
Pepi, Peta

Perdita (per-DĒ-tuh)
Latin— *Lost*
Literature: Perdita in *The Winter's Tale*, by Shakespeare.

Perry (PAIR-ē)
French— *Pear tree*

Persis (PER-sis)
Greek— *Woman from Persia*
Literature: Wife of Silas Lapham in *The Rise of Silas Lapham*, by William Dean Howells.

Petra (PĒ-truh) or (PE-truh)
Latin— *Rock*
Feminine form of Peter.
Perrine, Pet, Peta, Petrina, Petronella, Petronia, Petronilla, Petronille, Pette, Pier, Pierette, Pierrette

Petula (pe-TOO-luh)
Latin— *Searcher*
Entertainment: Petula Clark, singer.
Pet, Petulah

Petunia (pe-TOON-yuh)
American Indian— *From the petunia flower*

Phedra (FĀ-druh)
Greek— *Bright*
Phaedra, Phaidra

Phenice (fa-NĒS)
Hebrew— *From a palm tree*
Phenica, Phenicia

Philana (fil-AN-uh)
Greek— *Lover of mankind*
Feminine form of Philander.
Philina, Philine, Phillane

Philippa (FIL-ip-uh)
Greek— *Lover of horses*
Feminine form of Philip.
Literature: Pippi Longstocking, character in children's stories.
Felipa, Filippa, Phil, Philipa, Philippe, Philippine, Phillida, Phillie, Philly, Pippa, Pippi, Pippy

Philomena (fil-ō-MĒN-uh)
Greek— *Loving friend*
Mena

Phoebe (FĒ-bē)
Greek— *Shining or brilliant*
Mythological: Goddess of the moon.
Phebe

Phyllis (FIL-is)
Greek— *Green bough*
Entertainment: Phyllis George, actress and former Miss America.
Filide, Filippa, Phil, Philippine, Philis, Phillie, Phillis, Philly, Phyl, Phylis, Pippa, Pippy

Pia (PĒ-uh)
Italian— *Devout*

Pierrette (PĒR-et)
French— *Steady*

Pilar (PĒ-lar)
Spanish— *Pillar*

Pinga (PEN-guh)
Hindi— *Dark*

Piper (PĪ-per)
Old English— *Player of the pipe*
Entertainment: Piper Laurie, actress.

Placidia (pla-SI-dē-uh)
Latin— *The serene*
Placida

Polii (PŌ-lē)
Polynesian— *Younger sister*

PHILIPPA — *Lover of horses*

Polly (POL-ē)
Hebrew — *Bitter*
Literature: Pollyanna, character in
children's stories.
Entertainment: Polly Bergen,
actress.
**Pol, Poll, Pollie,
Pollyanna, Pollyannie**

Pomona (po-MŌ-nuh)
Latin — *Fertile*

Poppy (POP-ē)
Latin — *Poppy flower*

Portia (POR-shuh)
Latin — *Offering*
Literature: Heroine in *Merchant of Venice* and wife of Brutus in *Julius Caesar,* both by Shakespeare.

Prane (PRĀN)
Lithuanian, Latin — *Free one*
Pranele, Pranute

Prima (PRĒ-muh)
Latin — *The first born*

Primalia (prē-MĀ-lē-uh)
Latin — *The first*

Primavera (prē-ma-VAIR-uh)
Latin — *Spring's beginning*

Primrose (PRIM-roz)
Latin — *First rose*

Priscilla (pri-SIL-uh)
Latin — *Of ancient time*
Biblical: Priscilla was helper to Apostle Paul.
Literature: Heroine in *The Courtship of Miles Standish,* by Henry Wadsworth Longfellow.
Cilla, Pris, Prisca, Priscell, Priscellia, Prisilla, Prissie, Prissy, Sil

Prudence (PROO-dens)
Latin — *Prudent*
Pru, Prud, Pruddie, Prudi, Prudy, Prue

Prunella (proo-NEL-uh)
French, Latin — *Plum color*

Psyche (SĪ-kē)
Greek — *The soul*
Mythological: Mortal loved by Cupid.

Queenie (KWĒ-nē)
See Regina.
Queena, Queenie, Queeny

Quenby (KWEN-bē)
Scandinavian — *Womanly*

Quenie (KWĒ-nē)
Old English — *Queen*
Quenna

Querida (ker-RĒ-duh)
Spanish — *Beloved*

Quinta (KWIN-tuh)
Latin — *Fifth*
Quentin, Quintilla, Quintina

Quirita (ker-RĒ-tuh)
Latin — *Citizen*
Quartilla

Rabi (RĀ-bē)
Arabic— *Breeze*
Rabiah

Rachel (RĀ-chel)
Hebrew— *Ewe*
Biblical: Wife of Jacob and mother
of Joseph.
Entertainment: Raquel Welch,
actress.
**Rachele, Rachelle, Rae, Rahel,
Rakel, Raquel, Raquela, Ray,
Raya, Rochell, Rochelle,
Shell, Shelley, Shelly, Tey**

Radmilla (rad-MIL-uh)
Slavic— *Worker for the people.*

Raizel (RĀ-zel)
Hebrew— *Rose*
Rayzel, Razil

Ramla (RAM-luh)
Swahili— *Fortuneteller*

Ramona (ruh-MŌ-nuh)
Spanish— *Mighty or wise*
Feminine form of Raymond.
Rama, Romona, Romonda

Rana (RĀ-nuh)
Sanskrit— *Royal*
Mythological: Goddess of the sea.
Rani, Rania, Rayna

Ranita (ra-NĒ-tuh)
Hebrew— *Song*
Ranice, Ranit

Raphaela (ra-fī-EL-uh)
Hebrew— *Blessed healer*
Feminine form of Raphael.
Rafaela, Rafaelia

Rawnie (RAW-nē)
English— *Lady*

Razilee (RA-zi-lē)
Hebrew— *My secret*
Razili

Rebba (RĒ-buh)
Hebrew— *Fourth-born*
Reba, Rebah

Rebecca (re-BEK-uh)
Hebrew— *The captivator*
Biblical: Wife of Isaac.
Literature: Heroine of *Ivanhoe,* by
Sir Walter Scott; Becky Sharp in
Vanity Fair, by Thackeray; book
Rebecca of Sunnybrook Farm.
**Beba, Becca, Becka, Becki,
Beckie, Becky, Bekki, Rebeca,
Rebeka, Rebekah, Ree, Reeba,
Riba, Rikah, Riva, Rivalee,
Rivi, Rivy**

Regina (re-JĒN-uh)
Latin— *Queen*
**Raina, Regan, Reggi, Reggie,
Regine, Reina, Reine, Reyna,
Rina**

Rei (RĒ-uh)
Japanese— *Gratitude*
Reiko

Remy (RĀ-mē)
French— *From Rheims*

Rena (RĒ-nuh)
Greek— *Peace*
Eirene, Eirni, Ereni, Nitsa

Renata (re-NAT-uh)
Latin— *Reborn*
Entertainment: Renata Tebaldi,
opera singer.
**Renae, Renate, Rene, Renee,
Renie, Rennie**

Reseda (re-SĒ-duh)
Latin — *Healing*
Interesting: Reseda is also the
Latin word for the flower
mignonette.

Rhea (RĒ-uh)
Greek — *Earth or motherly*
Mythological: In Greek
mythology, Rhea is the mother of
Zeus. In Roman mythology,
Rhea is the mother of Romulus
and Remus.

Rhoda (RŌ-duh)
Greek — *A garland of roses*
Entertainment: Rhonda Fleming,
actress; character in TV show
Rhoda.
**Rhonda, Roda, Rodi, Rodie,
Rodina, Ronda**

Rica (RĒ-kuh)
See Frederica.
**Ricca, Ricki, Rickie, Ricky,
Riki, Rikki, Rycca**

Ricarda (ri-KAR-duh)
Teutonic — *Powerful ruler*
Feminine form of Richard.
Erica, Frederica, Ricky, Roderica

Rida (RĒ-duh)
Arabic — *Favor*

Rihana (RĒ-an-uh)
Muslim — *Sweet basil*

Rimona (ri-MŌ-nuh)
Hebrew — *Pomegranate*
Mona

Risa (RĒ-suh)
English — *Laughter*

Rita (RĒ-tuh)
See Margaret.
Entertainment: Rita Hayworth,
actress; Rita Coolidge, singer.

Ritsa (RĒT-suh)
Greek — *Helper and defender*

Riva (RĒ-vuh)
French — *Shore*
**Ree, Reeva, Rivalee,
Rivi, Rivy**

Roanna (rō-AN-uh)
Latin — *Sweet*
Roana, Roanne

Roberta (rō-BER-tuh)
Teutonic — *Of shining fame*
Entertainment: Roberta Peters,
opera singer; Roberta Flack, pop
singer.
**Bobbe, Bobbette, Bobbi, Bobbie,
Bobby, Bobbye, Bobina, Bobine,
Bobinette, Robbi, Robbie, Robby,
Robena, Robenia, Robin, Robina,
Robinette, Robinia, Rubert,
Ruperta**

Robin (RO-bin)
Old English — *Robin*
**Robbin, Robena, Robenia,
Robina, Robinet, Robinett, Robyn**

Rochelle (rō-SHEL)
French — *Little rock*

Roderica (rod-RĒ-kuh)
Teutonic — *Famous ruler*
Feminine form of Roderick.
**Rica, Roch, Rochella,
Rochette, Roshelle, Shell,
Shelley, Shelly**

Rohana (rō-AN-uh)
Hindi — *Sandalwood*

Rolanda (rō-LAN-duh)
Teutonic — *Fame of the land*

Rolla (RŌ-luh)
See Rolf.

Roma (RŌ-muh)
Latin — *Eternal city*
**Romaine, Romelle, Romilda,
Romina**

RONA — *Mighty power*

Romilda (rō-MIL-duh)
Teutonic — *Glorious battle-maiden*

Romola (rō-MŌ-luh)
Latin — *The Roman*

Rona (RŌ-nuh)
Norwegian — *Mighty power*
Entertainment: Rona Barrett,
Hollywood columnist.
Rhona, Ronalda

Ronli (RON-lē)
Hebrew — *Joy in mine*
**Rona, Roni, Ronia,
Ronice, Ronit**

Ronni (RON-ē)
See Roanna.
**Roanna, Roni, Ronnie,
Ronny, Rowena, Veronica**

Rosa (RŌ-suh)
Latin — *A rose*
Famous: Rosalyn Carter, wife of
President Jimmy Carter.
**Rosabel, Rosabella, Rosabelle,
Rosalyn**

Rosalba (rō-SAL-buh)
Latin — *White rose*

Rosalia (rō-SĀ-lē-uh)
Italian — *Melody or tune*
**Rosaleen, Rosalie, Rozalia,
Rozalie, Rozele**

141

Rosalind (ROZ-uh-lind)
Spanish, Latin—*Fair rose*
Entertainment: Rosalind Russell,
  actress.
**Ros, Rosalinda, Rosalinde,
Rosaline, Rosalyn, Rosalynd,
Roselin, Roseline, Roslyn,
Roz, Rozalin**

Rosamond (ROZ-uh-mund)
Teutonic—*Famous guardian*
**Ros, Rosamund, Rosamunda,
Rosemonde, Roz, Rozamond**

Rosanne (rō-ZAN)
Latin—*Gracious rose*
**Ranna, Roanna, Roanne,
Rosanna, Roseann, Roseanne**

Rose (RŌZ)
Greek—*Rose*
**Rasia, Rhada, Rhodie, Rhody,
Rois, Rosa, Rosaleen, Rosalia,
Rosalie, Rosel, Rosella,
Roselle, Rosena, Rosene,
Rosetta, Rosette, Rosie,
Rosina, Rosita, Rosy, Rozalie,
Roze, Rozele, Rozella, Rozina,
Zita**

Roselani (rō-ze-LAN-ē)
English, Polynesian—*Heavenly rose*
Roselane, Roseline

Rosemary (RŌZ-mair-ē)
Latin—*Mary's rose*
Entertainment: *Rose Marie*, light
  opera; Rosemary Clooney,
  singer; Rose Marie, actress.
Rosemaria, Rosemarie

Rosetta (rō-ZE-tuh)
Italian—*Little rose*
Entertainment: Rosina Lhevinne,
  concert pianist.
Rosett, Rosette, Rosina

Rowena (rō-WE-nuh)
Celtic—*White mane*
Literature: Heroine of *Ivanhoe*, by
  Sir Walter Scott.
**Ranna, Rena, Ro, Ronni,
Ronnie, Ronny, Row, Rowe**

Roxanne (roks-AN)
Persian—*Dawn*
Historical: Persian wife of
  Alexander the Great.
**Rosana, Rox, Roxana, Roxane,
Roxi, Roxie, Roxine, Roxy**

Rozele (rō-ZEL)
Lithuanian—*Rose*
Roz, Roze, Rozyte

Rozene (rō-ZEN)
North American Indian—*Rose*

Ruby (ROO-bē)
Latin—*Precious stone*
**Rubetta, Rubi, Rubia,
Rubie, Rubina**

Rue (ROO)
Greek—*Herb of grace*

Ruth (ROOTH)
Hebrew—*A friend*
Biblical: Friend of Naomi.
Entertainment: Ruth Buzzy,
  comedienne.
**Ruthann, Ruthanna, Ruthanne,
Ruthe, Ruthi, Ruthie**

Sabina (sa-BĒN-uh)
Latin— *Sabine woman*
Interesting: Poppaea Sabina,
Roman empress.
Bina, Sabine, Sabrina

Sabra (SĀ-bruh)
Hebrew— *Thorny cactus*
Zabra

Sabrina (suh-BRĒ-nuh)
Latin— *From the border*
Brina, Zabrina

Sachi (SA-shē)
Japanese— *Bliss child*
Sachiko

Sada (SĀ-duh)
Japanese— *The chaste*
Sadie

Sadie (SĀ-dē)
Hebrew— *Princess*
Entertainment: Sadie Hawkins in
Li'l Abner comic strip.
**Sada, Sadye, Saidee,
Sarah, Sydel, Sydelle**

Sadira (sa-DĒR-uh)
Arabic— *Ostrich returning to water*

Sadzi (SAD-zē)
Indian— *Sun heart*

Sagara (sa-GAIR-uh)
Hindi— *Ocean*

Sakari (sa-KAR-ē)
Indian— *Sweet*

Saki (SA-kē)
Japanese— *Cape*

Sakti (SAK-tē)
Hindi— *Energy*
Interesting: Hindi goddess.

Sakura (sa-KOOR-uh)
Japanese— *Cherry blossom*
Interesting: Japanese symbol of
wealth and prosperity. In China,
a cherry blossom symbolizes
good education.

Salama (suh-LAW-muh)
Arabic— *Safety*

Salena (sa-LEN-uh)
Latin— *Salty*

Sally (SAL-ē)
Hebrew— *Princess*
Entertainment: Sally Fields, Sally
Struthers, actresses.
**Sal, Salina, Sallee, Salli,
Sallie**

Salome (suh-LŌ-me) or
(SAL-ō-mā)
Hebrew— *Peaceful*
Biblical: Daughter of Herodias and
Herod.
Literature: *Salome,* play by Oscar
Wilde.
Entertainment: Salome Jens,
actress.
Sam, Samara, Sammy, Samuela

Samala (suh-MĀ-luh)
Hebrew— *Asked of God*
Samale

Samantha (suh-MAN-thuh)
Arabic— *Listener*
Entertainment: Samantha Eggars,
actress.
Sam, Sammy

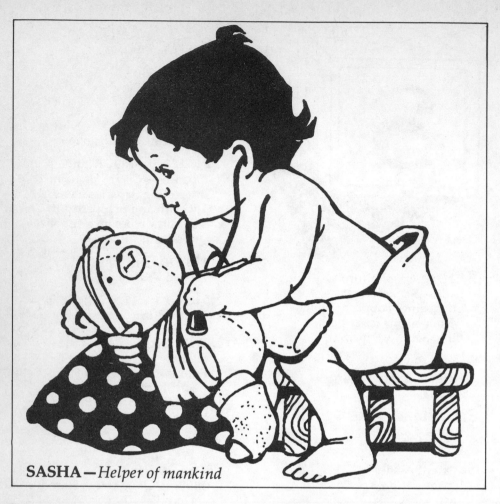

SASHA — *Helper of mankind*

Samara (suh-MA-ruh)
Hebrew — *From Samaria*
Interesting: Samaria, a city in
   Palestine.
Sam, Samaria, Sammy

Samuela (sam-ū-EL-uh)
Hebrew — *Name of God*
Feminine form of Samuel.
Samantha, Samella, Samuella

Sandra (SAN-druh)
Greek — *Helper of mankind*
Entertainment: Sandra Dee,
   actress.
Sandi, Sandie, Sandy, Sandye

Sanuye (SAN-u-ā)
Indian — *Red cloud coming with
   sundown*

Sapphire (SA-fīr)
Greek — *Sapphire*
Hebrew — *The beautiful*
Biblical: Wife of Ananias.
Literature: *Sapphira and the Slave
   Girl*, novel by Willa Cather.
Sapphira

Sappho (SA-fo)
Greek — *Unknown*
Literature: *Sapho*, novel by Daudet.
Sapho

Sarah (SAIR-uh)
Hebrew—*Princess*
Biblical: Wife of Abraham, mother of Isaac.
Entertainment: Sarah Bernhardt, Sarah Miles, actresses.
Sadella, Sadie, Sadye, Sahri, Saidee, Sal, Salaidh, Sallee, Salli, Sallie, Sally, Sara, Sarena, Sarene, Sarette, Sari, Sarine, Sarita, Sayre, Serita, Shara, Sharai, Sharon, Sharona, Sher, Sheree, Sheri, Sherie, Sherri, Sherrie, Sherry, Sherye, Soralie, Sorcha, Sorella, Sydel, Sydelle, Zara, Zarah, Zaria

Saril (suh-RIL)
Turkish—*Sound of running water*

Sasha (SA-shuh)
Russian—*Helper of mankind*
Sacha, Sascha

Satinka (sa-TEN-kuh)
North American Indian—*Magic dancer*

Sawa (SAW-wa)
Japanese—*Marsh*
Indian—*Rock*

Scarlett (SKAR-let)
English—*Scarlet red*
Literature: Heroine in *Gone with the Wind,* by Margaret Mitchell.
Scarlet, Scarllet, Scarllett

Secunda (se-KOON-duh)
Latin—*The second*

Seda (SĒ-duh)
Armenian—*Echo through the woods*
Zelda

Seema (SĒ-muh)
Hebrew—*Treasure*
Cyma, Seena, Simah

Sela (SĒ-luh)
Hebrew—*A rock*

Selena (suh-LĒ-nuh)
Greek—*Moon*
Mythological: Selene, goddess of the moon.
Celene, Celie, Celina, Celinda, Celine, Sela, Selene, Seleta, Selia, Selie, Selina, Selinda, Seline, Sena

Selima (suh-LĒ-muh)
Hebrew—*Peaceful*
Feminine form of Solomon.

Selma (SEL-muh)
Celtic—*Fair*
Teutonic—*Divine helmet*
Anselma, Zelma

Senalda (se-NAL-duh)
Spanish—*A sign*

Seraphina (sair-uh-FĒN-uh)
Hebrew—*Burning ardent*
Sera, Serafina, Serafine

Serena (suh-RĒN-uh)
Latin—*Tranquil*
Reena, Rena, Serene

Serilda (suh-RIL-duh)
Teutonic—*Armored warrior-maid*

Setsu (SET-soo)
Japanese—*Fidelity*
Setsuko

Shada (SHAW-duh)
North American Indian—*Pelican*

Shahar (sha-HAR)
Muslim—*The moon*

Shaina (SHĀ-nuh)
Hebrew—*Beautiful*
Shaine, Shane, Shanie, Shayna, Shayne

Shani (SHA-nē)
African—*Marvelous*

Shannon (SHA-non)
Gaelic—*Small or wise*
Channa, Shana, Shane, Shauna, Shawna

Shappa (SHAW-puh)
North American Indian—*Red thunder*

Sharon (SHĀR-on)
Hebrew—*Level plain*
**Shara, Sharai, Shari,
Sharma, Sharmin, Sharona,
Sherri, Sherrie, Sherry, Sherye**

Sheba (SHĒ-buh)
Hebrew—*From the Sheba*
Biblical: Queen of Sheba.
Interesting: The Southwestern part of Arabia.
Saba

Shehan (SHĒ-han)
Hebrew—*Request, petition*

Shela (SHĒ-luh)
Celtic—*Musical*
Literature: Shelagh Delany, playwright.
Entertainment: Sheila Graham, Hollywood columnist.
**Celia, Selia, Sheela, Sheelagh,
Sheelah, Sheila, Sheilah, Shelagh,
Shelley, Shelli, Shellie, Shelly**

Shelley (SHEL-ē)
Old English—*From the meadow on the ledge*
Entertainment: Shelley Winters, actress.
**Rachel, Shelby, Shell,
Shelli, Shellie, Shelly**

Shera (SHAIR-uh)
Hebrew—*Song*

Sherry (SHAIR-ē)
See Cher.
Entertainment: Sheree North, actress.
**Sheree, Sheri, Sherri,
Sherrie, Sherye, Sheryl**

Shina (SHĒ-nuh)
Japanese—*Good or virtue*
Sheena

Shiri (SHIR-ē)
Hebrew—*My song*
Shira, Shirah

Shirley (SHER-lē)
Old English—*From the white meadow*
Literature: Heroine of *Shirley*, by Charlotte Bronte.
Entertainment: Shirley Temple, Shirley Booth, Shirley MacLaine actresses.
**Sher, Sheree, Sheri, Sherill,
Sherline, Sherri, Sherrie,
Sherry, Sherye, Sheryl, Shir,
Shirl, Shirlee, Shirleen,
Shirlene, Shirline**

Shoshannah (shō-SHA-nuh)
Hebrew—*Rose*
Shoshana

Shulamith (SHOO-luh-mith)
Hebrew—*Peace*
Sula, Sulamith

Shumana (shoo-MAN-uh)
Hopi Indian—*Rattlesnake girl*

Sibley (SIB-lē)
Greek—*Prophetess*
Literature: *Sybil*, novel by Benjamin Disraeli.
Entertainment: Dame Sybil Thorndike, actress.
**Sib, Sibbie, Sibby, Sibeal,
Sibel, Sibella, Sibelle,
Sibilla, Sibylla, Sibylle,
Sybil, Sybila, Sybilla,
Sybille**

Sidonia (si-DON-ē-uh)
Hebrew—*To ensnare*
Sadonia, Sidney, Sidonie, Sydney

Sidra (SID-ruh)
Latin—*Related to the stars*

Silva (SIL-vuh)
Latin—*Woodland maid*
Silvia, Silvie, Sylvia

SHUMANA—*Rattlesnake girl*

Silver (SIL-ver)
Anglo-Saxon— *White*

Simone (sē-MŌN)
Hebrew— *Heard by the Lord*
Feminine form of Simon.
Literature: Simone de Beauvoir,
French author.
Entertainment: Simone Signoret,
actress.
**Simona, Simonetta, Simonette,
Simonne**

Sirena (si-RĒN-uh)
Greek— *A siren*

Situla (si-TOOL-uh)
Indian— *Valley quail running uphill*
Latin— *Well bucket*

Sivia (SIV-ē-uh)
Hebrew— *Doe or beautiful woman*
Sivie

Sofi (SŌ-fē)
Greek — *Wisdom*
Sofia, Sofya, Sophia, Sophey, Sophi, Sophie, Sophron, Sophy

Solana (sō-LA-nuh)
Spanish — *Sunshine*

Solite (SŌ-lēt)
Latin — *Accustomed*

Sondra (SAWN-druh)
See Alexandra.

Sonia (SŌN-yuh)
See Sophia.
Literature: Heroine of *Crime and Punishment,* by Dostoyevsky.
Sofia, Sonia, Sonja, Sonni, Sonnie, Sonny, Sonya, Soph, Sophey, Sophi, Sophie, Sophy, Sunny

Sophia (sō-FĒ-uh)
Greek — *Wisdom*
Literature: Heroine of *Tom Jones,* by Henry Fielding.
Entertainment: Sophie Tucker, Sophia Loren, actresses.
Sofia, Sofie, Sonia, Sonja, Sonni, Sonnie, Sonny, Sonya, Sophie, Sophronia, Sophy, Sunny

Spring (SPRING)
Old English — *Spring time*

Stacy (STĀ-sē)
Greek — *One who shall rise again*
Stace, Stacey, Stacia, Stacie

Star (STAR)
English — *A star*
Starr

Stella (STEL-uh)
Latin — *Star*
Entertainment: Stella Stevens, Stella Adler, Estelle Parsons, actresses.
Estelle

Stellara (STEL-ar-uh)
Zodiac — *Child of the stars*

Stephanie (STE-fuh-nē)
Greek — *Crowned*
Feminine form of Stephen.
Entertainment: Stephanie Powers, actress; Stevie (Stephanie) Nicks, singer.
Stefa, Steffi, Steffie, Stepha, Stephani, Stephanna, Stephi, Stephie, Stesha, Stevana, Stevanna, Stevena, Stevie

Stesha (STESH-uh)
Russian — *Crowned one*

Stina (STĒ-nuh)
German — *Christian*

Storm (STORM)
Old English — *Stormy*
Stormi, Stormie, Stormy

Sue (SOO)
Hebrew — *A lily*
Suki, Susan, Susey

Sula (SOO-luh)
Icelandic — *Large sea bird*
Ursola, Ursula

Summer (SUM-er)
Old English — *Summer*

Sunny (SUN-ē)
English — *Cheerful*

Surata (sur-AT-uh)
Hindi — *Blessed joy*

Susan (SOO-zan)
Hebrew— *Lily*
Biblical: Accused adultress, saved by Daniel.
Historical: Susan B. Anthony, fighter for women's rights.
Literature: Susan Glaspell, founder of Provincetown Playhouse.
Entertainment: Susan Hayward, Susan St. James, Suzanne Pleshette, Suzanne Somers, Susie Wong, actresses.
Sasanna, Sue, Suisan, Sukey, Suki, Susana, Susanetta, Susanette, Susanna, Susannah, Susanne, Susette, Susi, Susie, Susy, Suzanna, Suzanne, Suzette, Suzi, Suzie, Suzy, ZsaZsa

Suzu (SOO-zoo)
Japanese— *Little bell*
Suzue, Suzuki, Suzuko

Svetla (SVET-luh)
Czech— *Light*
Famous: Svetlana Stalin, author and daughter of Joseph Stalin.
Svetlana

Swanhilda (swan-HIL-duh)
Teutonic— *Swan-maiden*

Sydney (SID-ne)
French— *From the city of St. Denis*

Sylvia (SIL-ve-uh)
Latin— *Forest-maiden*
Literature: Sylvia Porter, author and columnist.
Silva, Silvan, Silvana, Silvia, Silvie, Sylvana, Sylvanna, Zilva, Zilvia

Tabia (TAB-e-uh)
Swahili— *Talents*

Tabitha (TA-bi-thuh)
Arabic— *A gazelle*
Tab, Tabbi, Tabbie, Tabby

Taci (TA-ke) or (TA-se)
Zuni Indian   *Washtub*

Tadita (ta-DE-tuh)
Omaha Indian— *To the wind*

Taffy (TAF-fe)
Welsh— *Beloved*

Taima (TA-ma)
North American Indian— *Crash of thunder*

Takara (ta-KAR-uh)
Japanese— *Precious object*

Talasi (ta-LAW-se)
Hopi Indian— *Corn-tassel flower*

Talia (TAL-e-uh)
Greek— *Blooming*
Entertainment: Talia Shire, actress.
Tallie, Tally, Thalia

Tallulah (tuh-LOO-luh)
Choctaw Indian— *Leaping water*
English— *Vivacious*
Entertainment: Tallulah Bankhead, actress.
Tallie, Tallow, Tallula, Tally

Tama (TĀ-muh)
American Indian— *Thunderbolt*
Japanese— *Jewel*

Tamaki (ta-MAW-kē)
Japanese— *Armlet*
Tamako

Tamara (TAM-uh-ruh) or
(ta-MAR-uh)
Hebrew— *Palm tree*
**Tamar, Tamarah, Tamma,
Tammi, Tammie, Tammy**

Tami (TA-mē)
Japanese— *People*
Tamiko

Tammy (TAM-ē)
Hebrew— *Perfection*
Entertainment: Tammy Wynette,
country-western singer.

Tani (TAW-nē)
Japanese— *Valley*

Tansy (TAN-sē)
Greek— *Immortality*
Latin— *Tenacious*

Tanya (TAWN-yuh)
Russian— *Fairy queen*
Literature: Titania, name of fairy
queen in *A Midsummer's Night's
Dream,* by Shakespeare.
Entertainment: Tanya Tucker,
country-western singer.
**Tanechka, Tania, Tankya,
Tatiana, Tatiania, Titania**

Tara (TAIR-uh)
Celtic— *Tower or crag*

Tawnie (TAW-nē)
English— *Little one*

Tecla (TEK-luh)
Greek— *Divine fame*
Tekla, Telca, Telka, Thecla

Tedra (TED-ruh)
See Theodora.

Temina (te-MĒN-uh)
Hebrew— *Whole or honest*

Tempest (TEM-pest)
French— *Stormy*

Templa (TEM-pluh)
Latin— *A temple*

Teresa (tuh-RĒ-suh)
Greek— *The harvester*
Entertainment: Teresa Wright,
Terri Garr, actresses; Teresa
Brewer, pop singer.
**Rezi, Riza, Teca, Tera,
Terese, Teresina, Teresita,
Teressa, Terez, Teri, Terike,
Terri, Terrie, Terry, Terrye,
Terza, Treszka**

Terry (TAIR-ē)
See Theresa.
Feminine form of Terence.
Tera, Teri, Terra, Terrie, Terrye

Tertia (TER-shuh)
Latin— *The third*

Tesia (TES-shuh)
Polish, Greek— *Loved by God*
Fila, Hortenspa, Teofila

Tess (TES)
See Teresa.
Literature: *Tess of the D'Urbervilles,*
by Thomas Hardy.
Tessa, Tessi, Tessie, Tessy

Thadine (THĀ-dēn)
Hebrew— *The praised*
Feminine form of Thaddeus.

Thais (THĀ-is)
Greek— *The bond*
Interesting: *Thais,* an opera and
novel by Anatole France.

Thalassa (tha-LAS-suh)
Greek— *From the sea*

Thalia (THĀL-yuh)
Greek— *Joyful or blooming*
Mythological: Thalia, one of the
Three Graces.

THERESA—*Reaper*

Thea (THĒ-uh)
Greek—*Goddess*
Mythological: Thea, supernatural
being who opposed the
Olympian Gods.

Thecla (THEK-luh)
Greek—*Of divine fame*
Thekla

Theda (THĒ-duh)
See Theodora.
Entertainment: Theda Bara,
silent-movie actress.

Thelma (THEL-muh)
Greek— *Nursling*
Literature: *Thelma,* by Marie
   Corelli.
Entertainment: Thelma Ritter,
   comedienne.
Telma

Themis (THĒ-mis)
Greek— *Order, custom and justice*

Theodora (thē-ō-DOR-uh)
Greek— *Divine gift*
Feminine form of Theodore.
**Dora, Fedora, Feodora, Ted,
Tedda, Teddi, Teddie, Teddy,
Tedi, Tedra, Teodora, Theda,
Thekla, Theodosia, Theola**

Theone (THĒ-ō-ne)
Greek— *Godly*

Thera (THAIR-uh)
Greek— *The unmastered or wild*

Theresa (tuh-RĒ-suh)
Greek— *Reaper*
Literature: *Thérèsa Raquin,* novel
   by Emile Zola.
**Tera, Teresa, Terese, Teresita,
Teressa, Teri, Terri, Terrie,
Terry, Terrye, Tess, Tessa,
Tessi, Tessie, Tessy, Theda,
Therese, Tracey, Tracie, Tracy,
Tresa, Trescha, Tressa, Zita**

Thirza (THIR-zuh)
Hebrew— *Delight, pleasantness*
Thyrza, Tirtzah, Tirza

Thisbe (THIZ-be)
Greek— *Region of doves*
Literature: Pyramus and Thisbe, in
   A Midsummer Night's Dream, by
   Shakespeare.

Thomasine (TOM-uh-sēn)
Hebrew— *The twin*
Feminine form of Thomas.
Literature: Heroine in *The Return
   of the Native,* by Thomas Hardy.
**Tammi, Tammie, Tamzin,
Thomasa, Thomasin, Thomasina,
Toma, Tomasina, Tomasine,
Tommi, Tommie, Tommy**

Thora (THOR-uh)
Teutonic— *Thunder*
Mythological: Scandinavian
   goddess and friend of mankind.
Thordia, Thordis, Tyra

Tia (TĒ-uh)
Greek, Egyptian— *Princess*
Historical: Princess Tia was the
   sister of the pharaoh, King
   Ramses.

Tiffany (TI-fuh-ne)
Greek— *Appearance of God*
Interesting: Tiffany's, famous
   jewelry store in New York City.
Tiff, Tiffi, Tiffie, Tiffy

Tilda (TIL-duh)
See Mathilda.
Tillie, Tilly

Timothea (tim-ō-THĒ-uh)
Greek— *Honoring God*
Feminine form of Timothy.
**Thea, Tim, Timmi, Timmie,
Timmy**

Tina (TĒ-nuh)
Unknown.
Entertainment: Tina Louise,
   actress; Tina Turner, singer.
Teena, Tine

Tirtha (TIR-thuh)
Hebrew— *Ford*

Tirza (TIR-zuh)
Hebrew— *Cypress tree or desirable*

Tivona (ti-VON-uh)
Hebrew— *Lover of nature*
Von

Tobey (TŌ-bē)
German— *Dove*
Hebrew— *Good*
**Tobe, Tobi, Tobias, Tobit,
Toby, Tobye, Tova, Tove,
Tybi, Tybie**

Toni (TŌ-nē)
See Antoinette.
Entertainment: Toni Tennille,
    singer.
Toinette, Tonia, Tonie, Tony

Tracy (TRĀ-sē)
Gaelic— *Battler*
Latin— *Courageous*
Sports: Tracy Austin, tennis
    champion.
Tracey, Tracie

Tricia (TRI-shuh)
See Patricia.
Famous: Tricia Nixon, daughter of
    President Richard M. Nixon.
Trisha

Trina (TRĒ-nuh)
See Katherine.
Trenna

Trista (TRIS-tuh)
Latin— *Woman of sadness*

Trixie (TRIKS-ē)
See Beatrice.
Trix, Trixy

Troth (TROTH)
Anglo-Saxon— *Truth or pledge*

Trudey (TROO-dē)
See Gertrude.
**Truda, Trude, Trudel,
Trudi, Trudie**

Truly (TROO-lē)
English— *Truly*

Tuesday (TOOS-dā)
Old English— *Tuesday*
Entertainment: Tuesday Weld,
    actress.

Udele (Ū-del)
Anglo-Saxon— *Prosperous*

Ula (Ū-luh)
Celtic— *Sea jewel*
Eula, Ulla

Ulalume (u-LA-loo-ma)
Latin— *Wailing*

Ulani (Ū-la-nē)
Polynesian— *Cheerful*
Ulane

Ullah (Ū-luh)
Hebrew— *A burden*
Ulla, Ullia

Ulrica (ool-RĒ-kuh)
Teutonic— *Ruler of all*
Feminine form of Ulric.
Rica, Ulrika

Umeko (Ū-mē-kō)
Japanese— *Plum-blossom child*
Umekio

Una (OO-nuh)
Gaelic, English, Latin— *One*
Entertainment: Una Merkel,
    actress.
Euna

Undine (un-DĒN)
Latin — *Of water*
Ondine

Unity (Ū-ni-tē)
English — *Unity*
Unus

Upala (ōō-PAL-uh)
Indian — *Opal*

Urania (ū-RĀ-nē-uh)
Greek — *Heavenly*
Uranie

Urbana (ur-BAN-uh)
Latin — *Courteous*
Urban

Uria (ū-RĒ-uh)
Hebrew — *Light of the Lord*

Urit (ŪR-ēt)
Hebrew — *Light*
Urice

Ursula (ER-suh-luh)
Latin — *Little she-bear*
Entertainment: Ursula Andress,
   actress.
**Orsa, Orsola, Sula, Ulla,
Ulli, Urmi, Ursa, Ursala,
Ursel, Ursulina, Ursuline**

Uta (Ū-tuh)
See Ottilie.
Entertainment: Uta Hagen, actress.

Utina (ū-TĒN-uh)
North American Indian — *Woman
of my country*

Valda (VAL-duh)
Teutonic — *Battle-heroine*
Val, Valdis

Valeda (va-LĒ-duh)
Latin — *The strong or healthy*

Valentina (val-en-TĒN-uh)
Latin — *Vigorous and strong*
**Val, Vale, Valeda, Valencia,
Valentia, Valentin, Valerie,
Valli, Vally, Valore**

Valerie (VAL-er-ē)
Latin — *Strong*
Entertainment: Valerie Harper,
   actress.
Val, Vale, Valera, Vally

Valeska (va-LES-kuh)
Polish, Russian — *Glorious ruler*
Vladislav

Valonia (va-LŌN-ē-uh)
Latin — *Of the vale*
Mythological: Latin goddess of
   valleys.
Vallonia

Valora (va-LOR-uh)
Latin — *The valorous*

154

VANESSA — *Butterfly*

Vanessa (va-NE-suh)
Greek — *Butterfly*
Entertainment: Vanessa Redgrave,
  Vanessa Brown, actresses;
  Vanessa, American opera by
  Samuel Barber.
**Nania, Van, Vanna, Vanni,
Vannie, Vanny**

Vania (va-NĒ-uh)
Hebrew — *God's gracious gift*
Van

Vara (VAIR-uh)
Greek — *The stranger*

Vashti (VASH-tē)
Persian — *Beautiful*
Vashta, Vasti

Veda (VĀ-duh)
Sanskrit— *Wise*
Vedette, Velda, Veleda

Vedia (VĀ-dē-uh)
Teutonic— *Sacred spirit of the forest*

Velma (VEL-muh)
See Wilhelmina.
Entertainment: Vilma Banky,
silent-movie actress.
Vilma

Velvet (VEL-vet)
English— *Velvety*
Literature: *National Velvet,* novel
by Enid Eagnold.

Venus (VĒ-nus)
Latin— *Venus*
Mythological: Goddess of beauty.
**Venita, Vin, Vinita, Vinnie,
Vinny**

Vera (VIR-ruh)
Latin— *True*
Russian— *Faith*
Entertainment: Vera Miles,
actress; Vera Zorina, ballet
dancer.
**Veradis, Vere, Verena,
Verene, Verina, Verine,
Verla, Vernice, Vernita**

Veradis (VĒR-uh-dis)
Latin— *Truthful, genuine*

Verda (VER-duh)
Latin— *Young and fresh*
Verdie

Verena (va-RĒ-nuh)
Teutonic— *Defender*
Vera, Verna

Verity (VAIR-i-tē)
Latin— *Truth*
Verita

Verna (VER-nuh)
Latin— *Spring-born*

Veronica (vuh-RON-i-kuh)
Latin— *True image*
Entertainment: Veronica Lake,
actress.
**Ranna, Vera, Veronika,
Veronike, Veronique, Vonni,
Vonnie, Vonny**

Vesta (VES-tuh)
Sanskrit, Latin— *Guardian of the
sacred fire*
Mythological: Goddess of hearth
and home.
Vest

Victoria (vik-TOR-ē-uh)
Latin— *Victory*
Historical: Name given to the
queen of England.
Entertainment: Victoria de los
Angeles, opera singer; Vicki
Carr, singer; Victoria Principal,
actress.
**Vick, Vicki, Vickie, Vicky,
Victorie, Victorine, Vikki, Vikkii,
Vikky, Vitoria, Vittoria**

Vida (VĒ-duh)
Hebrew— *Beloved*
Veda, Vita, Vitia

Vidonia (vi-DŌN-yuh)
Portuguese— *Vine branch*

Violet (VĪ-uh-let)
Latin— *Violet flower*
**Eolande, Iolande, Iolanthe,
Vi, Viola, Violante, Viole,
Violetta, Violette, Yolanda,
Yolande, Yolane, Yolanthe**

Virginia (VER-jin-yuh)
Latin— *Virgin maiden*
Historical: Colony of Virginia.
Literature: Virginia Woolf,
novelist.
Entertainment: Virginia Mayo,
actress.
**Ginger, Ginni, Ginnie, Ginny,
Jimmy, Virg, Virgie,
Virgilia, Virginie, Virgy**

Viridis (vi-RĒ-dis)
Latin— *Youthful and blooming*

Vita (VĒ-tuh)
Latin— *Life*

Vivian (VI-vē-un)
Latin— *Full of life*
Literature: Vivian, imprisoned by
  Merlin in King Arthur legend.
Entertainment: Vivien Leigh,
  actress.
**Vevay, Vi, Viv, Vivi, Vivia,
Viviana, Vivianne, Vivie, Vivien,
Vivienne, Vivyan, Vivyanne**

Voleta (vō-LĒ-tuh)
French— *The veiled*

Wakanda (wa-KAN-duh)
Sioux Indian— *Inner magical power*

Wallis (WAL-lis)
Teutonic— *Girl of Wales*
Feminine form of Wallace.
Historical: Wallis Simpson, who
  married the Duke of Windsor
  after he gave up the throne of
  England for her.
Walli, Wallie, Wally

Wanda (WAN-duh)
Teutonic— *Wander*
Entertainment: Wanda
  Landowska, harpsichordist.
**Vanda, Wandie, Wandis, Wenda,
Wendeline, Wendi, Wendie,
Wendy, Wendye**

Wendy (WEN-dē)
See Wanda.
Literature: Wendy, character in
  children's classic, *Peter Pan*.
Entertainment: Wendy Barrie,
  Wendy Hiller, actresses.
**Wendelin, Wendeline, Wendi,
Wendie, Wendye, Windey,
Windy**

Wenona (wē-NŌ-nuh)
North American Indian—
  First-born daughter
Wenonah

Wesley (WES-lē)
English— *From the west meadow*
Wesla

Whitney (WIT-nē)
English— *From the white island*

Wilhelmina (wil-hel-MĒ-nuh)
Teutonic— *Determined guardian*
Feminine form of William.
Sports: Billie Jean King, tennis
  champion.
**Billi, Billie, Billy, Guglielma,
Guillema, Guillemette, Min,
Mina, Minna, Minni, Minnie,
Minny, Valma, Velma,
Vilhelmina, Vilma, Wileen,
Wilhelmine, Willa, Willabel,
Willabella, Willabelle,
Willamina, Willetta, Willette,
Willi, Willie, Willy, Wilma,
Wilmet, Wilmette, Wylamina,
Wylma**

Willette (wil-LET)
See William.
Literature: Willa Cather, novelist.
Willa

Willow (WIL-ō)
English — *Freedom*

Wilma (WIL-muh)
See Wilhelmina.
Sports: Wilma Rudolph Ward,
Olympic sprinter.

Wilona (wi-LŌ-nuh)
Anglo-Saxon — *The desired*
Wilone

Winema (wi-NĒ-muh)
Indian — *Chieftainess*

Winnie (WIN-nē)
See Gwyneth.
Literature: *Winnie the Pooh,* by
A.A. Milne.
Winni, Winny

Winnifred (WI-ni-fred)
Teutonic — *Friend of peace*
Entertainment: Winifred Lenihan,
actress.
**Freddi, Freddie, Freddy,
Fredi, Ona, Oona, Una,
Winifred, Winnie, Winny**

Winola (wi-NŌ-luh)
Teutonic — *Gracious friend*

Winona (wi-NŌ-nuh)
Sioux Indian — *First-born daughter*
**Wenona, Wenonah, Winnie,
Winny, Winonah**

Winter (WIN-ter)
Old English — *Winter*

Wisia (WI-shuh)
Polish — *Victory*
**Wicia, Wikitoria, Wikta,
Wiktorja**

Wynne (WIN)
Welsh — *Fair*
Winne, Winny, Wyanet

Xanthe (ZAN-thē)
Greek — *Golden yellow*
Historical: Wife of Socrates.
Xantha, Xanthus

Xaviera (za-vē-AIR-uh)
Arabic — *Brilliant*

Xenia (ZĒ-nē-uh)
Greek — *Hospitable*
Xena, Zena, Zenia

Ximena (zi-MĒ-nuh)
Spanish — *Unknown*
Literature: Heroine of *El Cid,* by
Corneille.
Ximenes

Xylia (ZĪ-luh) or (ZĪ-lē-uh)
Greek — *Of the wood*
Xylina

Yachi (YA-chē)
Japanese— *Eight thousand*

Yachne (YAWK-nē)
Lithuanian, Hebrew— *Gracious*

Yamka (YAM-kuh)
Hopi Indian— *Flower budding*

Yasmeen (YAS-mēn)
Arabic— *Jasmine flower*

Yasu (YAW-sōō)
Japanese— *The tranquil*
Yasuko

Yepa (YĒ-puh)
North American Indian— *The snow-maiden*

Yesmina (yez-MĒ-nuh)
Hebrew— *Right hand, strength*

Yetta (YET-tuh)
Old English— *Giver*

Yeva (YĀ-vuh)
Russian, Hebrew— *Life-giving*

Yolanda (yō-LAN-duh)
Greek— *Violet flower*
Eolande, Iolande, Iolnathe, Yolande, Yolane, Yolanthe

Yoluta (yō-LŌŌ-tuh)
North American Indian— *Farewell to the spring flower*

Yonina (yō-NĒ-nuh)
Hebrew— *Dove*
Jona, Jonati, Jonina, Yona, Yonit, Yonita

Yoshiko (yō-SHĒ-kō)
Japanese— *Good*
Yoshi

Yovela (yō-VĒ-luh)
Hebrew— *Rejoicing*

Yseult (Ē-zōōlt)
Celtic— *The fair*

Yuri (Ū-rē)
Japanese— *Lily*

Yvonne (ē-VON)
French— *Archer*
Entertainment: Yvonne De Carlo, Yvonne Printemps, Yvette Mimieux, actresses.
Evonne, Yevette, Yvette

Zada (ZĀ-duh)
Syrian— *Lucky one*

Zahara (za-HAR-uh)
Swahili— *Flower*

Zaltana (zal-TA-nuh)
North American Indian— *High mountain*

Zaneta (za-NĒ-tuh)
  Hebrew— *God's gracious gift*

Zara (ZAIR-uh)
  Hebrew— *Dawn*
  Zarah, Zaria, Zarie

Zel (ZEL)
  Turkish— *A bell*

Zelda (ZEL-duh)
  See Griselda.
  Famous: Zelda Fitzgerald, wife of
    F. Scott Fitzgerald.
  Selda, Zelde

Zenia (ZE-nē-uh)
  Greek— *The hospitable*
  **Xenia, Zenecia, Zeni, Zenija,
  Zenobia, Zina**

Zenobia (ze-NŌ-bē-uh)
  Arabic— *Her father's ornament*

Zerdali (zer-DĀ-lē)
  Turkish— *Wild apricot*

Zia (ZĒ-uh)
  Latin— *Kind of grain*
  Zea

Zina (ZĒ-nuh)
  African— *Name*

Zipparah (zi-PAW-ruh)
  Hebrew— *Sparrow*
  Biblical: Wife of Moses.
  Zifarah, Zifora, Zippora

Zita (ZĒ-tuh)
  Greek, Spanish— *Little rose*
  Zitela, Zitella

Zizi (ZĒ-zē)
  Hungarian, Hebrew— *Dedicated to
    God*
  **Beti, Boske, Boski, Bozsi,
  Eresike, Erqsbet, Erzsi,
  Erzsok, Liszka, Liza, Zsoka**

Zoe (ZŌ) or (ZŌ-uh)
  Greek— *Life*
  Literature: Zoe Akins, author of
    the play *The Old Maid.*

Zoheret (ZŌ-her-et)
  Hebrew— *She shines*

Zola (ZŌ-luh)
  Italian— *Ball of the earth*

Zona (ZŌ-nuh)
  Greek, Latin— *Girdle belt*
  Literature: Zona Gale, author.

Zora (ZOR-uh)
  Greek— *Dawn*
  Zorah, Zorana, Zorina, Zorine

Zuleika (ZOO-lē-kuh)
  Arabic— *The fair one*

Zuri (ZOO-rē)
  Swahili— *Beautiful*

BOYS' NAMES

Aaron (AIR-un)
Hebrew— *Light or mountain*
Biblical: First high priest of Israel,
brother of Moses.
**Aharon, Ari, Arnie, Arny,
Aron, Haroun, Ron, Ronnie,
Ronny**

Abasi (uh-BĀ-sē)
Swahili— *Stern*
Abbas

Abbotson (A-but-sun)
Hebrew— *Son*

Abbott (A-but)
Arabic— *Father*
**Ab, Abba, Abbe, Abbey,
Abbie, Abbot, Abby**

Abdel (AB-del)
Arabic— *Servant*
Abdul, Abdullah

Abel (Ā-bel)
Hebrew— *Breath*
Biblical: Second son of Adam and
Eve, slain by Cain.
Literature: Hero of *Green
Mansions,* by W. H. Hudson.
Abe, Abey, Abie

Abelard (A-bel-ard)
Teutonic— *Nobly resolute*
Ab, Abbey, Abby, Abel

Abi (A-bē)
Turkish— *Elder brother*

Abijah (a-BĒ-juh)
Hebrew— *The Lord is my father*
Abisha

Abner (AB-ner)
Hebrew— *Father of light*
Biblical: Commander of King
Saul's army.
Literature: *Li'l Abner,* comic strip
by Al Capp.
Abbner

Abraham (Ā-bruh-ham)
Hebrew— *Father of multitude*
Biblical: First Hebrew patriarch.
Historical: Abraham Lincoln,
President.
Entertainment: Civil war song *We
Are Coming, Father Abraham.*
**Abe, Abey, Abie, Abrahan,
Abram, Abramo, Abran,
Avram, Avrom, Bram**

Abram (Ā-brum)
Hebrew— *Exalted father*
Famous: James Abram Garfield,
President.
Avram, Avrom, Bram

Absalom (AB-suh-lom)
Hebrew— *Father of peace*
Literature: *Absalom, Absalom,* by
William Faulkner.

Acayib (a-KĀ-yib)
Turkish— *Wonderful and strange*

Ace (ĀS)
Latin— *Unity*
Acey, Acie, Ase

ADLER — *Eagle*

Achilles (a-KIL-ēz)
Unknown
Mythological: Hero of Homer's
Iliad.

Ackerley (A-ker-lē)
Old English — *From the oak-tree
meadow*
Ackley

Adair (uh-DAIR)
Celtic — *From the oak-tree ford*

Adal (Ā-dal)
German — *Noble*

Adalbert (Ā-dal-bert)
German — *Noble bright*
**Adalard, Adelard, Dalbert,
Delvert**

Adam (AD-um)
Hebrew — *Man of the red earth*
Biblical: First man created by God.
Literature: Adam Smith, author of
The Wealth of Nations; novel
Adam Bede, by George Eliot.
**Ad, Adamo, Adams, Adan,
Adao, Addie, Addis, Addy,
Ade, Adem, Adham**

Adamson (AD-um-sun)
Hebrew — *Son of Adam*

Adar (Ā-dar)
Syrian — *Prince or ruler*

Addison (A-di-sun)
Anglo-Saxon — *Adam's descendant*
Ad, Addie, Addy

Adel (Ā-del)
German— *Noble*
Adelar, Adelard, Adelbern, Adelhart

Adelbert (Ā-del-bert)
Teutonic— *Nobly bright*
Adelburt, Bert

Adelric (Ā-del-rik)
Teutonic— *Noble commander*
Adalric

Adigun (A-di-gun)
Nigerian— *Righteous*

Adin (Ā-din)
Hebrew— *Voluptuous or sensual*

Adir (Ā-dir)
Hebrew— *Majestic*

Adlai (AD-lā)
Hebrew— *Justice of Jehovah*
Famous: Adlai E. Stevenson, U.S. Ambassador to the United Nations and candidate for President.

Adlar (AD-lar)
Teutonic— *Noble and brave*

Adler (AD-ler)
Teutonic— *Eagle*
Ad

Adley (AD-lē)
Hebrew— *The just*

Adolph (Ā-dolf)
Teutonic— *Noble wolf or noble hero*
Historical: Adolph Hitler, German dictator.
Ad, Adolf, Adolpha, Adolphe, Adolpho, Adolphus, Dolf, Dolph

Adon (Ā-don)
Hebrew— *Lord*
Adomis, Adonis, Adonnis

Adri (AD-rē)
Hindi— *Rock*

Adrian (Ā-drē-un)
Latin— *Black earth*
Entertainment: Sir Adrian Boult, conductor.
Ade, Adriano, Adrien, Hadrian

Adriel (Ā-drē-el)
Hebrew— *Of God's flock*
Adrial

Agler (AG-ler)
Greek— *Gleaming*

Agustin (aw-GUS-tin)
Spanish— *The exalted one*
Austin

Ahab (Ā-hab)
Hebrew— *Uncle*
Literature: Captain Ahab, character in Herman Melville's *Moby Dick.*

Ahanu (a-HAW-noo)
North American Indian— *He laughs*

Aharon (a-HAR-on)
Hebrew— *Exalted*

Ahearn (Ā-hern)
Celtic— *Lord of the horses*
Ahern

Aidan (Ā-dan)
Celtic— *Fire or warmth of the home*

Ainsley (ĀNS-lē)
Old English— *From Ann's meadow*
Ainslie

Ainsworth (ĀNS-werth)
Old English— *From Ann's estate*

Airell (AR-el)
Celtic— *Chief*

Ajax (Ā-jaks)
Greek— *Eagle*
Turkish— *Frost on a clear winter night*
Literature: Hero in Homer's *Iliad.*

Ala (AW-luh)
Arabic— *Glorious*

Alabi (AL-uh-bē)
Yoruban— *A boy born after many girls*

Alan (AL-an)
Gaelic— *Handsome or cheerful*
Literature: Allen-a-Dale, character in *Ivanhoe,* by Sir Walter Scott.
Entertainment: Alan Ladd, Alan Alda, Allen Stewart Konigsberg (Woody Allen), Alan Arkin, Alan Bates, Al Pacino, actors; Alan Jay Lerner, music composer.
Ailin, Al, Alain, Alair, Aland, Alano, Alanson, Alayne, Allan, Allayne, Allen, Alley, Alleyn, Allie, Allyn

Alaric (AL-ar-ik)
Teutonic— *Ruler of all*
Alric, Alrick

Alastair (AL-a-stair)
See Alexander.
Literature: Alistair McLean, novelist.
Entertainment: Alastair Sim, Alistair Cooke, actors.
Al, Alasdair, Alasteir, Alaster, Alistair, Alister, Alistir, Allister, Allistir

Alben (AL-ben)
Latin— *Fair-blond*
Al, Alban, Albie, Albin, Alby

Albern (AL-bern)
Teutonic— *Of noble valor*

Albert (AL-bert)
German— *Noble, bright*
Historical: Albert Luthuli, Zulu chief, Nobel-Peace-Prize winner.
Famous: Prince Albert, husband of Queen Victoria; Albert Einstein, scientist.
Literature: Albert Camus, French novelist.
Entertainment: Fat Albert, cartoon character created by Bill Cosby.
Adelbert, Ailbert, Al, Alberto, Albie, Albrecht, Aubert, Bert, Berty, Elbert

Albion (AL-bē-on)
Latin— *White or fair*

Alcott (AL-kot)
Old English— *From the old cottage*
Alcot

Alden (AWL-den)
Anglo-Saxon— *Old friend or protector*
Al, Aldin, Aldwin, Elden, Eldin

Aldis (AWL-dis)
Old English— *From the old house*
Al, Aldo, Aldous, Aldus

Aldous (AWL-dus)
German— *Old and wise*
Literature: Aldous Huxley, author of *Brave New World.*

Aldred (AWL-dred)
Anglo-Saxon— *Ancient counselor*

Aldrich (AWL-drich)
Teutonic— *Sage or noble ruler*
Al, Aldric, Aldridge, Alric, Eldridge, Rich, Rickie, Ricky

Aldwin (AWL-dwin)
Anglo-Saxon— *Old friend*
Allwin

Alein (AL-ēn)
Hebrew— *Alone*

Aleron (AL-er-on)
French— *Shoulder-badge or knight armor*
Aleren

Aleser (a-LĀ-ser)
Arabic— *Lion*

Alexander (al-eks-AN-der)
Greek— *Helper of mankind*
Famous: Alexander the Great;
Alexander Graham Bell, inventor
of the telephone; Sir Alexander
Fleming, discoverer of penicillin;
Sandro Botticelli, painter of *The
Birth of Venus;* Alessandro
Scarlatti, founder of modern
opera.
Literature: Alexandre Dumas,
Aleksandr Solzhenitsyn,
authors; Alex Haley, author of
Roots.
Entertainment: Alec Guinness,
Alejandro Rey, actors.
**Al, Alasdair, Alastair,
Alaster, Alec, Alejandro,
Alejo, Alek, Alekos,
Aleksandr, Alessandro, Alex,
Alexandr, Alexandre, Alexandro,
Alexandros, Alexio, Alexis,
Alic, Alick, Alik, Alisander,
Alistair, Alister, Alix,
Allister, Allistir, Lyaksandr,
Sander, Sandra, Sandro, Sandy,
Sanya, Sascha, Sasha, Saunder,
Shura, Shurik**

Alf (ALF)
Norwegian— *Elfin*
Entertainment: *Alfie,* movie
starring Michael Caine.
Alfie, Alfy, Alv

Alfred (AL-fred)
Old English— *Elf counselor*
Famous: Alfred the Great; Alfred
Bernhard Nobel, inventor of
dynamite and founder of the
Nobel prizes.
Entertainment: Alfred Drake,
actor; Alfred Hitchcock, film
director.
**Abery, Al, Alf, Alfie,
Alfredo, Alfy, Fred, Freddie,
Freddy**

Alger (AL-jer)
Teutonic— *Noble spear man*
**Al, Algar, Algernon,
Elgar, Elger, Elgernon**

Ali (A-lē)
Arabic— *Greatest*

Alim (al-IM)
Arabic— *Wise, learned*
Alem

Alison (AL-i-sun)
Teutonic— *Of holy fame*
Allison

Allan (AL-un)
See Alan.
Allen

Allard (AL-ard)
Teutonic— *Nobly resolute*
Alard

Allister (AL-i-ster)
See Alexander.
Alaster

Almon (AL-mon)
Hebrew— *Forsaken*

Almund (AL-mund)
Anglo-Saxon— *Protector of the
temple*

Alon (AL-on)
Hebrew— *Oak tree*

Alonzo (a-LON-zō)
See Alphonse.
Sports: Alonzo Stagg, football
coach.
Alfonso, Alonso, Lon

Aloysius (al-ō-WI-shus)
Teutonic— *Famous in war*

Alpheus (AL-fē-us)
Greek— *River god*

Alphonse (AL-fons)
Teutonic— *Eager for battle*
Literature: Alphonse Daudet,
author.
**Alf, Alfie, Alfons, Alfonso,
Alford, Alfy, Alphonse, Alonso,
Alonzo, Fons, Fonsie, Fonz,
Fonzie, Lon**

Alrik (AWL-rik)
Swedish, Teutonic— *Ruler of all*

Alroy (AWL-roi)
Spanish— *The king*

Alson (AL-son)
Old English— *Son of all*

Alston (AL-ston)
Anglo-Saxon— *From the old manor*

Alton (AL-ton)
Old English— *From the old manor*
Alten

Alvar (AWL-var)
Latin— *White or fair*

Alvin (AL-vin)
Teutonic— *Friend of all*
Famous: Thomas Alva Edison,
  inventor of the light bulb.
**Aloin, Aluin, Aluino, Alva,
Alvan, Alvie, Alvy, Alwin,
Alwyn, Elvin**

Alvis (AL-vis)
Scandinavian— *All-knowing*

Amadis (uh-MA-dis)
Latin— *Love of God*

Amado (uh-MA-dō)
Spanish, Latin— *Loving deity*
Amadeo, Amadis, Amando

Amasa (uh-MĀ-suh)
Hebrew— *Burden*

Ambert (AM-bert)
Teutonic— *Bright*

Ambrose (AM-brōz)
Greek— *Belonging to the immortals*
Literature: Ambrose Bierce, author.
**Ambee, Ambie, Ambros,
Ambrosi, Ambrosio, Ambrosius,
Amley, Brose**

Ameer (a-MĒR)
Arabic— *A prince*

Amiel (a-MĒL)
Hebrew— *Lord of my people*

Amin (a-MIN)
Indian— *Faithful*
Amitan, Amnon

Amory (Ā-mō-rē)
German— *Industrious*
Literature: Amory Blaine, hero of
  This Side of Paradise, by F. Scott
  Fitzgerald.
**Almericus, Amalric, Amelric,
Americus, Amerigo, Amery,
Emery, Emmerich, Emmery**

Amos (Ā-mos)
Hebrew— *Burden*
Biblical: Prophet of Old Testament.
Entertainment: Amos and Andy,
  comedy team.
Amoss

Amyas (a-MĒ-as)
Latin— *One who shall love God*

Anastasius (an-uh-STĀ-shus)
Greek— *One who shall rise again*
**Anastas, Anastasius, Anastatius,
Anstice**

Anatole (AN-uh-tōl)
Greek— *From the east*
Literature: Anatole France, French
  novelist.
Anatol, Anatolio

Anders (AN-ders)
See Andrew.
Anderson

André (ON-drā)
Russian, French— *Strong and manly*
Literature: André Maurosi, André
  Malraux, authors; André Gide,
  Nobel Prize winning author.
**Anders, Andi, Andor, Andras,
Andreas, Andres, Andrew,
Andrey, Andris, Andrius, Aniol,
Endre, Evagelos, Jedrek,
Jedrus, Ondra, Ondro**

ANDRE—*Strong and manly*

Andrew (AN-dr$\overline{oo}$)
Greek—*Manly*
Biblical: Apostle of Jesus Christ.
Famous: Andrea del Sarto, painter
of *The Faultless Painter*; Andrew
Young, former Ambassador to
the United Nations.
Entertainment: Andre Segovia,
guitarist; Andy Williams, singer.
**Anders, Andie, Andonis,
Andre, Andrea, Andreas, Andres,
Andrey, Andy, Dre, Dru,
Drud, Drugi**

Aneurin (a-N$\overline{U}$R-in)
Welsh—*Very golden*
Latin—*Honorable*
Famous: Aneurin Beva, British
labor leader.

Angell ($\overline{A}$N-jel)
Greek—*Messenger*

Angelo (AN-juh-l$\overline{o}$)
Greek—*Angel or saintly*
Literature: Angel Clare, hero of
Tess of the D'Urbervilles, by
Thomas Hardy.
Ange, Angel, Angie, Angy

Angus ($\overline{A}$NG-us)
Celtic—*Exceptionally strong*
Interesting: In Irish folklore,
Angus Og is the God of laughter,
love, wisdom and understanding.
Ennis, Gus

Ansel (AN-sel)
French—*Adherent of a nobleman*
Famous: Ansel Adams,
photographer.
Ancell, Ansell

Anselm (AN-selm)
Teutonic—*Divine helmet*
**Anse, Ansel, Anselma, Anselme,
Anselmi, Anselmo, Elmo, Selma**

Anson (AN-sun)
Old English — *Son of a nobleman*
Teutonic — *Son of John*
Entertainment: Anson Williams,
   actor in *Happy Days.*
Ansun, Hanson

Anthony (AN-thō-nē)
Latin — *Priceless*
Historical: Mark Antony and
   Cleopatra.
Famous: *The Temptation of St.
   Anthony,* painting by
   Hieronymus Bosch.
Entertainment: Anthony Quinn,
   Anthony Perkins, Tony Curtis,
   actors.
**Antoine, Anton, Antone,
Antoni, Antonin, Antonio,
Antonius, Antony, Toni, Tonie,
Tony**

Anton (AN-ton)
Latin — *Unestimable*
**Andonias, Andonis, Antal,
Antavas, Antek, Anthony, Anti,
Antin, Antinko, Antoine,
Antonen, Antonin, Antons,
Antos, Tolek, Tonda, Tonek,
Tonik, Tonis, Tony, Tosya,
Tusya**

Apang (a-PANG)
North American
   Indian — *First-place winner*

Apenimon (uh-PE-ni-mon)
North American Indian — *Trusty*

Apollo (uh-PAW-lō)
Greek — *Manly beauty*
Mythological: Greek god of light,
   healing and arts.
Apolo, Polio, Polo

Archer (AR-cher)
Old English — *Bowman*

Archibald (AR-chi-bald)
German — *Nobly or genuinely bold*
Literature: Archibald MacLeish,
   winner of three Pulitzer Prizes.
**Arch, Archaimbaud,
Archambault, Archer,
Archibaldio, Archibaldo,
Archibold, Archie, Archy**

Arden (AR-den)
Latin — *Ardent, fiery*
Ard, Ardean, Ardie, Ardin, Ardy

Ardon (AR-don)
Hebrew — *Bronze*
Ardean

Arel (AIR-el)
Hebrew — *Lion of God*

Aren (AIR-en)
Norwegian — *Eagle*

Argus (AR-gus)
Greek, Danish — *Watchful or vigilant*
Gus, Guss

Argyle (AR-gīl)
Celtic — *From the land of the Irish*

Aric (AIR-ik)
Teutonic — *Ruler*
Arick

Ariel (AIR-ē-el)
Hebrew — *Lion of God*
Biblical: Chief who followed Ezra.
   Ariel was the name given to
   Jerusalem by Isaiah.
Literature: *Ariel,* biography by
   Andre Maurois.
Airel

Aries (AIR-ēz)
Zodiac — *Ram*

Arkin (AR-kin)
Norwegian — *The eternal King's son*

Arkwright (ARK-rīt)
Old English — *Maker of chests*

Arlen (AR-len)
Gaelic — *Pledge*
Arlin

ARCHER—*Bowman*

Arley (AR-lē)
Zodiac—*The bowman*

Arlo (AR-lō)
See Harlow.
Entertainment: Arlo Guthrie, folksinger.

Arman (AR-man)
Russian, Teutonic—*Army man*
Armand, Armando, Armin, Armond, Armund

Armon (AR-mon)
Hebrew—*Castle or place*
Armoni, Armony

Armstrong (ARM-strong)
Old English—*With a strong arm*

Arne (AR-nē)
Norwegian—*Eagle*
Arney, Arni, Arnie

Arnold (AR-nuld)
German—*Eagle power*
Literature: Arnold Bennet, author of *The Old Wive's Tale.*
Sports: Arnold Palmer, golfer.
Arnaldo, Arnaud, Arney, Arni, Arnie, Arnoldo, Arny

Arnon (AR-non)
Hebrew—*Rushing stream*
Interesting: Name for an energetic child.
Arnan

Aron (AIR-on)
Czech, Polish— *Lofty or exalted*
Aaron

Arpiar (AR-pē-ar)
Armenian— *Sunny, of sunshine*

Arri (AR-ē)
Greek— *Seeking the positive results*

Arrio (AR-rē-ō)
Spanish— *Warlike*
Ario

Arslan (ARS-lan)
Turkish— *Lion*

Artemas (AR-tuh-mus)
Greek— *Safe and sound*
Biblical: Character in the New
Testament.
**Art, Artemis, Artemus,
Artie, Arty**

Arthur (AR-ther)
Celtic— *Noble*
Welsh— *Bear hero*
Literature: British king of the
Round Table in *Idylls of the King,*
by Lord Alfred Tennyson; *Morte
d'Arthur,* by Sir Thomas Malory;
Sir Arthur Conan Doyle, creator
of Sherlock Holmes; Arthur
Miller, playwright.
Entertainment: Artur Rubinstein,
pianist; Art Garfunkel, singer.
Sports: Arthur Ashe, tennis
champion.
**Art, Artair, Arte, Arther,
Artie, Artur, Arturo, Artus,
Arty, Aurthur, Aurthus**

Arundel (uh-RUN-del)
Old English— *From the eagle dell*

Arvad (AR-vad)
Hebrew— *Wander*
Arv, Arvid, Arvie

Arve (ARV)
Norwegian— *Heir*
Arvid

Arvel (AR-vel)
Welsh— *Wept over*

Arvin (AR-vin)
German— *People's friend*
Arv, Arvie, Arvy

Asa (Ā-suh)
Hebrew— *Physician or healer*
Ase

Asadel (Ā-suh-del)
Arabic— *Most prosperous*

Ashby (ASH-bē)
Scandinavian— *From the ash-tree
farm*
Ashton

Asher (ASH-er)
Hebrew— *Happy, blessed*

Ashford (ASH-ford)
Old English— *Dweller by the
ash-tree ford*
**Ash, Ashen, Ashlen,
Ashley, Ashlin, Ashton**

Ashur (ASH-er)
Swahili— *Month*

Asiel (Ā-sē-el)
Hebrew— *God has created him*

Asker (ASK-er)
Turkish— *Soldier*

Aswad (AS-wad)
Arabic— *Black*

Athmore (ATH-mor)
Old English— *From the moor*

Atman (AT-man)
Hindi— *The self*

Atuanya (a-TWAN-yuh)
Nigerian— *Unexpected*

Aubrey (AW-brē)
German, French— *Elf rule*
Famous: Aubrey Beardsley,
English painter.
Literature: Oberon, elf king in *A
Midsummer Night's Dream*, by
Shakespeare.
**Alberik, Aube, Auberon,
Avery, Oberon**

Audley (AWD-lē)
Anglo-Saxon— *Unknown*

Audric (AWD-rik)
French— *Old and wise ruler*
Aldrich, Aldrick

Audun (AWD-un)
Norwegian— *Deserted or desolate*

Audwin (AWD-win)
Teutonic— *Rich or prospering friend*

August (AW-gust)
Latin— *Majestic dignity*
**Agosto, Aguistin, Agustin,
Augie, Auguste, Augustine,
Augusto, Augustus, Augy,
Austen, Austin, Gus, Guss**

Augustus (aw-GUS-tus)
Latin— *The exalted, sacred or sublime*
Famous: Augustus Caesar, Roman
emperor.
**Aguistin, Agustin, Augie,
Augustin, Augy, Austen,
Austin, Gus**

Aurek (AW-rik)
Polish— *Golden-haired*
Aureli, Elek

Austin (AWS-tin)
See Augustine.
Literature: Austin Dobson,
novelist.
Austen

Avedig (AV-dig)
Armenian— *Good news*

Avel (Ā-vel)
Greek— *Breath*

Averill (Ā-ver-el)
Anglo-Saxon— *Boarlike*
Famous: Averill Harriman, former
Secretary of State.
Av, Ave, Averell, Averil

Avery (Ā-ver-ē)
Anglo-Saxon— *Ruler of the elves*
Sports: Avery Brundage,
Chairman of U.S. Olympic
Committee.

Avi (AW-vē)
Hebrew— *Father*
**Avidan, Avidor, Aviel,
Avital, Avner, Avniel**

Awan (A-wan)
North American Indian— *Somebody*

Axel (AKS-el)
Hebrew— *Man of peace*
Aksel, Ax, Axe, Axie

Aylmer (AL-mer)
German *Noble fame*
Aylmar, Aymar, Aymer

Azad (A-zad)
Turkish— *Born free*

Azim (A-zim)
Arabic— *Defender*

Azriel (Ā-zrē-el)
Hebrew— *God is my help*

Badem (buh-DĒM)
Turkish — *Almond*

Bailey (BĀ-lē)
Teutonic — *Able*
French — *Bailiff or steward*
**Bail, Bailee, Bailie,
Baillee, Baillie, Baily**

Bainbridge (BĀN-brij)
Gaelic — *Fair bridge*

Baird (BAIRD)
Gaelic — *Ballad singer*
Bar, Bard, Barde, Barr, Bart

Balder (BAL-der)
Scandinavian — *God of light*
Aldur

Baldwin (BALD-win)
Teutonic — *Bold friend*
Bald, Balduin, Baudoin

Balfour (BAL-for)
Scottish — *Pasture land*

Balin (BĀ-lin)
Hindi — *Mighty soldier*
Baline

Balint (BĀ-lint)
Hungarian, Latin — *Strong and
healthy*

Ballard (BAL-ard)
Teutonic — *Bold or strong*
Ball

Bancroft (BAN-kroft)
Old English — *From the bean field*

Baram (BAIR-am)
Hebrew — *Son of a nation*

Barclay (BAR-klā)
Old English — *From the birch tree
meadow*

Bardo (BAR-dō)
Danish — *Son of the earth*
**Barth, Barto, Bartoli, Bartolme,
Toli**

Barlow (BAR-lō)
Old English — *From the bare hill*
Bar, Barlie, Barly

Barnabas (BAR-nuh-bus)
Hebrew — *Son of prophecy*
Biblical: Friend of Apostle Paul.
**Barnaba, Barnabe, Barnaby,
Barnebas, Barney, Barnie,
Barny, Burnaby**

Barnaby (BAR-nuh-bē)
See Barnabas.
Entertainment: Barnaby Jones, TV
character played by Buddy Ebsen.
Barnabas, Barney

Barnett (bar-NET)
Old English — *Noble man*
**Barn, Barney, Baron,
Barron, Barry**

Barrett (BAIR-et)
Teutonic — *Bearlike*

Barry (BAIR-ē)
French — *Dweller at the barrier*
Entertainment: Barry Gibb, singer;
Barry Manilow, composer and
singer.
Barri, Barrie, Barris

172

Bartholomew
(bar-THAW-lō-mū)
Hebrew — *Son of the farrow*
Biblical: One of the 12 Apostles of Jesus Christ.
Bart, Bartel, Barth, Barthel, Barthelemy, Bartholomeo, Bartholomeus, Bartlet, Bartlett, Bartley, Bartolome, Bat

Baruch (ba-ROOK)
Greek — *Doer of good*
Famous: Baruch Spinoza, philosopher.

Basham (BA-sham)
Zodiac — *Rich soil*

Basil (BĀ-zel)
Greek — *Kingly*
Entertainment: Basil Rathbone, actor who played Sherlock Holmes.
Base, Basile, Basilio, Basilius, Vasibis, Vassily

Basir (BĀ-sir)
Turkish — *Intelligent and discerning*

Baul (BŌL)
English — *Snail*

Bavol (BĀ-vol)
English — *Wind*

Baxter (BAKS-ter)
Old English — *Baker*
Bax, Baxie, Baxy

BAXTER — *Baker*

Bayard (BĀ-ard)
Teutonic — *Red-brown hair*
Historical: Pierre du Terrail,
  known as Chevalier de Bayard, a
  French hero.
Bay

Beau (BŌ)
French — *Handsome*
Entertainment: Beau Bridges, actor.
**Beal, Beale, Bealle,
Beaufort, Bo**

Beauregard (BŌ-ruh-gard)
French — *Beautiful expression*
Beau, Bo, Gard

Beck (BEK)
Swedish — *Brook*

Bedrich (BED-rik)
Czech, German — *Peaceful leader*
Beda, Bedo, Bedric

Bela (BE-luh)
Hebrew — *Destruction*
Biblical: Name given to a city
  destroyed by earthquakes.

Beldon (BEL-don)
Old English — *Child of unspoiled or
  beautiful glen*
Belden

Belen (BĀ-len)
Greek — *An arrow*
Belan, Belon

Bellamy (BEL-uh-mē)
French — *Beautiful friend*
Belamy, Bell, Bellum

Bem (BEM)
Nigerian — *Peace*

Bemossed (BE-mos-ed)
North American Indian — *The
  walker*
Bemosed

Ben (BEN)
Hebrew — *Son*
Benn, Bennie, Benny, Benton

Benci (BEN-sē)
Hungarian — *Blessed*
**Bendek, Benedek, Benedict,
Benedik, Benedyk, Benek**

Benedict (BEN-e-dikt)
Latin — *Blessed*
Interesting: Benedict is a
  confirmed bachelor that finally
  marries later in life.
Historical: Benedict Arnold,
  Revolutionary War traitor.
**Ben, Bendick, Bendict, Bendix,
Benedetto, Benedick, Benedicto,
Benedikt, Bengt, Benito,
Bennie, Benny, Benoit**

Benjamin (BEN-ja-min)
Hebrew — *Son of the right hand*
Famous: Benjamin Harrison,
  President; Benjamin Franklin,
  statesman and inventor.
Entertainment: Benny Goodman,
  clarinet player; Benny Anderson,
  member of the pop group, ABBA.
**Ben, Beniamino, Benji, Benjie,
Benjy, Benn, Bennie, Benno,
Benny, Benson, Jamie**

Bentley (BENT-le)
Old English — *From the moor*
**Ben, Benn, Bennie, Benny,
Bent, Bentlee, Benton**

Benzi (BEN-zē)
Hebrew — *Excellent son*

Berdy (BER-dē)
Russian, German — *Brilliant mind*
Berdi, Berdie

Berg (BERG)
Hebrew — *Mountain*

Bergren (BER-gren)
Swedish — *Mountain stream*

Berkeley (BERK-lē)
Anglo-Saxon — *From the birch
  meadow*
**Berk, Berkie, Berkley, Berkly,
Berky**

Bern (BERN)
Teutonic— *Bear*
**Bern, Berne, Bernie,
Berny, Bjorn**

Bernard (BER-nard)
Teutonic— *Grim bear*
Literature: George Bernard Shaw,
  playwright.
**Barnard, Barne, Barney,
Barny, Bear, Bearnard, Bern,
Bernardo, Bernarr, Bernhard,
Bernie, Berny, Burnard**

Bernhard (BERN-hard)
Swedish— *Brave as a bear*
Bern

Bersh (BERSH)
English— *One year*
Besh

Bert (BERT)
Old English— *Bright*
Entertainment: Bert Lahr, Bert
  Lancaster, actors; Burt
  Bacharach, songwriter.
Sports: Bart Starr, football
  quarterback.
**Bart, Bertie, Berty, Burt,
Burty, Butch**

Berthold (BER-tōld)
Teutonic— *Brilliant ruler*
Literature: Bertold Brecht, author
  of *The Three Penny Opera*.
**Bert, Berthoud, Bertie, Bertold,
Bertolde, Berty**

Bertin (BER-tin)
Spanish— *Distinguished*

Berton (BER-ton)
Teutonic— *Glorious raven*
Famous: Bertrand Russell,
  philosopher and winner of the
  Nobel Prize.
**Bart, Beltran, Bert, Bertie,
Bertram, Bertrand, Bertrando,
Berty**

Berwin (BER-win)
Teutonic— *Warrior friend*

Bevan (BE-van)
Celtic— *Youthful warrior*
Bev, Bevon

Bevis (BĒ-vis)
Teutonic— *Bowman*
Bevus

Bialy (BĒ-al-ē)
Polish— *White-haired boy*
Bialas

Bildad (BIL-dad)
Hebrew— *Beloved*

Bill (BIL)
See William.
Famous: Buffalo Bill Cody; Billy
  Graham, evangelist.
Literature: *Billy Budd,* by Herman
  Melville.
Entertainment: Bill Cosby, Bill
  Bixby, Billy Dee Williams, actors;
  Billy Joel, singer.
Bil, Billee, Billie, Billy

Bing (BING)
Teutonic— *Kettle-shaped hollow*
Entertainment: Bing Crosby,
  singer and actor.

Birch (BIRCH)
Old English— *Birch tree*
Famous: Birch Bayh, Senator.
Birk, Burch

Bishop (BI-shop)
Old English— *Bishop*
Bish

Bjorn (bē-ORN)
Norwegian— *Bear*
Entertainment: Bjorn Ulvaeus,
  member of the pop group, ABBA.
Sports: Bjorn Borg, tennis
  champion.

Blaine (BLĀN)
Gaelic— *Thin or lean*
Blainey, Blane, Blayne, Blayney

Blair (BLAIR)
Gaelic— *Child of the fields*

BORIS — *Battler*

Blake (BLĀK)
  Old English — *Pallid*
  Entertainment: Blake Edwards,
    film producer.

Blaze (BLĀZ)
  Latin — *Stammerer*
  Biagio, Blaise, Blas, Blase,
  Blasius, Blayze, Bleasien

Bo (BŌ)
  See Beauregard.

Boaz (BŌ-az)
  Hebrew — *Swift and strong*

Bob (BOB)
See Robert.
Entertainment: Bob Hope, Bob
Newhart, actors; Bob Dylan,
singer; Bob Fosse, choreographer
and film director.
Sports: Bob Cousy, basketball
player.
Bobbie, Bobby

Bogart (BŌ-gart)
French — *Strong as a bow*
Bo, Bogery, Bogey, Bogie

Bohdan (BŌ-dan)
Ukrainian — *Given by God*
Bogdan, Bogdashka

Bolton (BŌL-ton)
Old English — *Of the manor farm*

Bond (BOND)
Old English — *Tiller of the soil*
Bondie, Bondon, Bondy

Boone (BOON)
French — *Good*
Bone, Bonnie, Booney

Booth (BOOTH)
Old English — *From the hut*
Boot, Boote, Boothe

Borden (BOR-den)
Old English — *From the valley of the
boar*
Bord, Bordie, Bordy

Borg (BORG)
Norwegian — *From the castle*

Boris (BOR-is)
Slavic — *Battler*
Literature: Boris Pasternak, author
of *Doctor Zhivago*.
Entertainment: Boris Karloff, actor.

Bowie (BOO-e)
Gaelic — *Yellow-haired*

Bowle (BŌL)
English — *Snail*
Baul

Bowman (BŌ-man)
Zodiac — *An archer*

Boyce (BOIS)
French — *From the woodland*
Boy, Boycey, Boycie

Boyden (BOI-den)
Anglo-Saxon — *A herald*
Boy, Boyer

Boynton (BOIN-ton)
Celtic — *White-cow river*

Brad (BRAD)
Old English — *Broad*
Bradley, Brady

Bradburn (BRAD-bern)
Zodiac — *Broad brook*

Braden (BRĀ-den)
Old English — *From the wide valley*
Bradan

Bradford (BRAD-ford)
Old English — *From the broad river
crossing*
Entertainment: Bradford Dillman,
actor.
Brad, Ford

Bradley (BRAD-le)
Old English — *From the broad
meadow*

Bradshaw (BRAD-shaw)
English — *Large virginal forest*

Brainard (BRĀ-nard)
Teutonic — *Bold raven*

Bram (BRAM)
Gaelic — *Raven*
Old English — *Famous*
Literature: Bram Stoker, author of
Dracula.
Bran

Bramwell (BRAM-wel)
Old English — *Of Abraham's well*
Entertainment: Bramwell Fletcher,
actor.

Brand (BRAND)
Old English— *Firebrand*
Bran, Brander, Brandy, Brant

Brandon (BRAN-don)
Teutonic— *Flaming hill*
Anglo-Saxon— *Sword*
Bran, Brand, Brandy

Brede (BRĒD)
Norwegian, Danish— *Glacier*

Brencis (BREN-sis)
Latin— *Crowned with laurel*

Brendan (BREN-dan)
Gaelic— *Little raven*
German— *Aflame*
Literature: Brendan Behan, author of *The Hostage.*
Bren, Brenden, Brendin, Brendis

Brent (BRENT)
Old English— *Steep hill*
Brentan, Brenton

Brett (BRET)
Celtic— *Native of Brittany*
Literature: Bret Harte, western short-story writer.
Entertainment: Bret Maverick, character played by James Garner.
Bret, Brit, Britt

Brewster (BRŌŌ-ster)
Old English— *Brewer*
Brew, Brewer, Bruce

Brian (BRĪ-an)
Celtic— *The strong*
Historical: Brian Boru, heroic king of Ireland.
Entertainment: Brian Aherne, Brian Keith, actors.
Briano, Briant, Brien, Brion, Bryan, Bryant, Bryon

Brice (BRĪS)
Celtic— *Quick moving*
Bryce

Brigham (BRI-gam)
Old English— *Dweller by the bridge*
Famous: Brigham Young, Mormon prophet and pioneer.
Brig, Brigg, Briggs

Brock (BROK)
Old English— *Badger*
Sports: Brock Yates, automotive journalist.
Brockie, Brocky, Brok

Broderick (BROD-er-ik)
Old English— *From the broad ridge*
Entertainment: Broderick Crawford, actor.
Brod, Broddie, Broddy, Broderic, Rick, Rickie, Ricky

Brody (BRŌ-dē)
Gaelic— *Ditch*
Brodie

Bromley (BROM-lē)
Old English— *From the broom-covered meadow*
Bromlee

Bronson (BRON-sun)
Old English— *Dark-skinned*

Brook (BROOK)
Old English— *From the brook*
Brooke, Brooks, Burne

Bruce (BRŌŌS)
French— *From the thicket*
Literature: Bruce Catton, author.
Entertainment: Bruce Dern, actor.
Brucie, Bruis

Bruno (BRŌŌ-nō)
Italian— *Brown-haired*
Bruna, Bruns

Bryant (BRĪ-ant)
Celtic— *Strong*
Entertainment: Bryant Gumbel, newscaster.
Bryan

Buck (BUK)
Old English — *Buck deer*
Entertainment: Buck Henry, actor;
Buck Rogers, space character.
Buckie, Bucky

Bud (BUD)
Old English — *Herald*
Entertainment: Buddy Hollie, rock
singer.
Budd, Buddie, Buddy

Burgess (BER-jes)
Old English — *Citizen of a fortified
town*
Entertainment: Burgess Meredith,
actor.
Burg, Burr

Burke (BERK)
French — *From the fortress*
Bark, Berk, Berke, Bourke

Burl (BERL)
Old English — *Cup-bearer*
Entertainment: Burl Ives, singer.
Burlie, Byrle

Burne (BERN)
Old English — *From the brook*
Bourn, Bourne, Burn, Byrne

Burris (BER-ris)
Anglo-Saxon — *Of the town*
Burr

Burton (BER-ton)
Old English — *From the fortress*
Entertainment: Burt Lancaster,
Burt Reynolds, actors.
Bert, Burt

Butch (BUTCH)
See Bert.
Famous: Butch Cassidy (Robert
LeRoy Parker), Western
bankrobber and outlaw.

Byrd (BERD)
Old English — *Birdlike*
Byrdie

Byron (BĪ-ron)
Anglo-Saxon — *Bear*
Teutonic — *From the cottage*
Literature: Lord Byron, poet.
Sports: Byron Nelson, professional
golfer.
**Biron, Buiron, Byran,
Byrann, Byrom**

Cadao (ka-DĀ-ō)
Vietnamese — *Folk song*

Cadell (ka-DEL)
Celtic — *Of material spirit*
Cadel, Cedell

Cadmar (KAD-mar)
Celtic — *Mighty in battle*
Cad, Mar

Caesar (SĒ-zer)
Latin — *Cut down*
Historical: Julius Caesar.
Famous: Cesar Chavez, organizer
of migrant farmworkers.
Entertainment: Cesar Auguste,
French organist; Cesare Siepi,
opera singer; Caesar Romero,
actor.
Casar, Cesar, Cesare, Kaiser

Cahil (KĀ-hil)
Turkish — *Young or naive*

Calder (KAL-der)
Old English — *Stream*
Cal, Caldwell

Caleb (KĀ-leb)
Hebrew — *Dog*
Cal, Cale

Calut (KAL-ut)
Turkish — *Goliath*

Calvert (KAL-vert)
Old English — *Herdsman*
Cal, Calbert

Calvin (KAL-vin)
Latin — *Bald*
Famous: John Calvin, Protestant
    reformer; Calvin Coolidge,
    President; Calvin Klein, designer.

Cam (KAM)
English — *Beloved*

Camden (KAM-den)
Scottish — *From the winding valley*
Camdan, Camdin

Cameron (KĀ-mer-un)
Celtic — *Crooked nose*
Entertainment: Cameron Mitchell,
    actor.
Cam, Camero, Camey, Cammy

Campbell (KAM-bel)
Scottish — *Crooked mouth*
Cam, Camp, Campy

Canute (ka-NŌOT)
Old Norse — *Knot*
Cnut, Knut, Knute

Cappi (KAP-ē)
English — *Good fortune*

Cardew (kar-DŌO)
Celtic — *From the black forest*

Carew (ka-RŌO)
Welsh — *From the fortress*

Carey (KAIR-ē)
Welsh — *From near the castle*
Entertainment: Cary Grant, actor.
Care, Cary

Carl (KARL)
Old English — *Farmer's town*
Literature: Carl Sandburg, poet.
Entertainment: Carl Reiner, actor;
    Carl Wilson, member of the rock
    group, The Beach Boys; Carlo
    Ponti, film producer and
    husband of Sophia Loren.
**Carl, Carleton, Carlo,
Carlton, Charlton**

Carlin (KAR-lin)
Gaelic — *Little champion*
Carl, Carlie, Carling, Carly

Carlisle (KAR-līl)
Old English, Latin — *From the walled
    city*
Carl, Carlie, Carly, Carlyle

Carmine (KAR-mīn)
Latin — *Song*

Carney (KAR-nē)
Celtic — *Warrior*
Car, Carney, Karney, Kearney

Carr (KAR)
Norwegian — *From the marsh*
Karr, Kerr

Carroll (KAIR-ul)
Gaelic — *Champion*
Entertainment: Carroll O'Connor,
    star of *All in the Family;* J. Carroll
    Nash, actor.
Carolus, Carrol, Cary, Caryl

Carson (KAR-sun)
Old English — *Dweller by the marsh*

Carswell (KARS-wel)
Zodiac — *Child of the watercress
    spring*
Karswell

Carter (KAR-ter)
Old English — *Cart driver*
Cart

Carvel (KAR-vel)
Old English — *From the villa by the
    marsh*
Carvell

CATALIN—*Magic wizard*

Carver (KAR-ver)
Old English—*Wood carver or sculptor*

Casey (KĀ-sē)
Gaelic—*Brave*
Sports: Casey Stengel, baseball manager.
Case

Casimir (KAZ-i-mir)
Slavic—*Proclamation of peace*
Casimire, Casper, Cass, Cassie, Cassy, Kazimir

Casper (KAS-per)
Persian — *Treasurer*
Famous: Casper Weinberger, of the
Reagan administration.
Entertainment: Casper the
Friendly Ghost, cartoon
character.
**Casimir, Caspar, Cass, Cassie,
Cassy, Gaspard, Gasparo,
Gasper, Jasper, Kaspar, Kasper**

Cassidy (KA-si-dē)
Gaelic — *Clever*
Cass, Cassie, Cassy

Cassius (KA-shus)
Latin — *Vain*
Famous: Cassius Jackson Keyser,
authority on philosophy of
mathematics.
Sports: Cassius Clay (Muhammad
Ali), heavyweight boxing
champion.
Cash, Cass, Cassie, Cassy, Caz

Catalin (KAT-lin)
Irish — *Magic wizard*

Caton (KĀ-ton)
Spanish, Latin — *Wise*

Cavell (ka-VEL)
Teutonic — *Boldly active*

Cecil (SĒ-sil)
Latin — *Blind*
Entertainment: Cecil Blount de
Mille, film producer and
director; Cecil Beaton,
photographer and stage designer.
Cece, Cecile, Cecilius

Cedric (SED-rik)
Celtic — *Chieftain*
Entertainment: Sir Cedric
Hardwicke, actor.

Cemal (SĒ-mal)
Arabic, Turkish — *Beauty*

Chad (CHAD)
Celtic — *Defender*
Entertainment: Chad Everett, actor.
Chaddie, Chaddy

Chadburn (CHAD-bern)
Old English — *From the wild catbrook*
Chadbern

Chadwick (CHAD-wik)
Old English — *From the warrior's
town*

Chaim (kī-AM)
Hebrew — *Life*
**Hayyim, Hy, Hyman, Hymie,
Mannie, Manny**

Chal (CHAL)
English — *Lad*
Chelovik, Chiel, Childe

Chale (CHĀL)
Spanish — *Strong and manly*
Chalie

Chalmers (CHAL-mers)
Scottish — *Son of the Lord*

Cham (CHAM)
Vietnamese — *Hard worker*

Chandler (CHAN-dler)
French — *Candlemaker*
Chan, Chane

Chane (SHĀN)
Swahili — *Tough leaf*
Chene

Chaney (SHĀ-nē)
French — *Oak wood*
Cheney

Channing (CHAN-ing)
Old English — *Knowing*
French — *Canon*
Chan, Chane, Chanely

Chanoch (CHA-nok)
Hebrew, Old English — *Clergyman*
Chano

Chapman (CHAP-man)
Old English — *Merchant*
**Chap, Chappie, Chappy,
Mannie, Manny**

Charles (CHARLZ)
Teutonic— *Manly or strong*
Famous: Prince Charles of
  England; Charles de Gaulle,
  President of France; Charles
  Schulz, cartoonist and creator of
  Peanuts; Charles Proteus
  Steinmetz, inventor.
Entertainment: Charles Boyer,
  Charlie Chaplin, Charlton
  Heston, Charles Bronson,
  Charles Laughton, actors.
**Carl, Carlo, Carlos, Carrol,
Carroll, Cary, Caryl, Chad,
Chaddie, Chaddy, Charley,
Charlie, Charlot, Charlton,
Chic, Chick, Chicky, Chuck,
Karel, Karl, Karoly**

Chase (CHĀS)
French— *Hunter*

Chatwin (CHAT-win)
Old English— *Warlike friend*
Chatvin

Chauncey (CHON-sē)
French, Latin— *Chancellor*

Chen (CHEN)
Chinese— *Vast or great*

Cheney (SHĀ-nē)
French— *From the oak wood*
Chen

Cheslav (CHES-lav)
Russian— *Lives in a fortified camp*
Chet

Chesmu (CHES-mū)
North American Indian— *Gritty*

Chester (CHES-ter)
English, Latin— *From the fortified
  camp*
Famous: Chester Alan Arthur,
  President.
Entertainment: Chet Huntley,
  newscaster; Chester, character
  on *Gunsmoke.*
Ches, Cheston, Chet

Chevalier (sha-VAL-yā)
French— *Knight*
Entertainment: Chevy Chase, actor
  and comedian.
Chev, Chevy

Chico (CHĒ-kō)
See Francis.

Chilton (CHIL-ton)
Old English— *From the farm by the
  spring*
Entertainment: Chill Wills, actor.
Chil, Chill, Chilt

Christian (KRIS-chun)
Greek— *Follower of Christ*
Interesting: Kris Kringle, another
  name for Santa Claus.
Famous: Christian Barnaard,
  surgeon to do first heart
  transplant; Christian Dior,
  clothes designer.
Literature: Hero in *Pilgrim's
  Progress,* by John Bunyan.
**Chretien, Chris, Chrisse,
Chrissie, Chrissy, Christiano,
Christie, Christy, Kit,
Kris, Krispin, Kristian**

Christopher (KRIS-tō-fer)
Greek— *Christ-bearer*
Famous: Christopher Columbus;
  Kit Carson.
Literature: Christopher Robin,
  character in children's books by
  A. A. Milne.
Entertainment: Christopher
  Willibald Gluch, composer;
  Christopher Cross, singer.
**Chris, Chrisse, Chrissy,
Christoffer, Christoforo,
Christoph, Christophe,
Christophorus, Cris, Cristobal,
Cristoforo, Kit, Kristo,
Kristofer, Kristoforo**

Cicero (SI-ser-ō)
Latin— *Chickpea*
Famous: Cicero, Greek
  philosopher.

Ciro (SĒ-rō)
Spanish — *The sun*

Clare (KLAIR)
Latin — *Famous*
Clair

Clarence (KLAIR-ens)
Latin — *Illustrious*
Clair, Clarance

Clark (KLARK)
French — *Scholar*
Entertainment: Clark Gable, actor;
Clark Kent, Superman's real
name.
Clarke, Clerc, Clerk

Claude (KLAWD)
Latin — *Lame*
Famous: Claude Monet,
impressionist painter.
Entertainment: Claude Debussy,
composer.
**Claudian, Claudianus, Claudio,
Claudius, Claus**

Clay (KLĀ)
Teutonic — *Born of the earth*
**Claiborn, Clayborn, Clayborne,
Claybourne, Clayton**

Clemens (KLEM-ens)
Danish — *Gentle or kind*

CHEVALIER — *Knight*

Clement (KLEM-ent)
Latin— *Merciful*
Literature: Clement E. Moore, author of *A Visit from St. Nicholas;* Samuel Clemens, real name of Mark Twain.
Chim, Clem, Clemens, Clemente, Clementius, Clemmie, Clemmy, Klemens, Klement, Kliment

Cleon (KLĒ-on)
Greek— *Famous*
Entertainment: Cleon Throckmorton, stage designer.
Kleon

Cletus (KLĒ-tus)
Greek— *Summoned*
Sports: Cletis Boyer, baseball player.
Cletis

Cleveland (KLĒV-land)
Old English— *From the cliffs*
Literature: Cleveland Amory, author of syndicated column, *Animal.*
Cleve, Cleaveland, Clevey, Clevie

Clifford (KLIF-erd)
Old English— *Dweller in the ford near the cliff*
Literature: Clifford Odets, playwright.
Entertainment: Clifton Webb, Cliff Roberts, Clifton Fadiman, actors.
Cliff, Clifton

Clinton (KLIN-tun)
Teutonic— *From the headland farm*
Literature: Clinton Scollard, American poet.
Entertainment: Clint Eastwood, actor.
Clint

Clive (KLĪV)
Old English— *From the cliff*

Clyde (KLĪD)
Scottish, Celtic— *Heard from afar*
Welsh— *Warm*
Cly, Clyd, Clyte

Cody (KŌ-de)
English— *Unknown*
Codi

Colby (KŌL-be)
Old English— *From the black farm*
Cole

Cole (KŌL)
See Nicholas.
Literature: Old King Cole, a nursery rhyme.
Entertainment: Cole Porter, songwriter.
Coleman, Colman

Colin (KAW-lin)
Gaelic— *Child*
Sports: Colin Chapman, race-car designer.
Cailean, Colan, Cole, Collin

Collier (KOL-yer)
Old English— *Miner*
Colier, Colis, Collayer, Collis, Collyer, Colyer

Colton (KŌL-ton)
Old English— *From the dark*

Coman (KŌ-man)
Arabic— *Noble*
Comen

Conal (KŌ-nal)
Celtic— *High and mighty*
Conall, Conan, Conant, Connel, Konal, Kynan

Conant (KŌ-nant)
Celtic— *Wise*
Con, Conal, Conn, Conney, Connie, Conny

Conn (KON)
Celtic— *Wise*
Con

Conrad (KON-rad)
Teutonic— *Brave counsel*
Famous: Conrad Hilton,
  hotel-chain owner.
Literature: *Conrad in Quest of His
  Youth,* by Leonard Merrick.
**Con, Conn, Conney,
Connie, Conny, Conrade,
Conrado, Cort, Koenraad,
Konrad, Kort, Kurt**

Conroy (KON-roi)
Irish— *Wise man*
**Commey, Con, Conn,
Connie, Conny, Roy**

Constantine (KON-stan-tēn)
Latin— *Firm*
Famous: Constantine the Great,
  Emperor of Rome.
**Con, Conn, Conney,
Connie, Conny, Constantin,
Constantino, Costa,
Konstantin, Konstantine**

Conway (KON-wā)
Gaelic— *Hound of the plain*
Entertainment: Conway Twitty,
  country-western singer.
**Con, Conn, Connie,
Conny**

Cooper (KOO-per)
Old English— *Barrel maker*
Coop

Corbett (KOR-bet)
Latin— *Raven*
**Corbet, Corbie, Corbin,
Corby, Cory**

Corbin (KOR-bin)
Latin— *The raven*
Corwin

Cordell (kor-DEL)
French— *Ropemaker*
**Cord, Cordie, Cordy,
Cory**

Corey (KOR-ē)
Irish— *From the hollow*
Cori, Cory

Cormac (KOR-mak)
Irish— *Charioteer*

Cornelius (kor-NĒL-ē-us)
Latin— *War horn*
Famous: Cornelius Vanderbilt,
  railroad tycoon.
**Conney, Connie, Conny,
Cornall, Cornell, Corney,
Cornie, Corny, Cory,
Neel, Nelly**

Cornell (kor-NEL)
See Cornelius.
Entertainment: Cornell Wilde,
  actor.
**Cornall, Corney, Cornie,
Corny, Cory**

Cort (KORT)
Teutonic— *Bold*
Norwegian— *Short*
Cortie, Corty, Kort

Corydon (KOR-i-don)
Greek— *Lark*
Coridon, Coryden

Cosmo (KOZ-mō)
Greek— *Well-ordered*
**Cos, Cosimo, Cosme,
Cozmo**

Courtland (KORT-land)
Anglo-Saxon— *From the enclosed
  land*
Court, Courtley, Courtly

Courtney (KORT-nē)
French— *From the court*
**Cort, Court, Courtnay,
Curt**

Cowan (KOW-an)
Gaelic— *Hillside hollow*
Coe, Cowey, Cowie

Craig (KRĀG)
Scottish— *Crag-dweller*
Sports: Craig Breedlove,
  land-speed record holder.
Craggie, Craggy

Crandall (KRAN-dal)
Old English — *From the crane's valley*
Can, Carndell

Crawford (KRAW-ford)
Old English — *From the ford of the crow*
Craw, Crow, Ford

Creighton (KRĀ-ton)
Old English — *From the farm*
Creight, Crichton

Crispin (KRIS-pin)
Latin — *Curly haired*

Crofton (KROF-ton)
Old English — *From the enclosed*

Crompton (KROMP-ton)
Old English — *From the winding farm*

Cromwell (KROM-wel)
Old English — *Dweller by the winding brook*

Crosby (KROZ-bē)
Norwegian — *From the shrine of the cross*
Cross

Culbert (KUL-bert)
Teutonic — *Cool and brilliant*
Colbert, Colvert

Cullen (KUL-en)
Celtic — *Young animal*
Cull, Cullan, Cullen, Culley, Cullie, Cullin, Cully

Culver (KUL-ver)
Old English — *Dove*
Colver, Cull, Cullie, Cully, Kullen, Kullie

Curcio (KER-sē-ō)
Spanish, French — *Courteous*
Curt

Curran (KER-en)
Gaelic — *Hero*
Curr, Currey, Currie, Curry

Curt (KERT)
Latin — *Short or little*
Sports: Curt Gowdy, sportscaster.
Curtie, Curty, Kurt

Curtis (KER-tis)
French — *Courteous*
Curcio, Curt, Curtice

Cutler (KUT-ler)
Old English — *Knife-maker*
Cut, Cuttie, Cuty

Cyril (SĒR-il)
Spanish, French — *Lordly one*
Entertainment: Cyril Ritchard, opera singer.
Cirillo, Cirilo, Cy, Cyrill, Cyrille, Cyrillus

Cyrus (SĪ-rus)
Persian, Greek — *Sun*
Famous: Cyrus Vance, former Secretary of State.
Ciro, Cy, Russ

Dabir (da-BĒR)
Algerian — *Teacher*

Dacey (DĀ-sē)
Gaelic — *Southerner*
Dace, Dacy

Dag (DAG)
Norwegian— *Day or brightness*
Famous: Dag Hammerskjold,
former Secretary-General of the
United Nations.
Dagny

Dagaim (da-GĪ-um)
Hebrew— *Two fishes*

Dagan (DĀ-gan)
Hebrew— *Corn or grain*
Entertainment: Dagwood,
comic-strip character.
Dagwood

Dale (DĀL)
Old English— *From the valley*
Entertainment: Dale Robertson,
actor.
Dael, Dal

Dalibor (DAL-i-bor)
Czech— *He dwells in the valley*

Dallas (DAL-as)
Celtic— *Wise*
Dal, Dall, Dallis

Dalston (DAL-ston)
Anglo-Saxon— *From Daegal's place*
Dalis

Dalton (DAL-ton)
Old English— *From the farm in the
dale*
Dal, Dalt, Tony

Damek (DĀ-mek)
Czech— *Man of the earth*
**Adamec, Adamek, Adamik,
Adamok, Adham**

Damon (DĀ-mon)
Greek— *Tamer*
Famous: Damon and Pythias of
Sicily.
Literature: Damon Runyon,
journalist and storyteller.
**Dame, Damian, Damiano,
Damien**

Dan (DAN)
Hebrew— *Judge*
Biblical: One of the 12 tribes of
Israel.
Entertainment: Dan Rather,
newscaster.
Sports: Dan Gurney, race-car
driver.
Dannie, Danny

Dana (DĀ-nuh)
Scandinavian— *From Denmark*
Entertainment: Dana Andrews,
actor.
Dane

Daniel (DAN-yel)
Hebrew— *God is my judge*
Biblical: Hebrew prophet who was
delivered from the lion's den.
Historical: Daniel Boone, explorer
and Indian fighter.
Famous: Daniel Webster,
politician and orator.
Literature: Hero in Shakespeare's
Merchant of Venice; Daniel Defoe,
author of *Robinson Crusoe.*
Entertainment: Danny Kaye, actor.
**Dan, Dani, Dannel,
Dannie, Danny, Dawnee**

Dante (DON-tē)
See Durante.
Literature: Dante Alighieri, poet.

Danya (DAN-yuh)
Ukrainian— *Given by God*
Bohdan, Dania

Dar (DAR)
Hebrew— *Pearl*

Darby (DAR-bē)
Gaelic— *Free man*
Norwegian— *From the deer estate*
Dar, Darb, Darbee, Darby

Darcy (DAR-sē)
Gaelic— *Dark*
D'Arcy, Dar, Darce

Dario (DAIR-e-ō)
Spanish, Greek— *Wealthy*
Darin

DAN—*Judge*

Darius (DAIR-ē-us)
Persian— *Wealthy*
Entertainment: Darius Milhaud,
   French composer.
Dare, Dario, Derry

Darnell (dar-NEL)
Old English— *From the hidden place*
Dar, Darn, Darnall

Darrel (DAIR-el)
French— *Beloved or dear*
Entertainment: Daryl Dragon, also
   known as Captain Tennille;
   Darryl F. Zanuck, film director
   and producer.
**Dare, Darrell, Darrill,
Darryl, Daryl, Daryle**

189

Darren (DAIR-en)
Gaelic — *Great*
**Dare, Daren, Daron,
Darrin**

Darrick (DAIR-ik)
Teutonic — *Ruler of the people*
Dare, Darick

Darton (DAR-ton)
Old English — *From the deer park*
Dart, Dartan, Darten

Dasan (DĀ-san)
Pomo Indian — *Leader of bird clan*

Daudi (DAW-dē)
Swahili — *Beloved one*
Daudy

David (DĀ-vid)
Hebrew — *Beloved*
Biblical: David, boy who killed
   Goliath and became king.
Historical: Admiral David
   Glasgow Farragut, explorer and
   leader.
Literature: *David Copperfield*, novel
   by Dickens; David Herbert
   Lawrence, author of *Lady
   Chatterley's Lover*.
Entertainment: David Niven,
   David Carradine, actors; David
   Crosby, member of Crosby, Stills
   and Nash singing group; David
   Bowie, rock star; David Brinkley,
   newscaster; David Hartman,
   anchorman; David Frost,
   talk-show host.
**Dav, Dave, Daven, Davey,
Davidde, Davide, Davie,
Davin, Davis, Davy, Dewey,
Dov**

Davis (DĀ-vis)
Scottish — *David's son*
Dave, Davie, Davy

Dean (DĒN)
Old English — *From the valley*
Entertainment: Dean Jones, Dean
   Jagger, actors; Dean Martin,
   singer.
Deane, Dene, Dino

Dearborn (DĒR-burn)
Old English — *Beloved child*

Dedrick (DĒ-drik)
Teutonic — *Ruler of people*
Dedric

Delbert (DEL-bert)
Old English — *Bright as day*
Entertainment: Delbert Mann,
   director.
Bert, Bertie, Berty, Del

Delmar (DEL-mar)
French, Latin — *Mariner*
Del, Delmer

Delmore (DEL-mor)
French — *At a marsh*
Literature: Delmore Schwartz,
   poet.
**Del, Delmar, Delmer,
Delmor**

Delsin (DEL-sin)
North American Indian — *He is so*
Delsen

Delwin (DEL-win)
Teutonic — *Valley friend*
Del, Delwyn

Demetrius (de-MĒ-trē-us)
Greek — *Of the earth*
Biblical: Silversmith of Ephesus.
Entertainment: Dmitri
   Shostakovich, Dmitri Tiomkin,
   composers.
**Demetri, Demetria, Demetris,
Demitry, Demmy, Dimetre,
Dimitri, Dmitri**

Dempsey (DEM-sē)
Gaelic — *Proud*
**Demp, Dempsey, Dempster,
Dempstor**

Denby (DEN-bē)
Norwegian — *From the village of the
Danes*
**Danby, Den, Denney,
Dennie, Denny**

Deniz (DEN-ez)
Turkish—*Sea*
Denyz

Dennis (DEN-is)
French, Latin—*Of Dionysus*
Entertainment: Dennis Wilson,
member of The Beach Boys
singing group; Dennis the
Menace, comic character; Dennis
Day, Dennis Weaver, actors.
**Den, Denis, Dennett,
Denney, Dennie, Dennison,
Denny, Denys, Denzil, Dion,
Dionisio, Dionysus**

Denton (DEN-tun)
Old English—*From the valley farm*
Dent, Denten

Denys (DEN-is)
Russian, Greek—*God of wine*
Denis, Dennis, Denya

Derek (DAIR-ik)
Teutonic—*Ruler of people*
**Darrick, Derick, Derk,
Derrick, Dirk**

Dermot (DER-mōt)
English, Gaelic—*Free from envy*
**Der, Dermott, Diarmaid,
Diarmid**

Derry (DER-rē)
Gaelic—*Red-haired*

Desmond (DES-mund)
Celtic—*Man from South Munster*
Literature: Desmond Young,
author.
Des, Desi, Desmund

Devin (DEV-in)
Celtic—*A poet*
Dev, Devy

Devlin (DEV-lin)
Gaelic—*Brave or fierce*
Dev, Devlen

Dewey (DOO-ē)
Welsh—*Prized*
Dew, Dewie

Dewitt (de-WIT)
Dutch—*White*
**DeWitt, Dewit, Dwight,
Wit, Wittie, Witty**

Dexter (DEKS-ter)
Latin—*Dexterous*
Decca, Deck, Dex

Dichali (dī-KĀL-ē)
North American Indian—*He speaks
often*
Dichaly

Dick (DIK)
See Richard.
Entertainment: Dick Cavett,
talk-show host; Dick Clark, host
of *American Bandstand;* Dick
Powell, actor; Dick Tracy,
comic-strip detective.
Dickie, Dicky

Diego (dē-Ā-gō)
Spanish—*The supplanter*
Famous: Diego Rivera, Mexican
painter.
Jaime, James, Jayme, Jaymie

Dieter (DĒ-ter)
See Theodoric.

Dietrich (DĒ-trik)
See Theodoric.

Dillon (DIL-on)
Gaelic—*Faithful*
Dill, Dillie, Dilly

Dima (DĒ-muh)
Russian—*Powerful warrior*
Vladimir

Dinos (DĒ-nōs)
Greek, Latin—*Firm and constant*
**Costa, Kastas, Konstandinos,
Konstantions, Kostas, Kostis,
Kotsos**

Dinsmore (DINZ-mor)
Celtic—*From the great hill fort*
Dins, Dinzmore

DOANE—*Dweller of the sand dune*

Dion (DĒ-on)
See Dionysos.
Entertainment: Dion, singer.

Dirk (DIRK)
Teutonic—*Ruler of the people*
Famous: Dirk J. Struik,
mathematician.
Entertainment: Dirk Bogarde,
actor.
Derek

Diverous (DĪ-ver-us)
English—*Unknown*
Diver

Doane (DŌN)
Celtic—*Dweller of the sand dune*

Dobry (DŌ-brē)
Polish—*Good*
Entertainment: *Doby Gillis* comedy
show.
Doby

Dodek (DŌ-dek)
Polish—*Noble hero*
**Adek, Adolf, Adolph,
Dolf, Dolfa, Dolfi**

Dodley (DOD-lē)
Old English — *From the people's meadow*
Entertainment: Dudley Moore, actor.
Dudley

Dohosan (dō-HŌ-san)
North American Indian — *Small bluff*
Dohosun

Dolf (DOLF)
See Adolph.
Dolph

Domingo (dō-MING-gō)
Spanish — *Born on Sunday*
Dom, Domingio, Dominic

Dominic (DOM-i-nik)
Latin — *The Lord's*
Entertainment: Dom Deluise, actor.
Dom, Dominick, Dominy, Nic, Nick, Nicky

Don (DON)
Celtic — *Dark or brown*
Latin — *Lord*
Entertainment: Don Knotts, actor; Donny Osmond, singer.
Sports: Don Drysdale, baseball pitcher; Don Meredith, football quarterback.
Donn, Donnee, Donnie, Donny

Donahue (DON-a-hū)
Gaelic — *Dark warrior*
Don, Donn, Donnie, Donny, Donohue

Donald (DON-ald)
Celtic — *Dark-haired stranger*
Entertainment: Donald Sutherland, Donald Pleasance, actors; Donald Duck, Walt Disney character.
Don, Donal, Donalda, Donall, Donalt, Donn, Donnell, Donnie, Donny

Donnelly (DON-el-lē)
Gaelic — *Brave, dark man*
Don, Donn, Donnie, Donny

Donovan (DON-a-van)
Gaelic — *Dark warrior*
Don, Donny

Doran (DOR-an)
Celtic — *Stranger*
Dorran, Dorren

Dorian (DOR-ē-an)
Greek — *From the sea*
Literature: *The Picture of Dorian Gray,* novel by Oscar Wilde.
Darren, Dore, Dorey, Dorie, Dory

Dorjan (DOR-jan)
Hungarian, Latin — *Dark man*
Adorjan, Adrian

Dory (DOR-ē)
French — *Golden-haired*
Dore

Dotan (DŌ-tan)
Hebrew — *Low*
Dothan

Douglas (DUG-las)
Scottish — *From the dark water*
Famous: Douglas MacArthur, Army general.
Entertainment: Douglas Fairbanks, Douglas Campbell, Doug McClure, actors.
Doug, Dougie, Douglass, Dougy, Dugald

Dovev (DŌ-vev)
Hebrew — *To whisper*

Doyle (DOIL)
Celtic — *Dark stranger*
Doy

Drake (DRĀK)
English — *Male duck or swan*

Dreng (DRENG)
Norwegian — *Hired farmhand*

Drew (DR$\overline{OO}$)
German, French — *Trusty*
Dru, Drud, Drugi

Driscoll (DRIS-kol)
Celtic — *Interpreter*

Druce (DR$\overline{OO}$S)
Celtic — *Wise man*

Dryden (DR$\overline{I}$-den)
Old English — *From the dry valley*
Dry, Drydan, Drydon

Duane (DW$\overline{A}$N)
Celtic — *Song*
Dewain, Dwayne

Dude (D$\overline{OO}$D)
English — *Moon*

Duer (D$\overline{OO}$-er)
Celtic — *Heroic*

Duke (D$\overline{OO}$K)
French — *Leader*
Dukey, Dukie, Dukker, Duky

Duncan (DUN-kan)
Scottish — *Dark-skinned warrior*
Literature: King of Scotland in
  Shakespeare's *Macbeth*.
Dun, Dunc, Dunn

Dunham (DUN-am)
Celtic — *Dark man*
Dun

Dunstan (DUN-stan)
Old English — *From the brown, stone
  hill*
Dun

Dur (DER)
Hebrew — *To pile up*

Durant (der-ANT)
Latin — *Enduring*
Dante, Dunte, Durand, Durante

Durriken (DER-i-ken)
English — *Fortune telling*

Durward (DER-ward)
Old English — *Gate-keeper*
Entertainment: Durward Kirby,
  announcer on *The Garry Moore
  Show*.

Durwin (DER-win)
Anglo-Saxon — *Beloved friend*

Dustin (DUS-tin)
German — *Brave fighter*
Entertainment: Dustin Hoffman,
  actor.
Dust, Dustie, Dusty

Dwight (DW$\overline{I}$T)
Old English — *A cutting or clearing*
Famous: Dwight David
  Eisenhower, President.
Dewit

Dyami (D$\overline{I}$-am-$\overline{e}$)
North American Indian — *An eagle*

Dylan (DIL-un)
Welsh — *The sea*
Literature: Dylan Thomas, poet.
Dilan, Dill, Dillie, Dilly

Dyre (D$\overline{I}$R)
Norwegian — *Dear or precious*

Earl (ERL)
Old English — *Nobleman*
Literature: Erle Stanley Gardner,
  creator of *Perry Mason* series.
**Earle, Earlie, Early, Erle,
Erly, Errol, Erroll, Rollo**

Eaton (Ē-tun)
Old English — *From the estate on the river*
Eatton

Ebenezer (eb-e-NĒ-zer)
Hebrew — *Rock of help*
Literature: Ebenezer Scrooge, character in Dickens' *A Christmas Carol.*
Eb, Eben, Ebeneser, Evenezer

Eberhard (eb-er-HARD)
German — *Boar-strong*
Everart, Everard, Everett, Evrard, Eward

Ed (ED)
See Edward.
Entertainment: Ed McMahon, co-host of *Tonight Show;* Ed Sullivan, host of TV variety show; Ed Asner, actor.

Eddy (ED-ē)
Scandinavian — *Unresting*
Entertainment: Eddy Arnold, country-western singer; Eddy Fisher, Eddie Albert, actors.
Edan, Eddie, Eden

Edgar (ED-ger)
Anglo-Saxon — *Happy warrior*
Literature: Edgar Allen Poe, poet and short-story writer; Edgar Rice Burroughs, author of Tarzan series.
Entertainment: Edgar Bergen, ventriloquist.
Ed, Eddie, Eddy, Edgard, Edgardo, Ned, Neddy, Ted, Teddy

Edik (ED-ik)
Russian — *Wealthy guardian*
Edward

Edison (ED-i-sun)
Old English — *Son of Edward*
Ed, Eddie, Eddy, Edson

Edmund (ED-mund)
Anglo-Saxon — *Fortunate protector*
Famous: Edmund Muskie, Senator; Eamon de Valera, President of Ireland.
Literature: Edmund Spenser, author of *The Faerie Queene.*
Entertainment: Edmund O'Brien, actor.
Eadmund, Eamon, Ed, Edd, Eddie, Edmon, Edmond, Edmondio, Edmondo, Ned, Neddie, Ted, Teddie

Edward (ED-ward)
Anglo-Saxon — *Happy protector*
Historical: Name given to kings in England and Saxon.
Literature: Edward Gibbon, author of *The Decline and Fall of the Roman Empire.*
Entertainment: Edward G. Robinson, Eddie Albert, Jr. actors; Edward R. Murrow, newscaster.
Ed, Eddie, Eddy, Edik, Edouard, Eduard, Eduardo, Edvard, Ewart, Ned, Ted

Edwin (ED-win)
Anglo-Saxon — *Rich friend*
Entertainment: Edwin Thomas Booth, Ed Winn, actors.
Ed, Eddie, Eddy, Edlin, Eduino

Egan (Ē-gan)
Celtic — *Ardent*
Teutonic — *Formidable*
Egon

Egbert (EG-bert)
Anglo-Saxon — *Sword bright*
Bert, Bertie, Berty

Egerton (EG-er-tun)
Old English — *From the town on the ridge*
Egerten

Einar (Ī-nar)
German — *Chief*
Ejnar

Elangonel (e-LANG-ō-nel)
North American Indian — *Friendly*

Elbert (EL-bert)
Teutonic — *Nobly brilliant*
Bert, El, Elli

Elden (EL-den)
Old English — *From the valley of the elves*
Eldo, Eldon, Elton

Eldred (EL-dred)
Anglo-Saxon — *Sage counselor*
Eldrid

Eldridge (EL-drij)
German — *Wise ruler*
Aldrich, Algridge, Eldrige

Eldwin (EL-dwin)
Anglo-Saxon — *Sage friend*

Eleazar (el-Ē-ā-zar)
Hebrew — *God has helped*
Elazaro, Eleazar, Eli, Elie, Eliezer, Ely

Eli (Ē-lī)
Hebrew — *Highest*
Biblical: High priest who trained the prophet Samuel.
Famous: Eli Whitney, inventor of the cotton gin.
Entertainment: Eli Wallach, actor.
Ely

Elijah (e-LĪ-juh)
Hebrew — *Jehovah is God*
Biblical: Prophet of God.
El, Eli, Elia, Elias, Elihu, Elijah, Eliot, Elliott, Ellis, Ely

Elisha (e-LĪ-shuh)
Hebrew — *God is salvation*
Biblical: Successor of Elijah.
Elish, Lisha

Ellard (EL-ard)
Teutonic — *Nobly brave*

Ellery (EL-er-ē)
Teutonic — *Dweller by the alder tree*
Literature: Ellery Queen, fictional detective.
Ellary, Ellerey

Elliott (EL-ē-ot)
Hebrew — *Close to God*
Famous: Eliot Janeway, economist and consumer advocate.
Entertainment: Elliott Gould, actor.
Eliot, Eliott, Elliot

Ellison (EL-i-son)
Old English — *Son of Ellis*
Elson

Ellsworth (ELS-worth)
Old English — *Nobleman's estate*
Famous: Ellsworth Bunker, politician.
Ellswerth, Elsworth

Elmen (EL-men)
German — *Like an elm tree*
Elman

Elmer (EL-mer)
Anglo-Saxon — *Noble and famous*
Literature: *Elmer Gantry,* by Sinclair Lewis.
Entertainment: Elmer Fudd, cartoon character in Bugs Bunny series.
Aylmar, Aylmer, Aymer

Elmo (EL-mō)
Greek — *Friendly*
Italian — *Helmet*
Entertainment: Elmo Lincoln, silent-movie *Tarzan.*
Elmore

Elrad (EL-rad)
Hebrew — *God rules*

Elroy (EL-roi)
Latin, French — *Royal*
Roy

ELLIOTT—*Close to God*

Elston (EL-ston)
Old English—*Nobleman's town*
Sports: Elston Howard, baseball
   player.
Elton

Elton (EL-ton)
Old English—*From the old town*
Entertainment: Elton John, rock
   singer.
**Alden, Aldon, Alton,
Eldon**

Elvis (EL-vis)
Norwegian—*All wise*
Entertainment: Elvis Presley,
   singer and actor.
Al, Alvis, El

Elwin (EL-win)
Anglo-Saxon—*Befriended by elves*
**Al, Alvis, El, Elven,
Elvis, Elvyn, Elwyn, Win**

Elwood (EL-wood)
Old English—*From the old wood*
Ellwood, Woody

Eman (Ē-man)
Czech, Hebrew — *God with us*
Manuel

Emanuel (ē-MAN-ū-el)
Hebrew — *God with us*
Famous: Immanuel Kant,
  philosopher and author of
  Critique of Pure Reason.
**Emmanuel, Immanuel, Mannie,
Manuel, Manny**

Emery (EM-er-ē)
Teutonic — *Industrious ruler*
Historical: Amerigo Vespucci,
  explorer.
**Amerigo, Amery, Amory,
Emerson, Emery, Emmerich,
Emory**

Emil (Ā-mēl)
Latin — *Flattering, winning*
Literature: Emile Zola, author.
**Emelen, Emile, Emilio,
Emlen, Emlyn**

Emlyn (EM-lin)
Welsh — *Cling to*
Sports: Emlin Tunnel, football player.
Emlin

Emmet (EM-et)
Anglo-Saxon — *Ant or industrious*
Famous: Emmet Kelly, circus
  clown.
Em, Emmit, Emmott, Emmy

Eneas (uh-NĒ-us)
Spanish, Greek — *Praised one*
Literature: Aeneas, hero of Virgil's
  epic poem.
Aeneas

Engelbert (ENG-el-bert)
Teutonic — *Bright as an angel*
Entertainment: Engelbert
  Humperdinck, singer.
**Bert, Bertie, Berty, Englebert,
Ingelbert**

Enoch (Ē-nok)
Hebrew — *Dedicated or consecrated*
Biblical: Father of Methusaleh.
Literature: Enoch Arden, hero of
  the poem by Tennyson.

Enos (Ē-nus)
Hebrew — *Man*
Enoss

Enrico (en-RĒ-kō)
See Henry.
Entertainment: Enrico Caruso,
  opera singer.

Enyeto (en-YĀ-tō)
Miowok Indian — *The bear's manner
  of walking*
Enieto

Ephraim (Ē-frē-um)
Hebrew — *Doubly fruitful*
Biblical: Second son of Joseph.
Entertainment: Efrem Zimbalist,
  Sr., violinist; Efrem Zimbalist, Jr.,
  actor.
Efrem, Ephrem

Erasmus (er-AS-mus)
Greek — *Loveable*
Erasme, Erasmo

Erastus (er-AS-tus)
Greek — *Beloved*
Elmo, Eraste, Ras, Rastus

Eric (AIR-ik)
Norwegian — *Ever ruler*
Historical: Eric the Red, viking
  hero.
Literature: Eric Ambler, author.
Entertainment: Eric Sevareid,
  newscaster; Eric von Stroheim,
  film director; Eric Clapton, rock
  singer; Erik Estrada, actor.
**Erek, Erhard, Erhart,
Erich, Erick, Erik, Rick,
Rickie, Ricky**

Erin (AIR-in)
Irish — *Peace*

Erland (ER-land)
Teutonic — *Stranger or foreigner*
Arlan, Arland, Erlan

Ernald (ER-nald)
Teutonic — *Noble eagle*
Erneld

Ernest (ER-nest)
Old English — *Earnest*
Literature: Ernest Hemingway,
  novelist.
Entertainment: Ernst Lubitsch,
  film director; Ernest Borgnine,
  Ernie Kovacs, actors.
**Erna, Ernestine, Ernestis,
Ernesto, Ernestus, Ernie,
Ernst, Erny**

Errol (AIR-ol)
Teutonic — *A nobleman*
Entertainment: Errol Flynn, actor.
Erroll, Rolls

Erskine (ER-skin)
Scottish — *From the height of the cliff*
Literature: Erskine Caldwell,
  novelist.
Kin, Kinnie, Kinny

Ervin (ER-vin)
Czech, Hungarian — *Friend of the sea*
Erwin

Eshcol (ESH-kol)
Hebrew — *A grape cluster*
Eshkoll

Esmond (ES-mond)
Anglo-Saxon — *Gracious protector*

Este (ES-tē)
Italian — *From the east*
Estes

Ethan (Ē-than)
Hebrew — *The strong or firm*
Historical: Ethan Allen,
  Revolutionary War hero.
Literature: *Ethan Frome,* by Edith
  Wharton.
Etan, Ethe

Ethelbert (ETH-el-bert)
Teutonic — *Of shining nobility*
Entertainment: Ethelbert Nevins,
  composer.
Adalbert, Edelbert, Ethelberta

Etu (Ē-tōō)
North American Indian — *The sun*

Eugene (ū-JĒN)
Greek — *Well-born*
Literature: Eugene O'Neill,
  playwright; Eugene Field,
  journalist and poet.
**Engenio, Eugen, Eugene,
Eugenius, Gene, Jean**

Eustance (Ū-stuns)
Greek — *Fruitful*
**Eustashe, Eustasius,
Eustatius, Eustazio, Eustis,
Stacie, Stacy**

Evan (E-vun)
Greek — *Well-born*
Celtic — *Young warrior*
Literature: Evan Hunter, author of
  The Blackboard Jungle.
**Ev, Even, Evin, Ewan,
Ewen, Owen**

Evelyn (E-vel-in)
French, Teutonic — *Ancestor*
Literature: Evelyn Waugh,
  novelist.
Evelin

Everett (E-ver-et)
Old English — *Strong as a boar*
Famous: Edward Everett Dirksen,
  Senator.
**Eberhard, Ev, Everard,
Evered, Eward, Ewart**

Evers (EV-ers)
Anglo-Saxon — *Wild boar*

Ezekiel (e-ZĒ-kē-ēl)
Hebrew — *Strength of God*
Biblical: Prophet of the Old
  Testament.
**Ezechiel, Ezequiel,
Eziechiele, Zeke**

Ezhno (EZ-nō)
North American Indian — *Solitary*

Ezra (EZ-ruh)
Hebrew — *Helper*
Literature: Ezra Pound, poet.
**Azariah, Azrikam, Azur,
Ezer, Ezera, Ezra, Ezri**

Faber (FĀ-ber)
German — *Bean grower*
Fabi, Fabian, Fabujan

Fabian (FĀ-bē-un)
Latin — *Bean grower*
Entertainment: Fabian, rock singer.
**Fabe, Faber, Fabiano,
Fabien, Fabio**

Fabron (FĀ-bron)
Latin — *Mechanic*

Fadey (FĀ-dē)
Ukrainian — *Stout-hearted or
courageous*
**Faddeyka, Faddi,
Fadeyka, Fadeyusha**

Fadil (FA-dil)
Arabic — *Generous*

Fairfax (FAIR-faks)
Anglo-Saxon — *Fair-haired*
Fair, Fax

Fairleigh (FAIR-lē)
Unknown — *From the meadow of the
bull*
**Fairlay, Fairlee, Fairlie,
Farlay, Farlee, Farley, Farly**

Falkner (FALK-ner)
Old English — *Trainer of falcons*
Faulkner, Fowler

Famous (FĀ-mus)
Old English — *Famous*
Interesting: Famous Amos,
popular cookie shop in
California.

Farand (FAIR-und)
Old English — *Attractive or pleasant*
Farant, Farrand, Ran

Farley (FAR-lē)
Old English — *From the sheep meadow*
Literature: Farley Mowat, author.
Entertainment: Farley Granger,
actor.
**Fairleigh, Fairlie, Far,
Farleigh, Farlie, Farly**

Farrell (FAIR-el)
Celtic — *The valorous*
Farr, Farrel, Ferrell

Fath (FĀTH)
Arabic — *Victory*

Favian (FĀ-vē-an)
Latin — *A man of understanding*

Faxon (FAKS-on)
Latin — *Blessed*
Entertainment: Felix
Mendelssohn, composer and
conductor; Felix the Cat, cartoon
character.
**Fee, Felic, Felicio,
Felike, Feliks, Felix,
Felizio**

Felton (FEL-ton)
Old English — *From the estate built
on the meadow*
Felten

FALKNER—*Trainer of falcons*

Feodor (FĀ-ō-dor)
See Theodore.
Literature: Fyodor Dostoyevsky, author of *Crime and Punishment*.
Entertainment: Feodor Chaliapin, opera singer.
Fyodor

Ferdinand (FER-di-nand)
German—*Bold venture*
Famous: Ferdinand de Lesseps, builder of the Suez and Panama canals.
Literature: Ferdinand, lover of Miranda in Shakespeare's *The Tempest*.
Entertainment: Fernando Lamas, actor.
Sports: Fernando Valenzuela, baseball pitcher.
Ferdie, Ferdy, Fergus, Fernando, Hernando

Fergus (FER-gus)
Gaelic—*Strong man*
Ferd

Fermin (FER-min)
Spanish—*Firm and strong*

Fernald (FER-nald)
Teutonic—*Dweller by the alder tree*

Ferris (FAIR-is)
Gaelic—*Peter, the rock*
Farris

Fidel (fa-DEL)
Latin—*Faithful*
Famous: Fidel Castro, Cuban President.
Fidele, Fidelio

Fielding (FĒL-ding)
Old English—*From the field*
Field

Filbert (FIL-bert)
Old English — *Brilliant*
**Bert, Filberte, Filberto,
Phil, Philbert**

Filmore (FIL-mor)
Old English — *Very famous*
**Filmer, Phil,
Pilmer, Pilmore**

Finlay (FIN-lē)
Gaelic — *Little fair-haired soldier*
**Fin, Findlay, Findley,
Finley, Finn**

Firman (FIR-man)
Old English — *Fair man*
Anglo-Saxon — *Traveler*

Fisk (FISK)
Scandinavian — *The fisherman*
Fiske

Fitzgerald (fitz-JAIR-ald)
Old English — *Son of the spear-mighty*
Famous: John Fitzgerald Kennedy,
President.
**Derrie, Fitz, Gerald,
Gerry, Jerry**

Fitzhugh (FITZ-hū)
Old English — *Son of the intelligent man*
Fitz, Hugh

Fitzpatrick (fitz-PAT-rik)
Old English — *Son of a nobleman*
Fitz, Pat, Patrick

Fleming (FLEM-ing)
Anglo-Saxon — *Dutchman*
Flem

Fletcher (FLE-cher)
English — *Arrow-maker*
Literature: Fletcher Knebel,
novelist.
Fletch

Flint (FLINT)
Old English — *Stream*

Florian (FLOR-ē-an)
Latin — *Flowering or blooming*
Flory

Floyd (FLOID)
Welsh — *Dark complexion*
Sports: Floyd Patterson, boxing
champion.

Flynn (FLIN)
Gaelic — *Son of the red-haired man*
Flin, Flinn

Forbes (FORBS)
Gaelic — *Prosperous or headstrong*

Ford (FORD)
Old English — *River crossing*
Bradford

Fordel (for-DEL)
English — *Forgives*

Forrest (FOR-est)
French — *Forest; woodsman*
Entertainment: Forrest Tucker,
actor.
**Forest, Forester, Forrester,
Forster, Foss, Foster**

Fortune (FOR-chun)
French — *Lucky*
Fortunato, Fortune, Fortunio

Foster (FOS-ter)
Latin — *Keeper of the woods*
Entertainment: Foster Brooks,
comedian.

Fowler (FOWL-er)
Old English — *Hunter of wild fowl*

Francis (FRAN-sis)

Latin—*Frenchman*
Biblical: St. Francis of Assisi.
Historical: Sir Francis Drake,
  explorer.
Famous: Francis Scott Key, author
  of *The Star-Spangled Banner.*
Entertainment: Franchot Tone,
  singer; Francis X. Bushman,
  actor.
**Chico, Fran, Francais,
Francesco, Franchot, Francisco,
Franciskus, Frangois, Frank,
Frankie, Franky, Frannie, Franny,
Frans, Frants, Franz, Pancho**

Francisco (fran-SIS-kō)

Latin—*Free man*
Entertainment: Chico Marx, actor.
**Chicho, Chico, Chilo, Chito,
Currito, Curro, Farruco, Frans,
Franz, Franzen, Frasco, Frascuelo,
Paco, Pacorro, Panchito, Pancho,
Paquito, Quico**

Frank (FRANK)

See Francis.
Famous: Frank Lloyd Wright,
  architect.
Entertainment: Frank Sinatra,
  singer and actor; Frankie
  Avalon, Frankie Lane, singers.
Sports: Frank Howard, baseball
  player.
Frankie, Franky

FRAZER—*Curly-haired*

Franklin (FRANK-lin)
German — *Free man*
Famous: Franklin Pierce,
  President; Franklin D. Roosevelt,
  President.
Literature: Franklin Pierce Adams,
  columnist and poet.
**Francklin, Francklyn, Frank,
Frankie, Franklyn, Franky**

Frazer (FRĀ-zer)
Old English — *Curly-haired*
French — *Strawberry*
**Fraser, Frasier, Fraze,
Frazier**

Fred (FRED)
See Frederick.
Entertainment: Fred Astaire,
  dancer and actor; Fred Gwynn,
  actor.
Freddie, Fredie, Fredy

Frederick (FRED-rik)
Teutonic — *Ruler in peace*
Historical: Frederick II of Prussia.
Famous: Frederic Remington,
  western artist.
Entertainment: Frederic Francois
  Chopin, composer; Fredric
  March, actor.
**Eric, Erich, Erick, Erik,
Fred, Freddie, Freddy, Fredek,
Frederic, Frederich, Frederico,
Frederigo, Frederik, Fredric,
Fredrick, Friedrick, Fritz,
Rick, Rickie, Ricky**

Fredi (FRE-dē)
German — *Peaceful ruler*
**Frederick, Fredrik, Friedel,
Friedrick, Fritz**

Freeman (FRĒ-man)
Anglo-Saxon — *One born free*
**Free, Freedman, Freeland,
Freemon**

Fremont (FRĒ-mont)
Teutonic — *Guardian of freedom*
Free, Monty

Friedrich (FRĒ-drik)
See Frederick.
Literature: Friedrich von Schiller,
  poet and dramatist.

Fritz (FRITZ)
See Frederick.
Entertainment: Fritz Kreisler,
  composer and violinist.

Fulton (FUL-ton)
Anglo-Saxon — *From a field*
Famous: Bishop Fulton J. Sheen,
  author and TV personality.
Fult

Gabriel (GĀ-brē-el)
Hebrew — *God is my strength*
Biblical: Archangel of the
  annunciation.
Entertainment: Gabe Kaplan,
  comedian.
**Gabbie, Gabby, Gabe, Gabi,
Gabie, Gabriele, Gabriello,
Gaby**

Gadi (GĀ-dē)
Hebrew — *My fortune*
Gadiel

Gage (GĀJ)
French — *Pledge*

Gale (GĀL)
Irish — *Stranger*
Scandinavian — *Ravine*
Norwegian — *To sing*
Sports: Gale Sayers, football player.
Gael, Gail, Gaile, Gayle

Galen (GĀ-len)
Gaelic — *Intelligent*
Greek — *Calm*
**Gael, Gaelan, Gail, Gale,
Gayle**

Galeno (ga-LĒ-nō)
Spanish — *Little bright one*

Gallagher (GA-luh-ger)
Gaelic — *Eager helper*

Galt (GALT)
Norwegian — *High ground*

Galvin (GAL-vin)
Gaelic — *Sparrow*
Gal, Galvan, Galven

Gamaliel (GA-ma-lel)
Hebrew — *Lord is vengeance or
recompense*
Famous: Warren Gamaliel
Harding, President.

Gan (GAN)
Vietnamese — *To be near*

Gannon (GAN-on)
Gaelic — *Fair-complected*
Gan, Gannie, Ganny

Garald (GAR-ald)
Russian — *Spear strong*
Garold, Garolds, Gerald

Gardell (GAR-del)
Teutonic — *Guardian*

Gardner (GARD-ner)
Anglo-Saxon — *A gardener*
**Gar, Gard, Gardener,
Gardie, Gardiner, Gardy**

Gareth (GAIR-eth)
Welsh — *Gentle*
Gar, Garth

Garfield (GAR-feld)
Old English — *Battlefield*
Entertainment: Garfield the Cat,
cartoon character.

Garibald (GAIR-i-bald)
Old English — *A welcome addition*

Garland (GAR-land)
Old English — *From the battlefield*
French — *Wreath*
Gar, Garlen

Garner (GAR-ner)
Teutonic — *Protecting warrior*
Famous: Garner Ted Armstrong,
leader of the Church of God
International.

Garnett (GAR-net)
Old English — *Armed with a spear*
Gar, Garnet

Garrett (GAIR-et)
Anglo-Saxon — *Powerful with the
spear*
Literature: Gerard Manley
Hopkins, religious poet.
Entertainment: Garrett Morris,
actor.
**Gar, Gareth, Garrard,
Garret, Garreth, Garrot,
Garrott, Gerard**

Garrick (GAIR-ik)
Teutonic — *Spear king*
Entertainment: Garrick Utley,
newscaster.
**Gar, Garek, Garik,
Garrik**

Garridan (GAIR-i-dan)
English — *You hid*

Garth (GARTH)
Norwegian — *Groundskeeper*
Literature: Hero in Maxwell
Anderson's *Winterset*.
Gar, Gareth, Gerth

Garvey (GAR-vē)
Gaelic — *Rough peace*
Garv, Garvy

Garvin (GAR-vin)
Teutonic— *Befriending warrior*
Gar, Garwin, Vin, Vinnie,
Vinny, Win, Winnie, Winny

Garwood (GAR-wood)
Old English— *From the fir-tree forest*
Gar, Wood, Woodie, Woody

Gary (GAIR-ē)
Old English— *Spear carrier*
Entertainment: Gary Cooper,
    Garry Moore, Gary Coleman,
    actors; Gary Crosby, singer, actor
    and son of Bing Crosby.
Gare, Garey, Garry

Gaspar (GAS-par)
Spanish— *Master of treasure*

Gasper (GAS-per)
See Jasper.
Gaspard

Gaston (ga-STON)
French— *From Gascony*

Gavin (GAV-in)
Scottish— *White hawk*
Literature: Gawain, nephew of
    King Arthur and knight of the
    Round Table.
Entertainment: Gavin McLeod,
    actor.
Gav, Gavan, Gaven,
Gawain, Gawen

Gavril (GAV-ril)
Russian— *Man of God*
Ganya, Gav, Gavrel

Gaylord (GĀ-lord)
French— *Jailor*
Sports: Gaylord Perry, baseball
    pitcher.
Gallard, Gay, Gayelord,
Gayler, Gaylor

Gaynor (GĀ-nor)
Gaelic— *Son of the fair-complected*
    man
Gainer, Gainor, Gay,
Gayner

Geber (gē-BAIR)
Hebrew— *Strong*

Gene (JĒN)
See Eugene.
Entertainment: Gene Kelly, actor
    and dancer; Gene Hackman,
    actor.

Geoffrey (JEF-rē)
See Godfrey.
Geoff, Jeff

George (JORJ)
Greek— *Farmer*
Famous: George Washington, first
    President; George Washington
    Carver, inventor of many uses
    for the peanut.
Literature: George Bernard Shaw,
    playwright; George Orwell,
    novelist.
Entertainment: George Harrison,
    one of the Beatles; George
    Benson, jazz singer and guitarist;
    George C. Scott, George Segal,
    actors; George Carlin, comedian;
    George M. Cohan, actor,
    playwright and composer.
Sports: George *(Babe Ruth)*
    Herman, baseball player.
Egor, Georas, Geordie,
Georg, Georges, Georgie,
Georgy, Giorgio, Goran,
Gorya, Jorgan, Jorge, Yurik

Gerald (JER-uld)
Teutonic— *Mighty with the spear*
Famous: Gerald Ford, President.
Garald, Garold, Gary,
Gearalt, Gearard, Gerard,
Gerrie, Gerry, Giraldo, Giraud,
Jerald, Jerrie, Jerrold, Jerry

Gerard (je-RARD)
Old English— *Spearhead*
Literature: Gerard Manley
    Hopkins, poet.
Gearard, Gerardo, Geraud,
Gerhard, Gerhardt, Gerrie,
Gerry, Gherardo

GEORGE—*Farmer*

Gerhard (GAIR-hard)
Scandinavian—*Spearbrave*
Gerri, Gerrie, Gerry

Gerik (GAIR-ik)
Polish—*Prosperous*
**Edek, Gerek, Geri,
Gerick, Gerrick**

Gershom (GER-shom)
Hebrew—*The expelled or exiled*

Gervase (jer-VĀ-sē)
Teutonic—*Honorable*
**Gervais, Jarv, Jarvey,
Jarvis, Jervis**

Giamo (jē-A-mō)
Italian—*The supplanter*
Entertainment: Giacamo Puccini,
composer of *Madam Butterfly.*
**Giacamo, Giacomo, Gian,
James**

Gibor (gi-BOR)
Hebrew—*Strong*
Gabor

Gideon (GID-ē-on)
Hebrew—*Feller of trees or destroyer*
Biblical: Judge of Israel.

Gifford (GIF-ord)
Teutonic— *Bold giver*
Giff, Giffard, Gifferd,
Giffie, Giffy

Gil (GIL)
Spanish— *Shield bearer*
Giles, Gill

Gilad (GIL-ad)
Hebrew, Arabic— *Camel hump*
Giladi, Gilead

Gilbert (GIL-bert)
Old English— *Trusted*
Famous: Gilbert Stuart, portrait
  painter.
Literature: Gilbert K. Chesterton,
  essayist and poet.
Bert, Bertie, Berty, Burt,
Burtie, Burty, Gib, Gibb,
Gibbie, Gibby, Gil, Gilberto,
Gilburt, Gill, Giselbert, Guilbert,
Wilbert

Gilchrist (GIL-krist)
Gaelic— *Servant of Christ*
Gil, Gill, Gilley, Gillie, Gilly

Giles (JĪLS)
Greek— *Shield bearer*
Literature: *Giles Goat-Boy*, novel by
  John Barth.
Egide, Egidio, Egidius,
Gide, Gil, Gill, Gilles,
Gilley

Gillie (GIL-ē)
English— *A song*

Gilmore (GIL-mor)
Gaelic— *Devoted to Virgin Mary*
Gillie, Gillmore, Gilly,
Gilmour

Gilroy (GIL-roi)
Celtic, Latin— *Servant of the king*
Gill, Gilley, Gillie,
Gilly, Roy

Gino (JĒ-nō)
See Ambrogio.

Ginton (GIN-ton)
Hebrew— *A garden*
Ginson

Giovanni (jē-ō-VAN-ē)
See John.
Famous: Giovanni Bellini,
  impressionist artist.
Gian, Gianni, Gioacchino,
Giovanna

Giuseppe (je-SEP-ē)
See Joseph.
Historical: Giuseppe Mazzini,
  Italian liberation fighter.
Entertainment: Giuseppe Verdi,
  composer.
Giuseppi, Seppi

Givos (GĒ-vōs)
Hebrew— *Heights*

Gladwin (GLAD-win)
Old English— *Cheerful*
Glad, Gladdie, Gladdy,
Win, Winnie, Winny

Glen (GLEN)
Celtic— *Valley*
Entertainment: Glen Campbell,
  singer; Glen Miller, orchestra
  leader; Glenn Gould, pianist;
  Glenn Ford, actor.
Glenn, Glyn, Glynn

Glendon (GLEN-dun)
Scottish— *From the glen fortress*
Glen, Glenden, Glenn

Goddard (GOD-erd)
Teutonic— *Divinely firm*
Literature: *Waiting for Godot*,
  existentialist play.
Godard, Godart, Goddart,
Godot, Gothart

Godfrey (GOD-frē)
German— *God's peace*
Entertainment: Godfrey
  Cambridge, comedian.
Godfree, Godfry

Godwin (GOD-win)
Old English — *Friend of God*
Godewyn, Goodwin, Win

Goel (JŌ-el)
Hebrew — *The redeemer*

Gordon (GOR-dun)
Anglo-Saxon — *From the cornered hill*
Famous: G. Gordon Liddy, of the Nixon administration.
Entertainment: Gordon Lightfoot, singer; Gordon McRae, actor.
Gordan, Gorden, Gordie, Gordy

Gorman (GOR-man)
Zodiac — *Man of clay*
Gormen

Gozal (GŌ-zal)
Hebrew — *A bird*

Grady (GRĀ-dē)
Gaelic — *Noble, illustrious*
Gradey

Graham (GRĀ-um)
Anglo-Saxon — *Warlike*
Famous: Alexander Graham Bell, inventor of the telephone; Graham Kerr, gourmet cook.
Literature: Graham Greene, novelist and playwright.
Sports: Graham Hill, race-car driver.
Graeme, Ham

Granger (GRĀN-jer)
Old English — *Farmer*
Grange, Gray

Grant (GRANT)
French — *Great*
Famous: Grant Wood, American Gothic painter.
Entertainment: Grant Tinker, TV producer.
Sports: Grantland Rice, football coach and benefactor.
Gran, Grantham, Granthem, Grantland, Grantley, Granville, Grenville

Grayson (GRĀ-son)
Old English — *Son of a bailiff*
Gray, Greerson, Greyson

Gregory (GRE-gor-ē)
Greek — *Vigilant*
Entertainment: Gregory Peck, actor.
Greg, Gregg, Gregoire, Gregoor, Gregor, Gregorio, Gregorius

Gresham (GRE-sham)
Old English — *From the grassland*

Griffin (GRI-fin)
Latin — *Griffin or mystical beast*
Griff, Griffie, Griffy

Griffith (GRI-fith)
Welsh — *Fierce chief; ruddy*
Griff, Griffie, Griffin, Griffy

Griswold (GRIS-wold)
Teutonic — *From the gray forest*
Gris, Grisold

Grosvenor (GRŌV-ner)
French, Latin — *Mighty huntsman*
Gros, Grosner

Grover (GRŌ-ver)
Anglo-Saxon — *Grove dweller*
Famous: Grover Cleveland, President.
Entertainment: Grover, character on *Sesame Street*, a children's program.
Grove

Guido (GWE-dō)
Spanish — *Life*

Gunther (GUN-ther)
Old Norse — *Battle army*
Entertainment: Guenther Gebel Williams, animal trainer with Barnum & Bailey Circus.
Guenther, Gun, Gunar, Gunnar, Gunner, Guntar, Gunter

Gus (GUS)
See Augustus.
Gusten, Gustin, Guston

Gustave (GOOS-tav)
Swedish — *Staff of the Gothe*
Famous: Gustaf Adolf, Swedish king.
Literature: Gustave Flaubert, French novelist.
Gus, Gustaf, Gustav, Gustave, Gustavo, Gustavus

Guthrie (GUTH-rē)
Celtic — *War serpent*
Guthrey, Guthry

Guy (GĪ)
Celtic — *Guide*
Literature: Guy de Maupassant, French novelist and short-story writer; *Guy Mannering,* novel by Sir Walter Scott.
Guido, Guyos, Wiatt, Wyatt

Guyapi (GĪ-a-pē)
North American Indian — *Candid*

Gyasi (JĪ-a-sē)
Ghanan — *Wonderful child*

Habib (ha-BĒB)
Muslim — *Beloved*

Hadden (HAD-un)
Old English — *From the heath or moor*
Hadan, Haddan, Haddon, Haden

Hadley (HAD-lē)
Old English — *From the heath*
Had, Hadlee, Hadleigh, Lee, Leigh

Hadrian (HĀ-drē-un)
See Adrian.
Literature: *The Memoirs of Hadrian,* by Marguerite Yourcenar.
Adok, Adorjan, Adrian, Adrik, Andrian, Andryan

Hadwin (HAD-win)
Teutonic — *Friend in war*

Hahnee (huh-NĒ)
North American Indian — *Beggar*

Haidar (HĀ-dar)
Indian — *Lion*
Asad, Hirsuma

Haines (HĀNZ)
Teutonic — *Dweller in the hedged enclosure*

Hakeem (ha-KĒM)
Arabic — *Wise*

Hakem (HĀ-kem)
Arabic — *Ruler*

Hakon (HĀ-kon)
Norwegian — *Of the chosen race*
Haakon, Hak, Hakan, Hako

Hal (HAL)
See Harold.
Entertainment: Hal Linden, Hal Holbrook, actors.

Halbert (HAL-bert)
Teutonic — *Gem*
Bert, Hal, Hulbert

Halden (HAL-den)
Teutonic — *Half-Dane*
Dan, Dannie, Hal, Haldan, Halfdan

Hale (HĀL)
Old English — *From sturdy stock*
Hail, Hal, Heal

HAMILTON—*From the mountain hamlet*

Haley (HĀ-lē)
Gaelic—*Ingenious*
Hal, Hale, Lee, Leigh

Halford (HAL-ford)
Old English—*From the hall or manor*
Hal, Halford, Halstead, Halsted

Hall (HAWL)
See Halford.

Hallam (HAL-um)
Teutonic—*From the hillside*
Halam

Halsey (HAWL-sē)
Old English—*From Hal's Island*
Entertainment: *Little Fauss and Big Halsey,* movie starring Robert Redford.
Hal, Hallsy, Halsy

Hamal (HAM-al)
Arabic—*Lamb*

Hamilton (HAM-il-tun)
Old English—*From the mountain hamlet*
Famous: Hamilton Jordan, politician in the Carter administration.
Ham, Hamel, Hamil

Hamish (HĀM-ish)
See James.

Hamlet (HAM-let)
French, German—*Little home*
Literature: Hamlet, one of
    Shakespeare's most famous
    characters.
Ham, Hamnet

Hamlin (HAM-lin)
Teutonic—*Ruler of the home*
**Ham, Hamlen, Lin, Lyn,
Lynn**

Hanan (HĀ-nan)
Hebrew—*Gracious*
Hanen, Hanin

Hanif (HA-nif)
Arabic—*True believer*
Hanef

Hank (HANK)
See Henry.
Sports: Hank Aaron, baseball
    player and home-run record
    holder.

Hanley (HAN-lē)
Anglo-Saxon—*Of the high meadow*
**Hanleigh, Henleigh, Henley,
Henry**

Hans (HONS)
See John.
Literature: Hans Christian
    Andersen, author of *The Silver
    Skates.*

Hansel (HAN-sel)
Scandinavian—*Gift from God*
Literature: Hansel and Gretel,
    characters in a children's story.

Harb (HARB)
Arabic—*War*

Harcourt (HAR-kort)
French—*Fortified dwelling*
Harry, Court, Courtney

Harden (HAR-den)
Old English—*From the hare valley*
Hardan, Hardin

Hardy (HAR-dē)
Teutonic—*Strong or hardy*

Harel (HAIR-el)
Hebrew—*God's mountain*
Haral, Haril

Harim (HAIR-im)
Hebrew—*Flat-nosed*
Harem

Harlan (HAR-lun)
Teutonic—*From the land of the
    warriors*
Famous: Harlan F. Stone, Chief
    Justice of the Supreme Court;
    Harlan Sanders, founder of
    Kentucky Fried Chicken
    restaurants.
Literature: Harlan Ellison, science
    fiction author.
Harland, Harlen, Harlin

Harley (HAR-lē)
Old English—*The stag's meadow*
**Arleigh, Arley, Arlie,
Harden, Harl, Harleigh,
Hart, Hartley**

Harlow (HAR-lō)
Old English—*Army hill*
Famous: Harlow Shapely,
    astronomer.

Harod (HAIR-ud)
Hebrew—*The loud terror*
Biblical: Jewish king at time of
    Christ's birth.
Hared, Harrod

Harold (HAIR-uld)
Anglo-Saxon—*Army power*
Historical: Last Saxon king of
    England.
Famous: Harold C. Urey,
    discoverer of heavy hydrogen.
Literature: Harold Robbins,
    novelist.
Entertainment: Harold Lloyd,
    comedian.
**Araldo, Hal, Harald, Harry,
Herald, Hereld, Herold, Herrick**

Harper (HAR-per)
Old English, German — *Harp player*
Harp, Harpor

Harrison (HAIR-i-sun)
Old English — *Son of Harry*
Entertainment: Harrison Ford,
actor.
Harris

Harry (HAIR-ē)
Old English — *Soldier*
Famous: Harry S. Truman,
President.
Entertainment: Harry Guardino,
actor; song *I'm Just Wild About
Harry.*
**Har, Harald, Hareld,
Harold, Hereld**

Hart (HART)
Old English — *Hart-deer*
Literature: Hart Crane, poet.
**Hart, Hartley, Hartwell,
Harwell, Harwill**

Harvey (HAR-vē)
Teutonic — *Army warrior*
Literature: Harvey Cheyne, hero of
Captains Courageous, by Rudyard
Kipling; *Harvey,* play by Mary C.
Chase.
Entertainment: Harvey Korman,
actor and comedian.
Harv, Harve

Hasad (ha-SOD)
Turkish — *Harvest*
Hassad

Hashim (ha-SHĒM)
Arabic — *Broker*

Hasin (ha-SĒN)
Indian — *Laughing*
Hasen, Hassin

Haskel (HAS-kel)
Hebrew — *Understanding*
Haskell

Haslett (HAS-let)
Old English — *From the hazel-tree
land*
**Hassal, Hassel, Hassell,
Haze, Hazel, Hazlet, Hazlett**

Hassan (ha-SON)
Arabic — *Handsome*
**Hasain, Hasan, Husseini,
Muhassan**

Hastin (HĀ-stin)
Hindi — *Elephant*

Hastings (HĀ-stings)
Old English — *Son of the stern man*
Hastie, Hasty

Havelock (HA-ve-lok)
Norwegian — *Sea battle*

Hayden (HĀ-den)
Old English — *From the hedged hill*
Haydon, Hayes, Hayward

Haywood (HĀ-wood)
Old English — *From the hedged forest*
Heywood, Woodie, Woody

Heath (HĒTH)
English — *From the hearth*

Hector (HEK-tor)
Greek — *Steadfast*
Literature: Hector, a hero of
Homer's *Iliad.*
Ettore, Heck

Henry (HEN-rē)
Teutonic—*Ruler of an estate*
Historical: Henry Hudson, navigator and explorer.
Famous: Henry Kissinger, former Secretary of State and winner of Noble Peace Prize.
Literature: Henry James, Henry Thoreau, novelists; Henry Wadsworth Longfellow, poet.
Entertainment: Henry Winkler, actor known as the Fonz; Henry Morgan, Henry Fonda, actors.
Enrico, Enrique, Hal, Hamlin, Hank, Harry, Heindrick, Heinrich, Heinrik, Hendrick, Hendrik, Henri, Henrik

Herbert (HER-bert)
Teutonic—*Glorious soldier*
Famous: Herbert C. Hoover, President; Herbert Spencer, English philosopher.
Bert, Bertie, Berty, Eberto, Habert, Havert, Hebert, Herb, Herbie, Herby, Heriberto

Hercules (HER-kū-lēz)
Greek—*Glorious gift*
Herc, Herculie, Herculies, Hersule

Herman (HER-man)
Teutonic—*War man*
Famous: Armond Hammer, businessman.
Literature: Herman Melville, author of *Moby Dick;* Herman Hesse, author of *Steppenwolf.*
Armand, Armando, Armin, Armond, Armyn, Ermanno, Ermin, Harman, Harmon, Herm, Hermann, Hermie, Hermon, Hermy

Hernando (her-NAN-dō)
See Ferdinand.

Herrod (HAIR-ud)
Hebrew—*Heroic conqueror*
Herod

Hersh (HERSH)
Hebrew—*A deer*
Hersch, Herschel, Hershel, Herzl, Hirsch

Hervey (HER-vē)
See Harvey.
Literature: Hervey Allen, author of *Israfel,* biography of Edgar Alan Poe.

Herwin (HER-win)
Teutonic—*A friend*

Hewett (HŪ-et)
French—*Little and intelligent*
Hew, Hewet, Hewie, Hewitt

Heywood (HĀ-wood)
Anglo-Saxon—*Forest enclosure*
Entertainment: Heywood Hale Broun, newspaper columnist and humanitarian.
Haywood, Hey, Wood, Woodie

Hezekiah (he-ze-KĪ-uh)
Hebrew—*God is my strength*
Hesketh

Hilary (HIL-a-rē)
Latin—*Cheerful*
Hi, Hilaire, Hilario, Hilarius, Hill, Hillary, Hillery, Hillie, Hilly, Ilario

Hillel (HIL-el)
Hebrew—*Greatly praised*
Biblical: Hillel, renowned Jewish scholar.
Hill, Hillier, Hilly, Hillyer

Hilliard (HIL-yard)
Teutonic—*War guardian*

Hilton (HIL-ton)
Old English—*From the house on the hill*

Hinun (HĪ-nun)
North American Indian—*God of clouds and rain*
Hunon

Hiram (HĪ-ram)
Hebrew — *Exalted*
Hi, Huran, Hy

Hiroshi (hir-RŌ-shē)
Japanese — *Generous*

Hisoka (hi-SŌ-kuh)
Japanese — *Reserved*

Ho (HŌ)
Chinese — *The good*

Hobart (HŌ-bart)
Teutonic — *Bright mind*
**Hobard, Hobe, Hobey,
Hobie, Hoebart**

Hod (HOD)
Hebrew — *Vigorous*

Hogan (HŌ-gan)
Gaelic — *Youth*

Holbrook (HŌL-brook)
Old English — *From the brook in the
hollow*
Brook, Holbrooke

Holden (HŌL-den)
Teutonic — *Kind*

Holleb (HOL-ub)
Polish, German — *Peace*
Hollub, Holub

Hollis (HOL-is)
Anglo-Saxon — *Dweller by the holly
tree*

Holman (HŌL-man)
Teutonic — *From the river island*

Holt (HŌLT)
Ecological — *Son of the unspoiled
forest*

Homer (HŌ-mer)
Greek — *Pledge*
Literature: Homer, author of *The
Iliad* and *The Odyssey*.
Homere, Homerus, Omero

Honovi (hō-NŌ-vē)
North American Indian — *Strong*

Horace (HOR-is)
Latin — *Keeper of the hours*
Famous: Horace, Greek
philosopher; Horatio Alger,
rags-to-riches success story;
Horace Mann, innovator of
teaching methods.
Literature: Horace Gregory, poet.
**Horacio, Horatio, Horatuis,
Orazio**

Horton (HOR-ton)
Old English — *From the gray estate*
Hort, Horten, Orten, Orton

Hosea (ho-SĀ-uh)
Hebrew — *Salvation*
Hoseia

Houston (HŪ-ston)
Anglo-Saxon — *Hill town*

Howard (HOW-ard)
Old English — *Watchman*
Famous: Howard Hughes, aviator
and businessman.
Literature: Howard Lindsay,
author of *Life with Father*.
Entertainment: Howard Barlow,
conductor.
Sports: Howard Cosell,
sportscaster.

Howe (HOW)
Teutonic — *High*
Howey, Howie

Howin (HOW-in)
Chinese — *A loyal swallow*

Howland (HOW-land)
Old English — *Of the hills*
Howey, Howie, Howlan

HOWARD — *Watchman*

Hubert (HŪ-bert)

Teutonic — *Bright mind*
Historical: Hubert Wilkins, polar
  explorer.
Famous: Hubert H. Humphrey,
  Senator and candidate for
  President; Hubert de Givenchy,
  designer.
**Bert, Bertie, Berty, Hobard,
Hobart, Hube, Huberto, Hubey,
Hubie, Hugh, Hugibert, Hugo,
Ugo, Ulberto**

Hugh (HŪ)

Old English — *Intelligence*
Literature: Hugh Hefner, founder
  of *Playboy* magazine.
Entertainment: Hugo Wolf,
  Austrian composer; Hugh
  O'Brien, actor.
Hugo, Ugo

Humbert (HUM-bert)

German — *Giant; brilliant*
Literature: Humbert Wolfe,
  English poet.
Bert, Bertie, Berty, Hum

Humphrey (HUM-frē)
Teutonic— *Peaceful Hun*
Famous: Sir Humphrey Davis,
  inventor of the miner's safety
  lamp.
Literature: *Humphrey Clinker*,
  novel by Tobias Smollett.
Entertainment: Humphrey Bogart,
  actor.
**Hum, Humfredo, Humfrey,
Humfrid, Humfried, Hump,
Humph, Onfoi, Onfre,
Onofredo**

Hunter (HUN-ter)
Old English— *Huntsman*
Literature: Hunter Thompson,
  novelist.
Hunt

Huntington (HUN-ting-ton)
Old English— *Hunting estate*
Hunt, Huntingdon, Huntingston

Huntley (HUNT-lē)
Old English— *Hunter's meadow*
Hunt, Huntlee, Lee, Leigh

Hurd (HERD)
Anglo-Saxon— *Hard, strong*

Hurley (HER-le)
Gaelic— *Sea tide*
Hurlee

Husain (hoo-SĀN)
Muslim— *Little beauty*
Hussein

Hussein (hoo-SĀN)
Arabic— *Little and handsome*
Famous: King Hussein of Syria.
Husein

Hute (ŪT)
North American Indian— *Star*

Hutton (HUT-ton)
Old English— *From the house on the
  jutting ledge*
Hut, Hutt, Huttan

Hyatt (HĪ-at)
Old English— *From the high gate*
Hy, Hyat

Hyman (HĪ-mun)
Hebrew— *Life*
Masculine form of Eve.
Literature: Admiral Hyman G.
  Rickover, author of *Education and
  Freedom;* Hy Gardner, syndicated
  columnist.
**Chaim, Hayyim, Hy,
Hymen, Hymie, Mannie, Manny**

Iago (Ē-a-gō)
See James.
Literature: Villain in
  Shakespeare's *Othello.*
Iagio

Ian (Ē-an)
See John.
Literature: Ian Fleming, creator of
  James Bond.

Innis (IN-is)
Celtic— *From the island*
Innes, Inness

Inteus (in-TĀ-us)
North American Indian— *He shows
  his face*

Ioakim (Ē-ō-kim)
Russian, Hebrew— *God will
  establish*
Akim, Iav, Jov, Yov

Ira (Ī-ruh)
Hebrew—*Descendants or watchful one*
Famous: Ira Hays, one of the flag-raisers on Iwo Jima.

Irvin (IR-vin)
Anglo-Saxon—*Sea friend*
Ervin, Ervine, Erwin, Irv, Irving, Irwin, Marv, Marvin, Merv, Mervin, Merwin

Irving (IR-ving)
Gaelic—*Beautiful*
Old English—*Sea friend*
Famous: Irving Langmuir, Nobel Prize winner for chemistry.
Literature: Irving Wallace, Irving Stone, authors.
Entertainment: Irving Berlin, Irving Caesar, composers.
Earvin, Erv, Ervin, Erwin, Irv, Irvin, Irvine, Irwin

Irwin (IR-win)
Anglo-Saxon—*Lover of the sea*
Entertainment: Irwin Allen, film producer; Professor Irwin Corey, actor and comedian.
Irwinn, Irwon

Isaac (Ī-zak)
Hebrew—*Laughing*
Biblical: Son of Abraham and Sarah.
Famous: Isaac Newton, discoverer of the law of gravity.
Literature: Isaac Asimov, science fiction author.
Entertainment: Isaac Stern, violinist; Isaac Hayes, singer and actor.
Ike, Ikey, Isaak, Isac, Isacco, Izaak, Izak

Isaiah (ī-ZĀ-uh)
Hebrew—*God is my helper*
Biblical: Hebrew prophet.
Isa, Isak

Isas (Ī-sas)
Japanese—*Meritorious*

Isidore (IZ-i-dor)
Greek—*A gift of Isis*
Famous: Isidor Isaac Rabi, atomic scientist.
Dore, Dorian, Dory, Isador, Isadore, Isidor, Isidoro, Isidro, Issy, Iz, Izzy

Israel (IZ-rē-ul)
Hebrew—*Ruling with the Lord*
Biblical: One of the 12 Hebrew tribes; another name for Jacob.
Isa

Ivan (Ī-van)
Hebrew—*Gracious gift of God*
Famous: Ivan Mestrovic, sculptor.
Literature: Ivan Turgenv, novelist.
Vania, Vanya

Ivar (Ī-var)
Scandinavian—*Military archer*
Famous: Ivor Novello, composer.
Ive, Iver, Ivers, Ives, Ivo, Ivon, Ivor, Yvon, Yvor

Iye (Ī-yuh)
North American Indian—*Smoke*

Jabez (yúh-BEZ)
Hebrew—*Cause of sorrow*
Jabe

Jacinto (ha-SEN-tō)
Spanish—*Hyacinth*

218

Jack (JAK)
See John.
Entertainment: Jackie Cooper, Jack
Paar, Jackie Gleason, Jack Benny,
Jack Klugman, Jack Lemmon,
Jack Nicholson, actors; Jackson
Brown, singer.
Sports: Jackie Robinson, baseball;
Jack Nicklaus, golf champion;
Jack Brabham, race-car driver.
**Jackie, Jackson, Jacky,
Jock, Jocko**

Jacob (JĀ-kub)
Hebrew — *Supplanter*
Biblical: Son of Abraham and
brother of Esau.
**Cob, Cobb, Cobbie, Cobby,
Giacobo, Giacomo, Giacopo,
Hamish, Iago, Jack, Jackie,
Jacky, Jacobo, Jacques,
Jaime, Jake, Jakie, Jakob,
James, Jamesy, Jamey,
Jamie, Jay, Jayme, Jim,
Jock, Seamus, Seumas, Shamus**

Jacques (ZHOK)
See James.
Masculine form of Jacqueline.
Historical: Jacques Cartier,
discoverer of the St. Lawrence
River.
Famous: Jacques Cousteau,
oceanographer and explorer.
Literature: Philosopher in
Shakespeare's *As You Like It.*
Entertainment: Jacques Offenbach,
light-opera singer.

Jael (JĀ-el)
Hebrew — *Mountain goat*

Jafar (YAW-far)
Muslim — *A little stream*

Jagger (JA-ger)
Unknown — *To carry in a cart*
Jaggar

Jahi (ya-HĒ)
Swahili — *Dignity*

Jaime (JĀ-mē)
See James.
Diego, Jayme, Jaymie

Jake (JĀK)
See Jacob.

Jal (JAWL)
English — *He goes*

James (JĀMZ)
Hebrew — *The supplanter*
Biblical: Disciple of Jesus Christ.
Famous: James Madison, James
Monroe, James Polk, James
Buchanan, James Garfield,
Presidents; James Watt, inventor
of the steam engine.
Entertainment: James Garner,
James Cagney, James Caan,
James Stewart, James Coburn,
actors.
**Diego, Giacomo, Hamish,
Iago, Jacques, Jaime, Jakie,
Jamesy, Jamey, Jamie, Jay,
Jayme, Jemmy, Jim, Jimmie,
Jimmy, Jock, Jocko, Seamus,
Seumas, Shamus**

Jamil (ja-MĒL)
Arabic — *Handsome*
Jamill

Jan (JAN)
See John.
Entertainment: Jan Peerce, opera
singer; Jan, singer in group, Jan
and Dean.
**Janek, Janko, Jano, Janos,
Jenda**

Jared (JAIR-ed)
Hebrew — *Descending*
Jarad, Jordan

Jarek (JAIR-ek)
Polish — *January*
**Janiuszck, Januarius,
Januisz, Jarek**

Jarlath (JAR-lath)
Latin — *Man of control*

JARON — *To sing*

Jaron (JAIR-un)
Hebrew — *To sing*

Jaroslav (JAR-ō-slav)
Czech — *Glory of spring*

Jarvis (JAR-vis)
Teutonic — *Keen as the spear*

Jascha (YAW-shuh)
See James.
Entertainment: Jascha Heifetz,
violinist.

Jason (JĀ-sun)
Greek — *Healer*
Mythological: Leader in search of
the Golden Fleece.
Entertainment: Jason Robards, Jr.,
actor.
Jasun, Jay

Jasper (JAS-per)
Persian — *Treasurer*
Caspar, Cass, Gaspar, Kaspar

Javas (JA-vas)
Indian — *Quick*

Javier (ha-VĒR) or (ha-VE-ar)
Spanish — *Owner of the new house*
Xavier

Jay (JĀ)
French — *Blue jay*
Literature: Jay Gatsby in F. Scott
Fitzgerald's *The Great Gatsby.*
Entertainment: Jay Gorney,
composer.
Jaye

Jean (JĒN)
See John.
Literature: Jean Valjean, hero of
Les Miserables, by Victor Hugo.
Entertainment: Jean Gabin, actor.

Jeconiah (je-KŌ-nē-uh)
  Hebrew—*Gift of the Lord*

Jed (JED)
  Hebrew—*Beloved of the Lord*
  **Jedd, Jeddy, Jedediah,
  Jedidiah**

Jedrek (JED-rek)
  Polish—*Manly*
  Jedrus

Jeff (JEF)
  See Godfrey.
  Entertainment: Jeff Bridges, actor.
  Jefferson, Jeffy, Jeffie

Jeffrey (JEF-rē)
  French—*Heavenly peace*
  Entertainment: Jeffrey Hunter,
    actor.
  **Geoff, Geoffrey, Godfrey,
  Gottfried, Jeff, Jefferey,
  Jeffie, Jeffy**

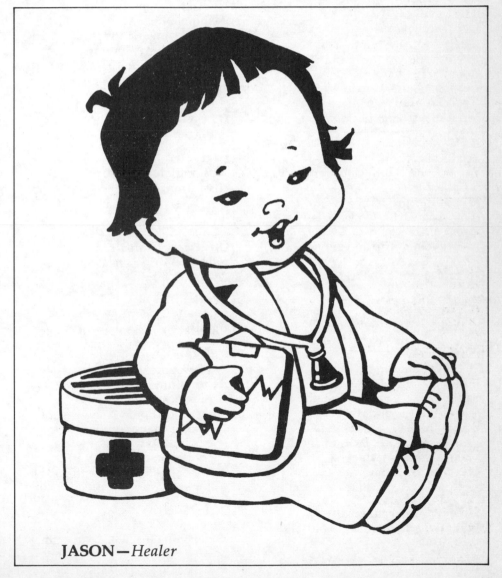

JASON—*Healer*

Jegar (YĀ-gar)
Hebrew — *Witness our love*
Jeggar, Jegger

Jeremiah (JER-uh-mī-uh)
Hebrew — *God is high*
Biblical: One of the great Hebrew
  prophets.
Famous: Jeremy Bentham, political
  philosopher.
**Germaine, Jer, Jere,
Jereme, Jeremias, Jeremy,
Jermyn, Jerry**

Jerome (je-RŌM)
Latin — *Holy name*
Entertainment: Jerome Kern,
  composer; Jerome Robbins,
  choreographer.
**Gerome, Gerri, Gerrie,
Gerry, Hieronymus, Jere,
Jereme, Jerrome, Jerry**

Jerry (JAIR-ē)
See Gerald.
Famous: Jerry Brown, governor of
  California.
Entertainment: Jerry Lewis, actor
  and comedian; Jerry Lee Lewis,
  rock singer; Jerry of *Tom and
  Jerry* comic strip and movies.
**Gerald, Gerard, Jere, Jerey,
Jerrald, Jerrold, Jerri, Jerry**

Jesper (JES-per)
French — *Jasper stone*
Jasper

Jesse (JES-ē)
Hebrew — *Grace or gift of God*
Biblical: Father of David.
Famous: Jessie Helms, Senator;
  Jessie James, outlaw.
Sports: Jesse Owens, Olympic
  champion; Jesse Jackson, football
  player and preacher.
Jess, Jessey, Jessie

Jethro (JETH-rō)
Hebrew — *Pre-eminence*
Biblical: Father-in-law of Moses.
Jeth, Row

Jibben (JIB-en)
English — *Life*
Jibvel

Jim (JIM)
See James.
Famous: Jim Bowie, frontiersman;
  Jim Bludso, inventor of the
  steamboat.
Literature: *Lord Jim*, novel by
  Joseph Conrad.
Entertainment: Jim Henson,
  creator of The Muppets; James
  Earl Jones, Jimmy Durante,
  Jimmy Stewart, actors; Jimmy
  Dean, singer and actor.
Sports: Jimmy Connors, tennis
  champion; Jim Clark, race-car
  driver.
James, Jimmie, Jimmy

Jin (JIN)
Chinese — *Gold*

Jivin (JIV-in)
East Indian — *To give life*
Jivanta

Joab (JŌ-ab)
Hebrew — *Praise the Lord*

Joachim (wah-KĒM)
Hebrew — *The Lord will judge*
Akim, Joaquin

Job (JŌB)
Hebrew — *The afflicted*
Biblical: Book in the Holy Bible.

Joe (JŌ)
See Joseph.
Entertainment: Joey Bishop, actor;
  Joe Cocker, singer.
Sports: Joe Louis, heavyweight
  boxing champion; Joe DiMaggio,
  baseball star; Joe Garagiola,
  sportscaster; Joe Namath,
  football player and actor.
Jo, Joey

Joel (JŌ-el)
Hebrew — *God is willing*
Entertainment: Joel Gray, actor.

John (JON)
Hebrew — *God is gracious*
Biblical: John the Baptist.
Historical: John Paul Jones, naval
ḥero; Johnny Appleseed, who
planted apple trees.
Famous: John Adams, John
Quincy Adams, John Fitzgerald
Kennedy, Presidents; John
Dewey, modern educational
practitioner.
Literature: John Milton, John
Keats, authors.
Entertainment: John Ritter, John
Belushi, John Travolta, actors;
Johnny Cash, country-western
singer; John Denver, singer and
actor; Johnny Carson, *Tonight
Show* host; John Barrymore, actor
and director.
Sports: Johnny Bench, baseball
catcher.
**Eoin, Evan, Ewan, Ewen,
Gian, Giavanni, Hanan,
Hanas, Hansel, Iaian, Iain,
Ian, Ivan, Jack, Jackie,
Jacky, Jan, Janos, Jean,
Jens, Jevin, Jock, Jocko,
Johan, Johann, Johannes,
Johnnie, Johnny, Johnston,
Johny, Jon, Jone, Juan,
Owen, Sean, Shane,
Shaughn, Shaun, Shawn, Zane**

Jonah (JŌ-nuh)
Hebrew — *Dove*
Biblical: Prophet swallowed by a
whale.
Jonas

Jonathan (JON-a-thun)
Hebrew — *Jehovah gave*
Biblical: A friend of David.
Literature: Jonathan Swift, author
of *Gulliver's Travels;* Richard
Bach's *Jonathan Livingston Seagull.*
Entertainment: Jonathan Winters,
comedian.
Jon, Jonathon

Jordan (JOR-dun)
Hebrew — *Descending*
**Giordano, Jared, Jerad,
Jori, Joudain**

Jose (hō-SĀ)
Hebrew — *God will increase*
Famous: Che Guevara, Cuban
Revolutionary War fighter.
Entertainment: Jose Ferrer, actor;
Jose Feliciano, singer; Jose Greco,
dancer.
**Che, Chepe, Chepito, Jose,
Josecito, Joseito, Pepe,
Pepillo, Pepito, Sodeph**

Joseph (JŌ-sef)
Hebrew — *He shall add*
Biblical: Husband of Mary, Jesus'
mother; Joseph was a ruler of
Egypt.
Famous: Joseph Lister, discoverer
of antiseptic.
Literature: Joseph Addison, poet;
Joseph Conrad, novelist.
**Che, Giuseppe, Iosep,
Jo, Joe, Joey, Jose, Jozef**

Joshua (JO-shōō-uh)
Indian — *Satisfaction*
Hebrew — *Jehovah saves*
Biblical: Led Israelites to the
promised land after the death of
Moses.
Entertainment: Joshua Logan, film
director and producer.
Josh, Josha, Joshia

Josiah (jo-SĪ-ah)
Hebrew — *Jehovah supports*
Josias

Jotham (JŌ-tham)
Hebrew — *Jehovah is perfect*

Juan (WAHN)
See John.

Judah (JŌŌ-duh)
Hebrew — *Praise*
Biblical: Judah was the son of
Jacob.
Judas, Judd, Jude

Jude (JOOD)
Hebrew — *Praise*
Biblical: Jude, one of the 12
apostles, also known as
Thaddeus.
Literature: *Jude the Obscure,* novel
by Thomas Hardy.
Entertainment: Song *Hey Jude,* by
the Beatles.
Juda, Judas, Judd, Judson

Julian (JOO-le-un)
Spanish — *Belonging to Julius*
Halian, Julio

Julius (JOO-le-us)
Greek — *Youthful and downy bearded*
Historical: Julius Caesar, Roman
emperor.
Sports: Julius Erving, also known
as *Dr. J,* basketball star.
**Giulio, Joliet, Jule,
Jules, Juley, Julian,
Julie, Julio**

Jumah (JOO-mah)
Muslim — *Friday*
Jimoh

Jun (JOON)
Chinese — *Truth*
Japanese — *Obedient*

Junius (JOO-ne-us)
Latin — *Born in June*

Juri (JOO-re)
Estonian — *Farmer*
**Juris, Juritis, Jurka, Jurkan,
Juss**

Justin (JUS-tin)
Latin — *The just*
**Giustino, Giusto, Just,
Justinian, Justino, Justis, Justus**

Kadar (KA-dar)
Arabic — *Powerful*
Kedar

Kadin (KA-din)
Arabic — *Companion*

Kalig (KA-lik)
Arabic — *Creative*

Kalil (ka-LIL)
Arabic — *Good friend*
Kahaleel, Kahlil

Kalman (KAL-man)
See Karl.
Karcsi, Kari, Karoly

Kane (KAN)
Celtic — *Bright or radiant*
Kayne

Kaniel (KAN-yel)
Hebrew — *Stalk*

Karl (KARL)
See Charles.
Famous: Karl Marx, founder of
Marxism.
Entertainment: Karl Malden, actor.
**Charles, Chuck, Kale,
Karel, Karlens, Karlik,
Karlis, Karol, Karolek**

Karsten (KAR-sten)
Greek — *Anointed*

Kasim (ka-SĒM)
Muslim — *Divided*
Kaseem

Kasimir (KAS-mir)
Slavic — *Commands peace*

Kass (KAS)
German — *Like a black bird*

Kay (KĀ)
Latin — *Rejoiced in*
Entertainment: Kay Kaiser, band leader.

Keahi (KĒ-a-hē)
Polynesian — *Fire*

Keane (KĒN)
Old English — *Sharp or keen*
Kean, Keen, Keene

Kearney (KER-nē)
See Carney.
Karney

Kedar (KĀ-dar)
Hindi — *Mountain lord*
Keady, Kedd, Keddie, Keddy

Keegan (KĒ-gun)
Gaelic — *Little and fiery one*
Kegan

Keenan (KĒ-nun)
Gaelic — *Little and ancient*
Entertainment: Keenan Wynn, actor.
Keen, Kienan

Keir (KĒR)
Celtic — *Dark-skinned*
Entertainment: Keir Dullea, actor.

Keith (KĒTH)
Scottish — *From the battle place*
Entertainment: Keith Carradine, actor, composer and singer.
Kenneth

Kelby (KEL-bē)
Teutonic — *From the farm by the spring*
Keelby, Kelbee, Kellby

Keleman (KEL-man)
Hungarian — *Gentle*
Kellman

Kelly (KEL-ē)
Gaelic — *Warrior*
Kele, Kelley

Kelsey (KEL-sē)
Norwegian — *From the ship-island*

Kelvin (KEL-vin)
Celtic — *From the narrow river*

Kendall (KEN-dul)
Old English — *From the bright valley*
Ken, Kendal, Kendell, Kenn, Kennie, Kenny

Kendrick (KEN-drik)
Anglo-Saxon — *Royal ruler*
Ken, Kendricks, Kenric, Rick, Rickie

Kenelm (ka-NĒL-em)
Anglo-Saxon — *Brave helmet*
Ken

Kenley (KEN-lē)
Old English — *From the king's meadow*
Kenleigh

Kenn (KEN)
Welsh — *Clear water*
Ken, Kennie, Kenny

Kenneth (KEN-eth)
Celtic — *Handsome*
Literature: Ken Kesey, author of *One Flew Over the Cuckoo's Nest.*
Entertainment: Kenny Loggins, singer; Kenny Rogers, composer and country-western singer.
Ken, Kennet, Kennett, Kenny, Kent

Kenton (KEN-tun)
Old English — *From the king's estate*
Ken, Kenn, Kennie, Kenny, Kent

KEEGAN—*Little and fiery*

Kenway (KEN-wā)
Anglo-Saxon—*The brave soldier*
Ken, Kenny

Kenyon (KEN-yun)
Celtic—*Fair-haired*
Ken, Kenny

Kerel (KAIR-el)
African—*Young man*

Kerem (ke-RĒM)
Turkish—*Nobility and kindness*

Kerey (KAIR-ē)
English—*Homeward bound*
Ker, Keri

Kermit (KER-mit)
Celtic—*Free*
Entertainment: Kermit the Frog,
star of *The Muppet Show.*
**Dermont, Ker, Kermie,
Kermy, Kerr, Kerry**

Kerr (KER) or (KAR)
Celtic—*Dark or mysterious*
Kerrie, Kerrin, Kerry, Kieran

Kerry (KAIR-ē)
Gaelic—*The dark*
Keary

Kersen (KER-sen)
Indonesian—*Cherry*

Kerwin (KER-win)
Gaelic—*Little jet-black one*
Kerwinn

Kevin (KEV-un)
Gaelic—*Handsome*
Interesting: St. Kevin is the patron
saint of Dublin.
Kev, Kevan, Keven

Khalil (ka-LIL)
Arabic—*Friend*

Kieran (KĒR-an)
Gaelic—*Little and dark-skinned*
Kierman, Kiernan

Kilby (KIL-bē)
Teutonic— *From the farmstead by the spring*
Kerby, Kirby

Killian (KIL-ē-un)
Gaelic— *Little and warlike*
Kilian, Killie, Killy

Kim (KIM)
Old English— *Chief or ruler*
Kimmie, Kimmy

Kimball (KIM-bul)
Old English— *Warrior chief*
Literature: Kimball O'Hara, hero of Kipling's *Life in India*.
Kim, Kimball, Kimble, Kimmie, Kimmy

King (KING)
Anglo-Saxon— *Wise or ruler*

Kingdon (KING-dun)
Old English— *From the king's hill*

Kingsley (KINGZ-lē)
Old English— *From the king's meadow*
King, Kingsly, Kinsley

Kingston (KING-ston)
Old English— *From the king's manor*
King, Kingsten

Kipp (KIP)
Old English— *From the pointed hill*
Kippar, Kipper, Kippie, Kippy

Kiral (KĒR-al)
Turkish— *King*

Kiril (KIR-il)
Greek, Bulgarian— *Lordly one*
Cirilo, Cyrek, Cyryl, Keereel, Kirila, Kirill, Kiryl, Kyrillos

Kiritan (KIR-i-tan)
Hindi— *Wearing a crown*

Kirk (KIRK)
Scottish— *Church*
Entertainment: Kirk Douglas, actor.
Kerk

Kistur (KIS-ter)
English— *A rider*

Kit (KIT)
See Christopher.
Famous: Kit Carson, pony-express rider and frontiersman.

Kliment (KLIM-ent)
Russian, Latin— *Gentle*
Klemenis, Klemens, Klemeny, Klemet, Klim, Klyment

Knoton (NOT-un)
North American Indian— *The wind*
Nodin

Knox (NOKS)
Old English— *From the hills*

Knud (NOOD)
Danish— *Kind*

Knut (NOOT)
Norwegian— *Knot*
Sports: Knute Rockne, football coach.
Canute, Cnut, Knute

Konrad (KON-rad)
Teutonic— *Able in counsel*
Conrad

Kontar (KON-tar)
Akan— *An only child*

Kris (KRIS)
Latvian— *Christian*
Famous: Kris Kringle, another name for Santa Claus.
Entertainment: Kris Kristofferson, singer and actor.
Kristafa, Krisus

Krister (KRIS-ter)
Swedish— *Anointed one*
Krist, Kristian

Kruin (KROO-in)
Afrikaans— *Mountain peak*

Kumar (KOO-mar)
Indian— *Prince*

Kurt (KERT)
German— *Bold counselor*
Entertainment: Kurt Weill,
  composer of *The Three Penny
  Opera;* Kurt Russell, actor.

Kyle (KĪL)
Gaelic— *Fair and handsome*
Sports: Kyle Rote, football player.
Kile, Ky

Kynan (KI-nan)
See Conal.
Ky, Kyn

Laban (LĀ-ban)
Hebrew— *White*

Lachlan (LAK-lan)
Celtic— *Warlike*

Ladd (LAD)
English— *Attendant*
Lad, Laddey, Laddie, Laddy

Laird (LAIRD)
Celtic— *Proprietor*

Lambert (LAM-bert)
Teutonic— *Land bright*

Lamont (luh-MONT)
Norwegian— *Lawyer*
Lammond, Lamond, Monty

Lancelot (LAN-suh-lot)
Anglo-Saxon— *Spear*
Literature: Greatest of King
  Arthur's knights.
**Lance, Lancelot, Lancey,
Lancy, Launce, Launcelot**

Landers (LAN-derz)
French— *From the long hill*
Langson

Landry (LAN-drē)
Anglo-Saxon— *Ruler of the place*

Lane (LĀN)
English— *From the narrow road*
Laney, Lanie

Lang (LANG)
Teutonic— *Tall man*

Langdon (LANG-don)
Old English— *From the long hill*
Landon, Langsdon, Langston

Langley (LANG-lē)
Old English— *From the long meadow*

Langundo (lan-GUN-dō)
North American Indian— *Peaceful*

Lani (la-NĪ)
Polynesian— *Sky*

Lanny (LAN-ē)
See Roland.
Entertainment: Lennie Bruce,
  comedian.
Sports: Lanny Watkins, golf
  champion.
Lannie, Lennie

Lashi (LA-shē)
English— *Famous warrior*
**Lajos, Lasho, Laszlo, Lazlo,
Lesley**

LAWTON—*Man of refinement*

Lathrop (LĀ-throp)
Old English—*From the barn-farmstead.*
Lathe, Lathrope, Lay

Latimer (LA-ti-mer)
English—*Interpreter*
Lat, Latie, Latiner, Lattey, Latty

Lavi (LĀ-vē)
Hebrew—*Lion*
Leib, Leibel

Lawrence (LOR-ens)
Latin—*Crowned with laurel*
Famous: Lawrence of Arabia.
Entertainment: Larry Hagman, Sir
  Lawrence Olivier, actors;
  Lawrence Welk, band leader.
**Larry, Lars, Lauren
Laurence, Laurens, Laurent,
Laurie, Lauritz, Lawry,
Lenci, Lon, Lonnie, Lonny,
Lorant, Loren, Lorens,
Lorenzo, Lori, Lorin,
Lorrie, Lorry, Lowrance, Rance**

Lawton (LAW-ton)
Old English—*Man of refinement*
Law, Laughton

Lazarus (LA-zuh-rus)
Hebrew—*God will help*
Biblical: Lazarus was raised from
  the dead by Christ.
Eleazar, Lazare, Lazaro, Lozar

Leander (lē-AN-der)
Greek—*Lionlike*
**Ander, Leander, Leandro,
Lee, Leigh, Leo**

Learoyd (LER-oid)
Teutonic—*From the cleared meadow*

Leben (LĒ-ben)
Hebrew—*Life*

Ledyard (LED-yard)
Teutonic—*The nation's guardian*
Entertainment: Led Zeppelin, rock
  group.
Led

Lee (LĒ)
Old English—*From the meadow*
Entertainment: Lee J. Cobb, Lee
  Majors, Lee Marvin, actors.
Leigh, Leo

Leif (LĒF)
Norwegian—*Beloved*
Famous: Leif Erickson, Nordic
  explorer.
Lief

Leighton (LĀ-ton)
Old English—*From the herb garden*
Lay, Layton, Leigh

Leland (LĒ-lund)
Old English—*Meadow land*
Famous: Leland Stanford, founder
  of Stanford University.
Lee, Leeland, Leigh

Lemar (luh-MAR)
Teutonic—*Close to the sea*
Lemar

Lemuel (LEM-ū-el)
Hebrew—*Consecrated to God*
Literature: Lemuel Gulliver, hero
  of *Gulliver's Travels*.
Lem, Lemmie, Lemmy

Leo (LĒ-ō)
Latin—*Brave as a lion*
Entertainment: Leo Sayer, singer.
Sports: Leo Durocher, baseball
  coach.
**Lee, Len, Lennie, Lenny,
Leon, Leonard, Leonardo, Lev,
Lion, Lionel, Lyon**

Leonard (LEN-erd)
Teutonic—*Bold lion*
Famous: Leonardo da Vinci,
  Renaissance inventor and
  painter of the *Mona Lisa* and *The
  Last Supper*.
Entertainment: Leonard Nimoy,
  actor; Leonard Bernstein,
  conducter and composer.
**Lee, Len, Lenard, Lennard,
Lennie, Lenny, Leo, Leon,
Leonardo, Leonerd, Leonhard,
Leonid, Leonidas, Lonnard,
Lonnie, Lonny, Lonya**

Leopold (LĒ-uh-pōld)
Teutonic—*Bold for the people*
Entertainment: Leopold
  Stakowski, conductor; Leopold
  Auer, violinist.
Leo, Leupold, Leupool

Leron (LAIR-un)
Hebrew — *Song is mine*
Lerone, Liron, Lirone

Leroy (LĒ-roi)
French — *King*
**Elroy, LeRoy, Lee, Leigh,
Leroi, Regis, Rex, Roi, Roy**

Leslie (LEZ-lē)
Celtic — *From the gray fort*
Entertainment: Leslie Howard,
actor.
**Lee, Leigh, Les, Lesley,
Lester, Lezlie**

Lester (LES-ter)
Latin — *From the chosen camp*
Leicester, Les

Levi (LĒ-vī)
Hebrew — *Joined in harmony*
Biblical: Son of Jacob and Leah.
Lev, Levey, Levy, Lewi

Lewis (LOO-is)
Teutonic — *Renowned in battle*
Famous: Clovis Ruffin, designer.
Sports: Lew Alcindor, now known
as Kareem Abdul Jabbar.
**Aloysius, Clovis, Lew,
Lewes, Lewie, Lou, Louie,
Louis, Ludovick, Ludvig,
Luigi, Luis**

Liam (LĪ-am)
See William
Literature: Liam O'Flaherty,
author of *The Informer.*

Liang (LĒ-ang)
Chinese — *Excellent*

Lincoln (LINK-un)
Old English — *From the place by the
pool*
Historical: Lincoln Ellsworth,
polar explorer.
Famous: Abraham Lincoln,
President.
Linc, Link

Lindsay (LIND-sē)
Old English — *From the linden-tree
island*
Lind, Lindsey

Linfred (LIN-fred)
German — *Gentle peace*

Linus (LĪ-nus)
Hebrew — *Flaxen-haired*
Entertainment: Linus, friend of
Charlie Brown in *Peanuts* comic
strip.
Lionello

Livingston (LIV-ing-stun)
Old English — *From Lyfing's place*
Literature: *Jonathan Livingston
Seagull,* by Richard Bach.

Liwanu (li-WAN-oo)
Miowok Indian — *Bear growling.*

Llewellyn (loo-EL-en)
Welsh — *Lionlike or lightning*
Lew, Lewis, Llywellyn

Lloyd (LOID)
Celtic — *Gray hair*
Famous: David Lloyd George,
Prime Minister of England
during World War I.
Entertainment: Lloyd Nolan,
Lloyd Bridges, actors.
Floyd, Loy, Loydie

Locke (LOK)
Old English — *From the forest*
Lock, Lockwood

Logan (LŌ-gun)
Gaelic — *From the hollow*
Literature: Logan Clendening,
author of *The Human Body.*

Lombard (LOM-bard)
Latin — *Long-bearded*
Brad, Lem, Lomberd

Lon (LON)
See Alonso.
Entertainment: Lon Chaney, actor.
Lonnie, Lonny

Lorant (LOR-ant)
Hungarian, Latin—*Crowned with laurel*
Lenci, Lorencz, Lorincs

Loren (LOR-en)
See Lawrence.
Entertainment: Lorin Maazel, conductor; Lorin Hollander, pianist.
Larin, Lauren, Lorin

Lorenzo (lor-EN-zō)
See Lawrence.
Loring, Lorry

Lorimer (LOR-i-mer)
Latin—*Harness-maker*
Lorrie, Lorrimer, Lorry

Lot (LOT)
Hebrew—*Veiled*
Biblical: Jewish patriarch whose wife was turned to a pillar of salt.

Lothar (LŌ-thar)
German—*Famous warrior*

Loudon (LOW-dun)
Teutonic—*From the low valley*
Lowdon

Louis (LOO-is)
German—*Renowned warrior*
Interesting: Name used for 18 French kings.
Famous: Louis Pasteur, French scientist and developer of method to purify milk.
Literature: Louis L'Amour, western writer.
Entertainment: Lou Rawls, singer; Louis Armstrong, jazz musician.
Sports: Lou Gehrig, baseball player.
Lew, Lewis, Lou, Louie, Loysius, Ludvig, Ludwig, Luigi, Luis

Lowell (LŌ-el)
French—*Little wolf*
Famous: Lowell Thomas, journalist and newscaster.
Lovell, Lowe

Lucius (LOO-shus)
Latin—*Bringer of light*
Literature: Lucius Morris Beebe, author of western folklore.
Luca, Lucais, Lucas, Luce, Lucian, Luciano, Lucias, Lucien, Lucio, Lukas, Luke

Ludlow (LUD-lō)
Old English—*From the prince's hill*

Ludwig (LUD-wig)
See Louis.
Famous: Ludwig van Beethoven, composer.
Luis

Luister (LOO-is-ter)
Afrikaans—*A listener*

Luke (LOOK)
Greek—*A person from Lucania.*
Biblical: Book in the Bible.
Lucais, Lucas, Lukas

Luther (LOO-ther)
Teutonic—*Famous warrior*
Famous: Martin Luther, religious reformer; Martin Luther King, civil rights leader.
Entertainment: Luther Adler, actor.
Lothaire, Lothario, Lutero

Lutherum (LOO-ther-um)
English—*Slumber*

Lyle (LĪL)
French—*From the island*
Lisle, Lothar, Lothario, Ly, Lyel, Lyell

LUISTER—*A listener*

Lyman (LĪ-man)
Old English—*Man from the valley*

Lyndon (LIN-dun)
Teutonic—*From the linden-tree hill*
Famous: Lyndon B. Johnson,
President.
**Lin, Lindon, Lindy,
Lyn, Lynn**

Lynn (LIN)
Anglo-Saxon—*From the waterfalls*
Lin, Linn, Lyn

Lyron (LĪ-ron)
Hebrew—*Lyrical*
Liron

Lysander (lī-SAN-der)
Greek—*Liberator*
Sander, Sandra

Mac (MAK)
Scottish—*Son of*
Entertainment: Mac Davis, singer.
Mack, Max

Mackenzie (ma-KEN-zē)
Gaelic—*Son of the wise leader*
Mac, Mack

Macnair (mak-NAIR)
Gaelic—*Son of the heir*
Macknair

Maddox (MAD-oks)
Celtic—*Beneficent*
Madoc, Maddock

Madison (MAD-i-son)
Old English—*Son of the powerful soldier*
Maddie, Maddy, Son, Sonnie, Sonny

Magnus (MAG-nus)
Latin—*Great one*
Manus

Mahir (MA-ir)
Hebrew—*Industrious*
Mahira

Mahlon (MĀ-lun)
Hebrew—*Sickness*
Biblical: First husband of Ruth.

Maimun (MĀ-mun)
Arabic—*Lucky*

Major (MĀ-jer)
Latin—*Greater*
Maje, Mauer, Mayor

Makis (MĀ-kis)
Greek—*Who is like God*
Mahail, Maichail, Mikhail, Mikhalis, Mikhos

Malachi (MAL-uh-kī)
Hebrew—*My messenger*
Biblical: Last book of the Old Testament.
Entertainment: Malachi Throne, actor.
Mal, Malachy

Malcolm (MAL-kom)
Celtic—*Dove*
Literature: Malcolm, son of King Duncan in Shakespeare's *Macbeth.*
Mal

Malik (MĀ-lik)
Muslim—*Master*

Mallory (MAL-ō-rē)
Teutonic—*Army counselor*
Mal, Mallery

Malvin (MAL-vin)
Celtic—*Chief*
Mal, Melvin

Manco (MAN-kō)
Peruvian—*King*

Mandek (MAN-dek)
Polish—*Army man*
Arek, Armand, Armandek

Mandel (MAN-del)
German—*Almond*
Mandal

Manfred (MAN-fred)
Old English—*Man of peace*
Entertainment: Manfred Mann, rock singer.
Fred, Mannie

Manipi (MAN-i-pē)
North American Indian — *A walking wonder*

Manton (MAN-tun)
Anglo-Saxon — *From the king's estate*

Manuel (man-WEL)
Hebrew — *God with us*
Entertainment: Manuel de Falla, Spanish composer.
Emmanuel, Emmanuil, Manuil, Manuyill

Manvel (MAN-vel)
Latin — *From the great estate*
Manvil

Marcel (mar-SEL)
Latin — *Little and warlike*
Literature: Marcel Proust, author of *Remembrance of Things Past.*
Entertainment: Marcel Marceau, pantomimist.
Marcello, Marcellus, Marcelo

Marcus (MAR-kus)
See Mark.
Famous: Marcus Aurelius, Roman emperor.
Entertainment: *Marcus Welby, M.D.*, television series starring Robert Young.

Mardon (MAR-dun)
Old English — *From the valley with the pool*
Marden

Marid (muh-RID)
Arabic — *Rebellious*

Marion (MAIR-ē-un)
See Mary.
Interesting: Name usually reserved for boys.
Marlin

Mark (MARK)
Latin — *Warlike*
Biblical: One of the 12 apostles of Christ.
Famous: Marco Polo, explorer.
Literature: Mark Twain (Samuel L. Clemens), author; Mark Van Doren, critic, novelist and poet; *Marco Millions*, play by Eugene O'Neill.
Entertainment: Mark Hamill, actor in *Star Wars.*
Sports: Mark Spitz, Olympic gold medal swimmer.
Marc, Marco, Marcos, Marcus, Mario, Marius, Markos, Markus

Marland (MAR-land)
Old English — *From the boundary*
Marlan

Marlon (MAR-lon)
French — *Little falcon*
Entertainment: Marlon Brando, actor; Marlin Perkins, narrator and host of *Wild Kingdom.*
Marlin, Merlin

Marlow (MAR-lō)
Old English — *From the hill by the lake*
Mar, Marlo, Marlot, Marlowe, Merlot

Marmaduke (MAR-muh-dūk)
Celtic — *Sea leader*
Duke

Marnin (MAR-nin)
Hebrew — *One who creates joy*

Marshall (MAR-shal)
French — *Steward*
Marsh, Marshal

MASON — *Worker in stone*

Martin (MAR-tin)
Latin — *The warlike*
Famous: Martin Van Buren,
  President; Martin Luther King,
  civil rights leader.
Literature: *Martin Chuzzlewit,*
  novel by Dickens.
Entertainment: Marty Feldman,
  comedian.
**Mart, Martain, Marten,
Martie, Martijn, Martino,
Marty, Martyn**

Marvin (MAR-vin)
Teutonic — *Sea friend*
Entertainment: Marvin Hamlisch,
  composer.
Marv, Marwin

Maska (MAW-skuh)
North American Indian — *Powerful*

Mason (MĀ-son)
Latin — *Worker in stone*
Entertainment: Mason Williams,
  composer and singer.
Maison, Mayson

Matthew (MA-thyōō)
Hebrew— *Gift of God*
Biblical: Matthew, one of the 12
apostles of Christ.
Famous: Matthew B. Brady,
Abraham Lincoln's
photographer.
Entertainment: Matt Dillon, old
west hero on television series,
Gunsmoke.
**Mata, Matei, Matek,
Mateo, Mathe, Mathian,
Mathias, Matias, Matt,
Matteo, Matthaeus, Matthaus,
Mattheus, Matthias, Matthiew,
Mattias, Mattie, Matty,
Matus, Matvey, Matyash, Motka**

Maurice (mor-ĒS)
Latin— *Dark-skinned*
Entertainment: Maurice Chevalier,
Morey Amsterdam, Maurice
Evans, actors; Maurice Ravel,
composer; Maurice Gibb,
member of the rock group, The
Bee Gees.
**Mauricio, Maurie, Maurise,
Maurits, Maurizio, Maury,
Morey, Morie, Moritz, Morris**

Max (MAKS)
See Maximillian.
Famous: Max Planck, winner of
Nobel Prize for physics.
Entertainment: Max Reinhardt,
film director and producer; Max
Baer, Jr., actor.
Maxie, Maxy

Maximillian (maks-i-MIL-ē-an)
Latin— *Most excellent*
Famous: Ferdinand Maximillian
Joseph, Archduke of Austria and
Emperor of Mexico.
Entertainment: Maximillian
Schell, actor.
**Mac, Mack, Massimiliano,
Massimo, Max, Maxie, Maxim,
Maximilianus, Maximilien,
Maximo, Maxy**

Maxwell (MAKS-wel)
Old English— *From the influential
man's well*
Literature: Maxwell Anderson,
author.
Entertainment: Maxwell Smart,
character on TV show, *Get Smart.*
**Mac, Mack, Max,
Maxie, Maxy**

Mayer (MĀ-er)
Austrian— *Farmer*

Maynard (MĀ-nerd)
Anglo-Saxon— *Mightily strong*
Entertainment: Maynard G.
Krebbs, character on *Doby Gillis*
TV show.

Mead (MĒD)
Old English— *From the meadow*
Meade

Medwin (MED-win)
Teutonic— *Strong friend*

Melbourne (MEL-born)
Old English— *From the mill stream*
Melborn, Melburn

Meldon (MEL-don)
Old English— *From the hillside mill*
Meldan, Melden

Melville (MEL-vil)
Old English— *From the estate of the
hard worker*
Mel, Melbille

Melvin (MEL-vin)
Celtic— *Chief*
Entertainment: Melvyn Douglas,
actor; Mel Brooks, actor and film
director.
Sports: Mel Allen, sportscaster.
Mal, Malvin, Mel, Melvyn

Mendel (MEN-del)
East Semitic— *Knowledge, wisdom*
Mendie, Mendy

Mendeley (MEND-lē)
Russian— *Comforter*
Latin— *Of the mind*
Menachem, Mendelly, Mendely

Mercer (MER-ser)
French, Latin — *Merchant*

Meredith (MAIR-e-dith)
Welsh — *Guardian from the sea*
Merideth, Merry

Merle (MERL)
French — *Blackbird*
Entertainment: Merle Haggard, country-western singer.
Merlin, Merrill

Merlin (MER-lin)
English — *Falcon*
Literature: Merlin, wizard in King Arthur legend.
Marlin, Marlon, Merle

Merrick (MAIR-ik)
Teutonic — *Industrious ruler*

Merrill (MAIR-il)
French — *Famous*
Merill, Merle, Merrel, Merrell, Meryl

Merripen (MAIR-i-pen)
English — *Life or death*

Merton (MER-ton)
Anglo-Saxon — *From the farm by the sea*
Entertainment: Merv Griffin, TV talk-show host.
Merv, Merwyn

Merwin (MER-win)
Teutonic — *Lover of the sea*
Merwyn

Mestipen (me-STIP-en)
English — *Life, fortune or luck*

Meyer (MĪ-er)
Belgian — *Farmer*
Mayeer, Mayer, Mayor, Meier, Meir, Myer

Micah (MĪ-kuh)
Hebrew — *Like unto the Lord*
Entertainment: Mick Jagger, singer.
Mic, Mick, Mike, Mikey

Michael (MĪ-kul)
Hebrew — *Who is like the Lord*
Biblical: An archangel.
Famous: Michelangelo Buonarrotti, painter and sculptor.
Literature: Michel Eyquem de Montaigne, essay writer.
Entertainment: Mike Love, of the rock group, The Beach Boys; Michael Jackson, singer and actor; Michelangelo Antonioni, actor and film director; Michael Caine, Michael Landon, Michael Douglas, Mike Nichols, Sir Michael Redgrave, actors; Michael Kitt, choreographer; Mike Douglas, host of *The Mike Douglas Show*.
Micah, Michael, Michail, Micheil, Michel, Michele, Mickey, Mickie, Micky, Mikael, Mike, Mikel, Mikey, Mikkel, Mikkell, Miquel, Mischa, Mitch, Mitchel, Mitchell, Mychal

Milap (MĪ-lap)
North American Indian — *He gives*

Milburn (MIL-bern)
Old English — *Of the stream by the mill*
Entertainment: Melburn Stone played Doc on TV series *Gunsmoke*.

Miles (MĪLS)
Greek — *Millstone*
Latin — *Soldier*
Mihiel, Milo, Myles

Millard (MIL-ard)
Old English — *Caretaker of the mill*
Famous: Millard Fillmore, President.
Millward, Milward

Milo (MĪ-lō)
See Miles.

Milton (MIL-ton)
Old English — *From the mill town*
Literature: John Milton, poet.
Entertainment: Milton Berle,
known as Uncle Milty and Mr.
TV.
Milt, Miltie, Milty

Minor (MĪ-ner)
Latin — *Junior or younger*
Miner

Mitchell (MITCH-el)
See Michael.
Entertainment: Mitch Miller, band
leader.
Mitch, Mitchel

Mohammed (mō-HAW-mud)
See Muhammad.

Mohan (MŌ-han)
Hindi — *Delightful*
Krishna

Mojag (MŌ-hag)
North American Indian — *Never
quiet*

Monroe (mon-RŌ)
Gaelic — *From the mouth of the Roe
River*
Monro, Munro, Munroe

Montague (MON-ta-gū)
French — *From the pointed mountain*
Monte, Monty

Monte (MON-tē)
Latin — *Mountain*
Entertainment: Monte Hall, host of
Let's Make A Deal.
Montgomery

Montgomery (MONT-gum-er-ē)
Old English — *From the rich man's
mountain*
Entertainment: Montgomery Clift,
actor.
Monte, Monty

Moore (MOR)
French — *Dark-complected*

Mordecai (MOR-de-kī)
Hebrew — *Belonging to Marduk*
Biblical: Cousin of Queen Esther.

Moreland (MOR-lund)
Old English — *From the moor*

Morgan (MOR-gun)
Celtic — *Born by the sea*
Morgun

Morley (MOR-lē)
Old English — *From the meadow on
the moor*
Entertainment: Morley Safer,
newscaster.
Morlee, Morly

Morrell (MOR-el)
Latin — *Swarthy*
Morel

Mortimer (MOR-ti-mer)
French — *Still water*
Entertainment: Mortimer Snerd,
character created by Edgar
Bergen, ventriloquist.
Mort, Mortie, Morty

Morton (MOR-tun)
Old English — *From the farm on the
moor*

Morven (MOR-ven)
Celtic — *Mariner*
Morvin

Moses (MŌ-zes)
Hebrew — *Saved*
Egyptian — *Child*
Biblical: Prophet that gave us the
Ten Commandments.
Famous: Moses Mendelssohn,
philosopher known as the
German Socrates; Moshe Dayan,
Israeli Defense Minister.
**Moe, Moise, Moises,
Mose, Moshe, Moss, Mozes**

Moulton (MŌL-tun)
Old English, Latin — *From the mule
farm*

Muhammad (mu-HAW-mud)
Arabic— *Praised*
Famous: Muhammad, founder of the Muslim religion.
Sports: Muhammad Ali, heavyweight boxing champion.
Ahmad, Amed, Hamdrenn, Hamdun, Hamid, Hammad, Humayd, Mahmoud, Mahmud, Mehamet, Mehemet, Mehmet, Mohammad

Muir (MŪR)
Celtic— *Moor*

Muraco (mer-AW-kō)
North American Indian— *White moon*

Murdock (MER-dok)
Celtic— *Wealthy sailor*
Murdoch, Murtach

Murray (MER-ē)
Celtic— *Seaman*
Murry

Musenda (mū-SEN-duh)
African— *Nightmare*

Myron (MĪ-ron)
Greek— *Fragrant ointment*
Entertainment: Myron Cohen, comedian.
My, Ron, Ronnie, Ronny

Nabil (na-BĒL)
Arabic— *Noble*

Nagid (na-GĒD)
Hebrew— *Ruler*

Nahele (na-HĒ-lē)
Polynesian— *Grove of trees*

Nahum (NĀ-hūm)
Hebrew— *Compassion*
Biblical: Prophet who predicted the fall of Nineveh.

Naldo (NAL-dō)
Teutonic— *Power*

Namir (nā-MĒR)
Hebrew— *Leopard or cunning swiftness*

Napoleon (na-PŌ-lē-on)
Greek— *Lion of the woodland dell*
Historical: Napoleon Bonaparte, French ruler.
Leon, Nap, Napoleon, Nappie, Nappy

Narcissus (nar-SIS-us)
Greek— *Self-loving*

Nathan (NĀ-than)
Hebrew — *Gift*
Biblical: Prophet who rebuked
  David for his treachery to Uriah.
Historical: Nathan Hale,
  Revolutionary War hero.
Literature: *Nathan The Wise,* play
  by Lessing.
Entertainment: Nathan Milstein,
  violinist; Nat King Cole, singer.
Nat, Nate

Nathaniel (na-THAN-yel)
Hebrew — *Gift of God*
Biblical: Nathaniel, one of the 12
  apostles of Christ.
Literature: Nathaniel Hawthorne,
  author of *The Scarlet Letter;*
  Nathanael West, author.
**Nataniel, Nate, Nathan,
Nathanael, Natie, Natty**

Neal (NĒL)
Celtic — *Champion*
Neale, Nealey, Nealon, Neil

Ned (NED)
See Norton.

Nehemiah (nē-uh-MĪ-uh)
Hebrew — *Comforted by the Lord*
Biblical: Prophet who helped
  rebuild Jerusalem.
Entertainment: Nehemiah Persoff,
  actor.
Hemiah

Neil (NĒL)
Irish — *Chief*
Latin — *Dark*
Literature: Neil Simon, playwright.
Entertainment: Neil Diamond,
  actor, songwriter and singer;
  Neil Sedaka, singer.
**Neal, Neale, Neall, Nealon,
Neel, Neil, Neill, Neils,
Nels, Nial, Niall, Niels,
Nil, Niles, Nils**

Nelson (NEL-son)
English — *Son of Neil*
Entertainment: Nelson Eddy,
  singer and actor.
**Nealson, Neils, Nels,
Niles, Nils, Nilson**

Neron (NER-on)
Spanish, Latin — *Stern*
Nero

Nestor (NES-ter)
Greek — *Wisdom*
Mythological: Chieftain of the
  seige of Troy.

Neville (NE-vil)
French — *From the new town*
Literature: Nevil Shute, author of
  On the Beach.
**Nebille, Nev, Nevil,
Nevile, Newton**

Nevin (NE-vin)
Gaelic — *Worshipper of the saints*
Anglo-Saxon — *Nephew*
Nevins

Newbold (NŌŌ-bōld)
Old English — *New building*

Newlin (NŌŌ-lin)
Celtic — *From the spring*
Newlyn, Newlynn

Nicholas (NI-kō-lus)
Greek — *Victory of the people*
Interesting: St. Nicholas, another
  name for Santa Claus.
Historical: Nicholas, Czar of
  Russia.
Famous: Nikita Kruschev, Russian
  Premier.
Literature: *Nicholas Nickleby,* novel
  by Dickens.
Entertainment: Nick Nolte, actor.
**Claus, Colas, Cole, Colet,
Colin, Colley, Klaus,
Niccolo, Nichol, Nicholl,
Nick, Nickie, Nickolaus, Nicky,
Nicol, Nicolai, Nicolas, Niki,
Nikita, Nikki, Nikolai, Nikolas,
Nikolaus, Nikolos, Nikos,
Niles, Nixo**

NORMAN — *Norseman*

Nicodemus (ni-kō-DE-mus)
Greek — *The people-conqueror*
Biblical: Jewish priest and member
of Sanhedrin.
Nick, Nicky

Nigel (NĪ-jel) or (NĒ-gel)
Latin — *Dark or black*
Literature: *The Fortunes of Nigel,* by
Sir Walter Scott; *Sir Nigel,* novel
by Arthur Conan Doyle.
Entertainment: Nigel Bruce, actor
who played the part of Watson in
Sherlock Holmes series.

Niles (NĪLS)
Danish — *Son of Neil*
Famous: Niels Bohr, scientist
known for his work with atoms.
Niel, Niels, Nils

Noah (NŌ-uh)
Hebrew — *Wandering or rest*
Biblical: Noah built the ark and
survived the Great Flood.
Literature: Noah Webster, author
of the Webster dictionary.
Entertainment: Noah Beery, actor.

242

Nobel (NŌ-bel)
Latin— *Well-born*
Nobe, Nobie, Noble, Noby

Nodin (NŌ-din)
North American Indian— *The wind*
Noton

Noel (NŎ-ul)
French— *Born at Christmas*
Entertainment: Noel Coward,
   actor and director.
Natal, Natale, Nowell

Nolan (NŌ-lan)
Gaelic— *Famous or noble*
Noland

Norbert (NOR-bert)
Norwegian— *Brilliant hero*
Famous: Norbert Wiener, scientist
   prominent in the field of
   cybernetics.
Norbie, Norby

Norman (NOR-man)
Anglo-Saxon— *Norseman*
Historical: Norman Thomas, six
   times a Presidential candidate.
Famous: Norman Rockwell,
   painter and illustrator.
Literature: Norman Mailer, author
   of *The Naked and the Dead*.
Entertainment: Norm Crosby,
   comedian.
**Norm, Normand, Normie,
Normy**

Norris (NOR-is)
French— *From the north*
Norrie, Norry, Norvin

Northrop (NORTH-rup)
Old English— *From the north farm*
North, Northrup

Norton (NOR-tun)
Anglo-Saxon— *From the north place*
Ned, Norty, Noton

Norward (NOR-ward)
Teutonic— *The guard at the northern
   gate*
Norwood, Norword

Noy (NOI)
Hebrew— *Beauty*

Nuri (NER-ē)
Hebrew— *Fire*
Nur, Nuriel, Nuris

Nye (NĪ)
English— *Islander*

Oakley (ŌK-lē)
Anglo-Saxon— *From the oak-tree
   meadow*
**Oak, Oakes, Oakie,
Oaks**

Obadiah (ō-buh-DĪ-uh)
Hebrew— *Servant of God*
**Obadias, Obed, Obediah,
Obie, Oby**

Octavio (ok-TĀ-vē-ō)
Latin— *Eighth*
**Octave, Octavian, Octavius,
Octavus, Tavey**

Odell (Ō-del)
Norwegian— *Little and wealthy*
**Dell, Ode, Odey,
Odie, Ody**

Odoric (Ō-dor-ik)
Latin— *Son of a good man*

243

Ogden (OG-den)
Old English— *From the oak valley*
Literature: Ogden Nash, humorist
poet.
Ogdan, Ogdon

Ohanko (ō-HAN-kō)
North American Indian— *Reckless*

Olaf (Ō-laf)
Norwegian— *Ancestor*
Famous: St. Olaf, first Christian
King of Norway.
**Olafur, Olav, Olen,
Olin**

Olery (Ō-ler-ē)
Teutonic— *Ruler of all*

Oliver (OL-i-ver)
Latin— *Olive tree*
Historical: Oliver Hazard Perry,
American officer at the battle of
Lake Erie.
Famous: Oliver Wendell Holmes,
Supreme Court Justice.
Entertainment: Oliver Hardy, of
comedy team Laurel and Hardy.
**Noll, Nollie, Nolly,
Olivero, Olivier, Oliviero,
Ollie, Olly, Olvan**

Olney (ŌL-nē)
Old English— *Unknown*

Omar (Ō-mar)
Arabic— *First son, highest follower of
the prophet*
Entertainment: Omar Sharif, actor.
Omer

Onan (Ō-nan)
Turkish— *Prosperous*
Onon

Orban (OR-ban)
Latin, Hungarian— *City boy*

Ordway (ORD-wā)
Anglo-Saxon— *Spear fighter*
Orway

Oren (OR-en)
Hebrew— *Pine tree*
Oran, Orin, Orren, Orrin

Orestes (or-ES-tez)
Greek— *Mountain man*
Mythological: Son of Agamemnon,
who avenged his father's murder
by slaying his mother.
Oreste

Orford (OR-ford)
Old English— *From the cattle ford*

Orion (or-Ī-on)
Greek— *Son of fire*

Orji (OR-jē)
Nigerian— *Mighty tree*

Orland (OR-land)
Old English— *From the pointed land*
**Land, Lannie, Lanny,
Orlan, Orlando**

Orman (OR-mun)
Teutonic— *Mariner or shipman*

Ormond (OR-mund)
English— *Bear or ravine mound*

Orson (OR-sun)
Latin— *Bearlike*
Entertainment: Orson Welles,
actor and director; Orson Bean,
actor; Sonny Bono, singer and
actor.
Sonnie, Sonny, Urson

Orton (OR-ton)
English— *Ravine town*
Horton

Orville (OR-vil)
French— *From the golden estate*
Famous: Orville Wright, one of the
inventors of the airplane.
Orv

Osbert (OZ-bert)
Anglo-Saxon— *Divinely bright*
**Bert, Bertie, Berty,
Oz, Ozbert, Ozzie**

Osborn (OZ-born)
Teutonic— *Divine bear*
Osborne, Osbourn, Osbourne

Oscar (OS-ker)
Celtic—*Leaping warrior*
Interesting: Oscar, award of the Academy of Motion Picture Arts and Sciences.
Literature: Oscar Wilde, author.
Entertainment: Oscar Hammerstein II, librettist for many of Richard Rodger's musicals.
Oshar, Ossie, Ossy, Ozzie, Ozzy

Osgood (OZ-good)
Teutonic—*Gift of our Lord*
Ozzie, Ozzy

Osmond (OZ-mund)
Teutonic—*Under divine protection*
Osmund

Oswald (OZ-wald)
Anglo-Saxon—*Divine power*
Ossie, Ossy, Oswell, Oz, Ozzie, Ozzy, Wald, Waldo

Otis ($\bar{O}$-tis)
Greek—*Keen of hearing*
Oates, Otes

Otman (OT-mun)
Teutonic—*Gift of our Lord*
Entertainment: Ozzie, character of *Ozzie and Harriett* TV show.
Ozzie, Ozzy

Otto (OT-t$\bar{o}$)
Teutonic—*Rich*
Literature: Othello, character in Shakespeare's play.
Entertainment: Otto Preminger, film producer and director.
Odo, Othello, Otho

ORSON—*Bearlike*

Otway (OT-wā)
Teutonic — *Fortunate in battle*

Outram (OT-ram)
Teutonic — *Prospering raven*

Ovid (Ō-vid)
Latin — *Shepherd*
Historical: Greek historian and
chronicler.
Ovidius

Owen (Ō-wen)
Celtic — *Lamb*
Greek — *Well-born*
Ewen

Oxford (OKS-ford)
Old English — *From the
river-crossing of the oxen*
Ford

Pablo (POB-lō)
See Paul.
Famous: Pablo Picasso, painter.
Entertainment: Pablo Cassals,
cellist.

Paco (PA-kō)
North American Indian — *Bald eagle*

Paddy (PA-dē)
See Patrick.

Padraic (pa-DRĀ-ik)
See Patrick.
Literature: Padraic Colum,
playwright and author.
Padrayc

Page (PĀJ)
French — *Servant to the royal court*
Padget, Padgett, Paige

Paine (PĀN)
Latin — *Country man*
Payne

Pal (PAL)
English — *Brother*

Pallaton (PAL-a-tun)
North American Indian — *Fighter*
Palladin, Pallaten

Palmer (POL-mer)
Latin — *The palm-bearer or pilgrim*
Palm, Palmer

Parker (PAR-ker)
English — *Guardian of the park*
Park, Parke

Parlan (PAR-lan)
Scottish — *Son of the earth*
Parlen

Parnell (par-NEL)
French — *Little Peter*
Entertainment: Pernell Roberts,
actor.
Parrnell, Pernell

Parrish (PAIR-ish)
English — *From the church yard*
Parrie, Parrisch, Parry

Parry (PAIR-ē)
French — *Guardian*

Pascal (PAS-kal)
Hebrew — *Passover*
Pascale, Pasquale

PAXTON—*A traveler*

Patrick (PAT-rik)
Latin—*Nobleman*
Interesting: St. Patrick, patron
saint of Ireland.
Historical: Patrick Henry,
Revolutionary War hero.
Literature: Sir Patrick Spens,
author of Scottish ballads;
Paddie Chayefsky, author.
Entertainment: Pat Boone, singer;
Pat Paulsen, comedian.
**Paddie, Paddy, Padraic, Padraig,
Pat, Paton, Patric, Patrice,
Patricio, Patrizio, Patrizius,
Patsy, Patten, Pattie, Patty, Peyton**

Patton (PAT-tun)
Old English—*From the warrior's
estate*
**Pat, Paten, Patin,
Paton, Patten, Pattin, Patty**

Paul (PAWL)
Latin—*Small*
Biblical: Saul, called Paul, was one
of the 12 apostles of Christ.
Historical: Paul Revere, known for
his ride to warn of the British
coming.
Entertainment: Paul Newman,
Paul Scofield, actors; Paul Anka,
singer and songwriter; Paul
McCartney, singer; Paul Lynde,
comedian.
**Pablo, Pall, Paolo,
Paulie, Pauly, Pavel, Poul**

Paxton (PAKS-tun)
Teutonic— *A traveler*
Packston, Paxon

Payat (PĀ-yat)
North American Indian— *He is coming*
Pay, Payatt

Paz (PAWZ)
Spanish— *Peace*

Peder (PĀ-der)
Danish— *Rock*
Panos, Pedro, Peet, Pero, Petr, Petras, Petros, Piero, Pierre, Pieter, Pietrek

Pembroke (PEM-brōk)
Celtic— *From the headland*

Penn (PEN)
Old English— *Enclosure*
Teutonic— *Commander*
Pen, Penny

Penrod (PEN-rod)
Teutonic— *Famous commander*
Pen, Penn, Pennie, Penny, Rod, Roddie, Roddy

Percival (PER-si-vul)
French— *Pierce the valley*
Interesting: Name invented by Chretien de Troyes.
Literature: Percival C. Wren, author of *Beau Geste;* Sir Percival, knight of King Arthur's Round Table.
Entertainment: Opera *Parsifal,* by Richard Wagner.
Parsifal, Perce, Perceval, Percy, Purcell

Percy (PER-sē)
English— *Pear tree*
French— *Little Peter*
Entertainment: Percy Grainger, pianist and composer.

Peregrine (PER-e-grin)
Latin— *Wander*
Perry

Perrin (PER-in)
See Peter.
Perren, Perryn

Perry (PER-ē)
French— *Pear tree*
Welsh— *Son of Harry*
Literature: Perry Mason, hero of Erle Stanley Gardner books.
Entertainment: Perry Como, singer.
Par, Parry, Perr

Peter (PĒ-ter)
Greek— *Rock*
Biblical: Simon, called Peter, was one of the 12 apostles of Christ.
Historical: Peter the Great, of Russia.
Literature: *Peter Ibbetson,* novel by George du Maurier; *Peter Pan,* by James Barrier; Peter Benchley, author of the novel *Jaws.*
Entertainment: Peter O'Toole, Peter Falk, Peter Graves, actors; Peter Ilyich Tchaikovsky, composer; Peter Duchin, orchestra leader.
Farris, Ferris, Parry, Peador, Pearce, Pearson, Peder, Pedro, Peerson, Peirce, Perkin, Perren, Perry, Pete, Peterus, Petey, Petr, Pierce, Pierre, Pierson, Pietrek, Pietro, Piotr

Peyton (PĀ-tun)
Old English— *From the warrior's estate*
Pate

Phelan (FĀ-lun)
Celtic— *Wolf or brave as a wolf*

Philander (FIL-an-der)
Greek— *Lover of mankind*

Philbert (FIL-bert)
Teutonic— *Illustriously brilliant*
Bert, Filbert

Philemon (FIL-e-mon)
Greek — *Loving*
Biblical: Greek to whom Paul wrote an Epistle.
Philemonn, Phillemon

Philip (FIL-ip)
Greek — *Lover of horses*
Biblical: One of the 12 apostles of Christ.
Historical: Father of Alexander the Great.
Famous: Prince Philip, husband of the Queen of England.
Literature: Philip Carey, hero in *Of Human Bondage*, by Somerset Maugham.
Entertainment: Phil Silvers, actor; Phil Donahue, host of *Donahue* talk show.
Felipe, Filip, Filippo, Phelps, Phil, Philipe, Philipp, Phillip, Phillipp

Philo (FĪ-lō)
Greek — *Friendly*
Philio

Phineas (FIN-ē-as)
Hebrew — *Oracle*
Famous: Phineas T. Barnum, founder of Barnum and Bailey Circus.

Pierce (PĒRS)
See Peter.
Famous: Pierre Cardin, clothes designer.
Literature: Pierre Corneille, author of *Golden Age of Louis*.
Pearce, Peirce, Pierre

Pierpont (PĒR-pont)
French, Latin — *Dweller by the stone bridge*
Pierre, Pierrepont, Pierrie, Pierrpont

Pius (PĪ-us)
Latin — *Pious*
Pyus

Plato (PLĀ-tō)
Greek — *Broad-shouldered*
Historical: Eminent Greek philosopher.
Platon

Pollard (POL-erd)
Teutonic — *Cropped hair*

Pomeroy (POM-e-roi)
French — *From the apple orchard*
Pom, Pommie, Pommy, Roy

Porter (POR-ter)
Latin — *Door keeper*
Port, Portie, Porty

Powell (POW-el)
Celtic — *Alert*

Prentice (PREN-tis)
Latin — *Learner or apprentice*
Pren, Prent, Prentiss, Prentiz

Prescott (PRES-kot)
Old English — *From the priest's collage*
Scott, Scottie, Scotty

Preston (PRES-ton)
Anglo-Saxon — *Of the priest's place*

Price (PRĪS)
Welsh — *Son of Rice*
Brice, Bryce, Phip, Pryce

Primo (PRĒ-mō)
Italian — *First born*

Prince (PRINS)
Latin — *Prince*

Prior (PRĪ-or)
Latin — *Superior*
Prior, Pry, Pryor

Proctor (PROK-tor)
Latin — *Manager or leader*
Procter

Putnam (PUT-nam)
Anglo-Saxon — *Dweller of the pond*
Putmen, Putnem

Quartus (KWAR-tus)
Latin— *Fourth son*

Quentin (KWEN-tin)
Latin— *The fifth*

Quillan (KWIL-an)
Gaelic— *Cub*

Quinby (KWIN-bē)
Scandinavian— *Of the womb of woman*

Quincy (KWIN-sē)
French— *From the fifth son's estate*
Famous: John Quincy Adams, President.
Literature: Quincy Howe, newspaper columnist.
Quin, Quinn, Quinzee

Quinlan (KWIN-lan)
Gaelic— *Physically strong*
Quinn

Quintus (KWIN-tus)
Latin— *Fifth*

Rabi (RA-bī)
Arabic— *Breeze*
Rabbi

Radburn (RAD-burn)
Old English— *From the red stream*
Rad, Radborne, Radbourne, Raddie, Raddy

Radcliffe (RAD-klif)
Old English— *From the red cliff*
Rad, Raddie, Raddy

Radman (RAD-man)
Slovak— *Joy*
Radmen

Radomil (RAD-ō-mil)
Czech— *Love of peace*
Rad, Radomill

Rafael (RA-fī-el)
Spanish— *God has healed*
Rafe, Raphael

Rafferty (RA-fer-tē)
Gaelic— *Rich, prosperous*
Rafe, Raff, Raffarty

Rafi (RĀ-fī)
Arabic— *Exalting*

Ragnar (RAG-nar)
Norwegian, Swedish— *Mighty army*
Ragnor, Rainer, Rayner, Raynor

Rahman (RAW-man)
Arabic—*Compassionate*
Abdul, Allah, Rahmet

Raleigh (RAW-lē)
Old English—*Of the deer field*
Lee, Leigh, Rawley

Ralph (RALF)
Old English—*Wolf counselor*
Famous: Ralph Nader, consumer
  advocate; Ralph Lauren, clothes
  designer.
Entertainment: Ralph Bellamy,
  actor.
**Rafe, Raff, Ralf, Raoul,
Rolf, Rolph**

Ralston (RAL-ston)
Old English—*Of the house of Ralph*
Ralfston, Rolfston

Ramon (ra-MŌN)
See Raymond.

Ramsay (RAM-sē)
Teutonic   *From the ram's island*
Famous: Ramsay MacDonald,
  Great Britain's first Labor Prime
  Minister.
Ram, Ramsey

Randall (RAN-dul)
See Randolph.
Literature: Randall Jarrell, poet.
Entertainment: Randy Newman,
  songwriter and singer.
**Rand, Randal, Randell,
Randi, Randy**

Randolph (RAN-dolf)
Anglo-Saxon—*Protected; advised by
  wolves*
Entertainment: Randolph Scott,
  actor.
**Raff, Raffaello, Ralph,
Rand, Randal, Randall,
Randell, Randolf, Randy**

Ranger (RĀN-jer)
French—*Guardian of the forest*
Rainger, Range

Ranon (RĀN-on)
Hebrew—*To be joyous*
Raman, Ranen

Ransom (RAN-som)
Old English—*Son of the shield*
Randsom, Ransum

Raphael (RA-fī-el)
Hebrew—*God has healed*
Biblical: An archangel.
Famous: Raffaello Sanzio, painter
  of Madonnas.
**Rafael, Rafaelle,
Rafaello, Rafe, Ray**

Ravi (RA-vī)
Hindi—*Conferring*
Famous: Ravi Shankar, guru.
Ravid, Raviv

Rawdon (RAW-don)
Teutonic—*From the roe or deer hill*

Ray (RĀ)
French—*Kingly or king's title*
Literature: Ray Bradbury, science
  fiction writer.
Entertainment: Ray Charles,
  singer; Ray Milland, Raymond
  Massey, actors; Ray Bolger,
  dancer and actor.
Ramon, Raymond, Raymund

Rayburn (RA-burn)
Old English—*From the deer brook*
Burn, Burnie, Burny, Ray

Raymond (RĀ-mund)
Teutonic—*Wise protection*
Entertainment: Raymond Burr,
  actor.
**Raimondo, Raimund, Raimundo,
Ramon, Ray, Raymund, Reamon,
Reamonn**

Raynor (RĀ-nor)
Norwegian—*Mighty army*
Ragnar, Rainer, Ray

Razi (RĀ-zē)
Hebrew—*My secret*
Raz, Raziel

Redford (RED-ford)
Old English— *From the red river crossing*
Entertainment: Redd Foxx, comedian and actor.
Ford, Red, Redd, Reddy

Reece (RĒS)
Welsh— *Enthusiastic*
Rees, Reese, Rice, Rip

Reed (RĒD)
Old English— *Red-haired*
Read, Reade, Reid

Reeve (RĒV)
English— *Steward*

Regan (RĀ-gan)
Gaelic— *Little king*
Reagan, Reagen, Regen

Reginald (REJ-i-nald)
Teutonic— *Mighty ruler*
Literature: *Reggie Fortune*, story by H. C. Bailey.
Entertainment: Reginald de Koven, composer.
Sports: Reggie Jackson, baseball player.
Reg, Reggie, Reggis, Reginauld, Reinald, Reinaldo, Reinaldos, Reinhold, Reinwald, Renault, Rene, Reynold, Reynolds, Rinaldo, Rinalldo, Ron, Ronald, Ronnie, Ronny

Remington (RE-ming-tun)
Old English— *From the raven estate*
Rem, Remming, Tony

Remus (RĒ-mus)
Latin— *Fast-moving*
Literature: Uncle Remus, teller of *Br'er Rabbit* stories.

Rendor (REN-dor)
Hungarian— *Policeman*

Rene (re-NĀ)
French— *Reborn*
Famous: Rene Descartes, philosopher and mathematician.
Renee

Reuben (ROO-ben)
Hebrew— *Behold a son*
Biblical: Eldest son of Jacob; one of the 12 tribes of Israel.
Reuven, Rouvin, Rube, Ruben, Rubin, Ruby

Rex (REKS)
Latin— *King*
Famous: Rex Whistler, English artist.
Literature: Rex Stout, author of Nero Wolfe detective novels.
Entertainment: Rex Harrison, actor; Rex Reed, critic; Rex Allen, singer and actor.
Rexir, Rexy

Reyhan (RĀ-an)
Arabic— *Favored by God*

Reynard (RĀ-nard)
French— *Fox*
Teutonic— *Mighty*
Ray, Raynard, Reinhard, Renard, Renaud, Rey

Rhys (RES) or (RĪS)
Celtic— *Hero*
Welsh— *Ardor or rush*
Rees, Rice

Richard (RICH-erd)
Teutonic— *Powerful ruler*
Famous: Richard I, known as The Lion-Hearted; Richard Nixon, President.
Literature: *Poor Richard's Almanac*, by Benjamin Franklin.
Entertainment: Richard Strauss, composer; Richard Carpenter, singer; Richard Rogers, composer of musicals; Rich Little, impressionist; Richard Burton, Richard Pryor, Richard Dreyfuss, Richard Chamberlain, Richard Benjamin, actors.
Dick, Dickie, Dicky, Ric, Ricard, Ricardo, Riccardo, Rich, Richart, Richi, Richie, Richy, Rick, Rickard, Rickert, Ricki, Rickie, Ricky, Rico, Riki, Ritch, Ritchie

RICHARD—*Powerful ruler*

Richmond (RICH-mond)
Teutonic—*Powerful protector*
Richmound

Rick (RIK)
See Richard.
Entertainment: Ricky Nelson,
actor and singer.

Rida (RĒ-duh)
Arabic—*Favor*
Rid, Ridd, Ridia

Rider (RĪ-der)
Old English—*Horseman*
Ridder, Rydder, Ryder

Ridgley (RIJ-lē)
Old English—*He lives by the
meadow's edge*
Ridley, Riddley

Riley (RĪ-lē)
Gaelic—*Valiant*
Reilly, Ryley

Rimril (RIM-ril)
Chinese— *Clan's name*
Hulen, Rimhel, Rimhen, Rimlal, Rimnir, Rimshu

Ring (RING)
Old English— *Ring*
Literature: Ring Lardner, novelist and short-story writer.
Entertainment: Ringo Starr, member of The Beatles.
Ringo, Ringio

Riordan (RĒ-or-dan)
Gaelic— *Bard or royal poet*
Dan, Dannie, Danny, Rio

Rip (RIP)
Dutch— *Ripe; full grown*
Literature: Rip Van Winkle, character created by Washington Irving.
Entertainment: Rip Torn, actor.
Lee, Leigh, Riplee, Ripley

Roald (RŌ-ald)
Teutonic— *Fame*

Roarke (RORK)
Gaelic— *Famous ruler*
Rorke, Rourke

Robert (ROB-ert)
Teutonic— *Of bright, shining fame*
Historical: Robert Fulton, designer of the first successful U.S. steamboat.
Famous: General Robert E. Lee, Confederate general.
Literature: Robert Frost, Robert Sherwood, Robert Stevenson, Robert Browning, writers and poets.
Entertainment: Robert Schumann, composer; Robert Redford, Robert Mitchum, Robert DeNiro, Robert Wagner, Robert Blake, actors.
Bob, Bobbie, Bobby, Riobard, Rip, Rob, Robb, Robbie, Robby, Robers, Roberto, Robin, Rupert, Ruperto, Ruprecht

Robin (RO-bin)
See Robert.
Famous: Robin Hood of Sherwood Forest.
Entertainment: Robby Benson, actor; Robin Williams, actor known as Mork; Robin Gibb, member of the Bee Gees.
Robby

Robinson (RO-bin-sun)
English— *Son of Robert*
Literature: Robinson Jeffers, poet; *Robinson Crusoe,* novel by Daniel Defoe.
Robert, Robin, Robinet, Robers, Roberto, Ruperto

Rochester (RO-ches-ter)
Old English— *From the stone camp*
Entertainment: Rochester, character on *The Jack Benny Show.*
Chest, Chester, Chet, Rock, Rockie, Rocky

Rockwell (ROK-wel)
Old English— *From the rocky spring*

Rocky (ROK-ē)
See Rochester.
Entertainment: Rock Hudson, actor; Rocky, movie character created by Sylvester Stallone.
Sports: Rocky Marciano, heavyweight boxing champion.
Rock, Rockwell, Rockey

Rodas (RŌ-das)
Spanish, Greek— *Place of the roses*

Roderick (ROD-rik)
German— *Famous ruler*
Literature: *Roderick Hudson,* novel by Henry James.
Entertainment: Roddy McDowall, Rod Steiger, actors; Rod McKuen, singer and poet; Rod Stewart, singer.
Rod, Rodd, Roddie, Roddy, Roderic, Roderich, Roderigo, Rodrick, Rodrigo, Rodrique, Rory, Rurik, Ruy

Rodmann (ROD-man)
Teutonic—*Red hair*
Old English—*One who rides with a knight*
Rod, Rodd, Roddie, Roddy, Rodman

Rodney (ROD-nē)
Teutonic—*Famous*
Anglo-Saxon—*Island clearing*
Entertainment: Rodney Dangerfield, comedian; Rodney Allen Rippy, child actor.
Rod, Rodd, Roddie, Roddy, Rodi, Rodie

Roger (ROJ-er)
Teutonic—*Famous spearman*
Historical: Rodger Williams, founder of Rhode Island.
Entertainment: Roger Daltrey, rock singer; Roger Smith, Roger Moore, actors.
Sports: Rogers Hornsby, Rodger Maris, baseball players.
Robers, Rodge, Rodger, Rog, Rogerio, Rogers, Rudiger, Ruggiero, Rutger, Ruttger

Roland (RŌ-lund)
German—*From the famous land*
Entertainment: Roland Petit, ballet dancer; Roland Young, actor.
Lannie, Lanny, Rolando, Roldan, Roley, Rolland, Rollie, Rollin, Rollins, Rollo, Rolly, Rowland

Rolf (ROLF)
Teutonic—*Famous wolf*
Historical: First Norman duke was the viking, Rollo.
Literature: Rolfe Humphries, poet.
Rolfe, Rollin, Rollo, Rolph

Rolon (RŌ-lon)
Spanish, Teutonic—*Famous wolf*

Roman (RŌ-man)
Latin—*Of Rome*
Literature: Romain Roland, author.
Sports: Roman Gabriel, football quarterback.
Roma, Romain

Romeo (RŌ-mē-ō)
Italian—*Pilgrim to Rome*
Literature: Hero in Shakespeare's *Romeo and Juliet.*
Rome, Romie

Romney (ROM-nē)
Welsh—*Curving river*

Romulus (ROM-ū-lus)
Latin—*Citizen of Rome*
Mythological: Romulus and Remus, twins nursed by wolves and founders of Rome.
Romulis

Ronald (RON-uld)
See Reginald.
Famous: Ronald Reagan, actor and President.
Entertainment: Ronald Coleman, Ron Howard, actors.
Ron, Ronn, Ronny

Rooney (ROO-nē)
Gaelic—*Red hair*
Rowan, Rowen, Rowney

Roper (RŌ-per)
Old English—*Rope maker*

Rory (ROR-ē)
Gaelic—*Red king*
Entertainment: Rory Calhoun, actor.
Ririk

Roscoe (ROS-kō)
Teutonic—*From the deer forest*
Sports: Roscoe Tanner, tennis star.
Rosco, Ross, Rossie, Rossy

Rosmer (ROS-mer)
Zodiac—*Sea horse*

RYAN—*Little king*

Ross (ROS)
French—*Red*
Scottish—*Headland*
Rosse, Rossie, Rossy

Roswald (ROZ-wald)
Teutonic—*Mighty steed*
Roz, Rozwald

Roth (ROTH)
German—*Red hair*

Rouvin (ROO-vin)
Greek, Hebrew—*Behold a son*
Famous: Rouvin, sculptor.

Roy (ROI)
Celtic—*Red-haired*
French—*King*
Entertainment: Roy Rogers, singer
and actor; Roy Clark, singer.
**Roi, Royce, Rufe, Rufo,
Rufus, Ruy**

Royal (ROI-ul)
French—*Kingly*
Roy, Royall

Royden (ROI-den)
French—*From the king's hill*
Roy, Royd

Rudd (RUD)
Old English — *Ruddy-complected*
**Ruddie, Ruddy, Rudy,
Rudyard**

Rudolph (ROO-dolf)
Teutonic — *Famous wolf*
Entertainment: Rudolf Nureyev,
  ballet dancer; hero of Puccini's
  opera *La Boheme*; Rudolph
  Valentino, actor; Rudy Vallee,
  singer and actor.
**Raoul, Rodolfo, Rodolph,
Rodolphe, Rolf, Rolfe, Rollin,
Rollo, Rolph, Rudie,
Rudolf, Rudolfo, Rudy**

Ruford (ROO-ford)
Old English — *From the red ford*

Rufus (ROO-fus)
Latin — *Red-haired*
**Griffin, Griffith, Grigg,
Rufe**

Rupert (ROO-pert)
Teutonic — *Of shining fame*
Historical: Prince Rupert of
  Bavaria.
Literature: *Rupert of Hentzau*, novel
  by Anthony Hope; Rupert
  Brooke, poet.

Ruskin (RUS-kin)
French — *Red-haired*
Rush, Russ

Russell (RUS-el)
French — *Red-haired or fox-colored*
Literature: Russell Crouse, author
  of *Life with Father.*
Russ, Rustie, Rusty

Ruthford (RUTH-ford)
Old English — *From the cattle ford*
Famous: Rutherford B. Hayes,
  President.
**Ford, Fordie, Ruther,
Rutherford**

Rutledge (RUT-lej)
Old English — *From the red pool*
Rutherford, Rutter

Ryan (RI-un)
Gaelic — *Little king*
Entertainment: Ryan O'Neal, actor.
Ryun

Sabin (SA-bin)
Latin — *A man of the sabine people*
Interesting: Name comes from the
  Sabines, an Italian tribe.

Sahale (sa-HAL-e)
North American Indian — *Above*

Sahen (SA-en)
Indian — *Falcon*

Sailsbury (SALS-bur-e)
Old English — *From the guarded
  palace*

Sakima (suh-KE-muh)
North American Indian — *King*
Sakim

Salim (SA-lim)
Arabic — *Safe*

Salvador (SAL-va-dor)
Italian — *Savior*
Famous: Salvador Dali, surrealist
  painter.
**Sal, Sallie, Sally,
Salvidor, Sauveur**

Sam (SAM)
See Samuel.
Interesting: Uncle Sam, symbol of the U.S. Government.
Famous: Sam Rayburn, Speaker of the House of Representatives.
Literature: Sam Weller, character in *Pickwick Papers,* by Dickens.
Entertainment: Sammy Davis, Jr., singer and actor.
Sammie, Sammy, Shem

Samson (SAM-son)
Hebrew— *Like the sun*
Biblical: Samson had great strength until Delilah betrayed him.
Sam, Sammie, Sammy, Sampson, Sanson, Sansone, Shem, Sim, Simpson, Simson

Samuel (SAM-ūl)
Hebrew— *Heard or asked of God*
Biblical: Prophet who anointed Saul, the first king of Israel.
Historical: Samuel Adams, Revolutionary War hero and a founder of the United States.
Famous: Samuel Finley Breese Morse, inventor of Morse code.
Literature: Samuel Butler Yeats, poet.
Sam, Sammie, Sammy, Samuele, Samura, Shem

Sanat (sa-NOT)
Hindi— *Ancient*

Sanborn (SAN-born)
Old English— *From the sandy brook*
Sand, Sandi, Sandy

Sancho (SAWN-chō)
Latin— *Sanctified*
Literature: Sancho Panza, sidekick of Don Quixote.
Sauncho, Sanjo

Sanders (SAN-ders)
Greek— *Son of Alexander*
Entertainment: Sander Vanocur, newscaster.
Sander, Sanderson, Sandi, Sandor, Sandy, Saunders, Saunderson

Sandy (SAN-dē)
See Alexander.
Sand, Sander, Sandi, Sandon, Sandor

Sanford (SAN-ford)
Old English— *From the sandy hill*
Ford, Sand, Sandford, Sandi, Sandy

Sarad (sa-RAWD)
Hindi— *Autumn-born*

Sargent (SAR-jent)
French— *Army officer*
Famous: Sargent Shriver, cabinet member in the Kennedy Administration.
Sarge, Sergeant, Sergent

Sarojin (SAIR-ō-hin)
Hindi— *Lotuslike*

Sartan (SAR-tan)
Hebrew— *House of the moon*

Saul (SAWL)
Hebrew— *Asked for*
Biblical: King of Israel; Apostle Paul was known as Saul of Tarsus.
Literature: Saul Bellow, novelist.
Sol, Sollie, Solly, Zollie, Zolly

Sawyer (SOI-er) or (SAW-yer)
Old English— *Sawer of wood*
Saw, Saxe

Saxon (SAKS-un)
Old English— *Swordsman*
Sax, Saxe

Sayer (SĀ-er)
Welsh— *Carpenter*
Say, Sayers, Sayre, Sayres

SCOTT—*Scotsman*

Schuyler (SKĪ-ler)
Dutch—*A shelter*
Sky, Skylar, Skyler

Scott (SKOT)
Old English—*Scotsman*
Famous: Scott Carpenter,
astronaut; Francis Scott Key,
composer of *The Star-Spangled
Banner.*
Literature: F. Scott Fitzgerald,
novelist.

Seabrook (SĒ-brook)
Old English— *From the brook by the sea*
Seabrooke, Brook, Brooke

Seadon (SĒ-don)
Old English— *From the hill by the sea*
Seaden, Seedon

Seamus (SHĀ-mus)
See James.
Seumas, Shamus

Sean (SHAWN)
See John.
Literature: Sean O'Casey, short-story writer.
Entertainment: Sean Connery, actor.
Shane, Shaughn, Shaun, Shawn

Searle (SERL)
Teutonic— *Armed or wearing armor*
Serle

Seaton (SĒ-tun)
Old English— *From the place by the sea*
Seton, Seeton

Seaver (SĒ-ver)
Anglo-Saxon— *Victorious stronghold*
Seever

Sebastian (se-BAS-chun)
Greek— *Respected or reverenced*
Famous: Johann Sebastian Bach, composer.
Entertainment: Sebastian Cabot, actor.
Bastian, Bastien, Sebastiano, Sebastien

Sedgewick (SEJ-wik)
Old English— *From the valley of victory*
Sedgewin, Sedgewinn, Sedgwick

Selby (SEL-bē)
Teutonic— *From the manor farm*
Selbey, Shelby

Seldon (SEL-dun)
Teutonic— *From the manor valley*
Selden, Shelden, Sheldon

Selig (SĀ-lig)
German— *Blessed*
Zelig

Selwyn (SEL-win)
Old English— *Friend from the palace*
Selwin, Winnie, Winny, Wyn, Wynn

Sepp (SEP)
Hebrew— *God will increase*
Entertainment: Zeppo Marx, one of the Marx brothers.
Josef, Jupp, Peppi, Zeppi, Zeppo

Serge (SERJ)
Latin— *Attendant*
Entertainment: Sergei Rachmaninoff, composer.
Sergei, Sergio

Serle (SERL)
Teutonic— *Bearing arms*

Seth (SETH)
Hebrew— *The appointed*
Biblical: Son of Adam and Eve.

Seton (SĒ-tun)
Anglo-Saxon— *From the place by the sea*
Seetan, Seeten, Setan

Sevilen (SEV-len)
Turkish— *Beloved*

Seward (SOO-werd)
Old English— *Victorious defender*
Siward

Sewell (SOO-el)
Teutonic— *Victorious on the sea*
Sewel, Suwell

Seymour (SĒ-mor)
French— *Follower of St. Maur*
Morey, Morie, Morrie

Shalom (sha-LOM)
Hebrew— *Peace*
Sholom

Shandy (SHAN-dē)
Old English— *Rambunctious*

Shane (SHĀN)
Hebrew — *God's gracious gift*
Literature: *Shane*, western novel by Zane Grey.
Entertainment: Shaun Cassidy, actor and pop singer.
Sean, Shaun, Shawn

Shannon (SHAN-un)
Gaelic — *Small and wise*
Shanan, Shannan

Sharif (sha-RĒF)
Arabic — *Honest*

Shaw (SHAW)
Old English — *From the grove*

Sheehan (SHĒ-an)
Gaelic — *Little and peaceful*

Sheffield (SHEF-fēld)
Old English — *From the crooked field*
Field, Fields, Sheff, Sheffie, Sheffy

Shelby (SHEL-bē)
Old English — *From the ledge estate*
Shell, Shelley, Shelly

Sheldon (SHEL-dun)
Old English — *From the farm on the ledge*
Entertainment: Sheldon Leonard, producer.
Shell, Shelley, Shelly, Shelton

Shelley (SHEL-ē)
Anglo-Saxon — *From the ledge meadow*
Shel, Shell, Shelly

Shepherd (SHEP-erd)
Anglo-Saxon — *Sheep tender*
Entertainment: Shepperd Strudwick, actor.
Shep, Shepard, Sheply, Sheppard, Shepperd

Sherard (SHAIR-ard)
Anglo-Saxon — *Brave soldier*
Sherrard

Sherborn (SHUR-burn)
Old English — *From the clear brook*
Sherborne, Sherburn

Sheridan (SHAIR-i-dun)
Celtic — *Wild man or savage*
Dan, Dannie, Danny, Sherrie, Sherry

Sherlock (SHUR-lok)
English — *Fair-haired*
Literature: Sherlock Holmes, fictional detective.
Sherlocke, Shurlock, Shurlocke

Sherman (SHUR-mun)
Anglo-Saxon — *Wool-shearer*
Man, Manny, Sherm, Shermie, Shermy

Sherwin (SHUR-win)
English — *Swift runner*
Sherwyn, Sherwynd, Win, Winnie, Winny, Wyn, Wynn

Sherwood (SHUR-wood)
Old English — *From the bright forest*
Interesting: Sherwood Forest in England.
Literature: Sherwood Anderson, novelist and short-story writer.
Sher, Shurwood, Wood, Woodie, Woody

Sibley (SIB-lē)
Anglo-Saxon — *Friendly or related*
Sibly, Sibyl

Sidney (SID-nē)
French — *From Sidon*
Interesting: Sidon, oldest city of ancient Phoenicia.
Literature: Sydney Carlton, hero of Dickens' *A Tale of Two Cities*; Sidney Kingsley, author of *Men in White*.
Entertainment: Sidney Poitier, actor; Sid Caesar, actor and comedian.
Sid, Sidnee, Syd, Sydney

Sidwell (SID-wel)
Old English — *From the broad well*
Sid, Syd, Sydwell, Well

Siegfried (SIG-frēd)
German — *Glorious peace*
Literature: Siegfried Sassoon,
   satirist.
**Siffre, Sig, Sigfrid,
Sigfried, Sigvard**

Sigmund (SIG-mund)
Teutonic — *Victorious protector*
Famous: Sigmund Freud, father of
   psychoanalysis.
Entertainment: Sigmund
   Romberg, composer.
**Sig, Sigismondo, Sigismund,
Sigismundo, Sigsmond,
Sigsmondo, Sigurd**

Silas (SĪ-lus)
Latin — *Man of the forest*
Biblical: Companion of Paul on his
   missionary treks.
Literature: *Silas Marner,* novel by
   George Eliot; *The Rise of Silas
   Lapham,* novel by William Dean
   Howells.
**Silvain, Silvan, Silvanio,
Silvano, Silvanus, Silvester,
Silvie, Silvio, Sylas, Sylus,
Sylvain, Sylvan, Sylvano**

Simen (SĪ-men)
English — *Alike*
Interesting: Name means
   resemblance between newborn
   and parent.

Simon (SĪ-mun)
Hebrew — *He who hears*
Biblical: One of the 12 apostles of
   Christ.
Historical: Simon Bolívar, known
   as the George Washington of
   South America.
Literature: Simple Simon,
   character in the nursery rhyme.
**Si, Sim, Simeon, Simone,
Sy, Syman, Symen, Symon**

Simpson (SIMP-sun)
See Samson.
Simpsen, Simson

Sinclair (SIN-klair)
French — *From St. Clair*
Latin — *The illustrious*
Literature: Sinclair Lewis, author.
Clair, Clare, Sinclare

Sion (SĪ-on)
Hebrew — *Exalted*

Skelly (SKEL-ē)
Gaelic — *Storyteller*
Skell

Skip (SKIP)
Norwegian — *Shipmaster*
Skipp, Skipper, Skippie, Skippy

Slade (SLĀD)
Old English — *Child of the valley*

Slane (SLĀN)
Czech — *Salty*

Slevin (SLE-vin)
Gaelic — *Mountaineer*
Slaven, Slavin, Sleven

Sloan (SLŌN)
Celtic — *Warrior*

Smitty (SMIT-ē)
Old English — *Blacksmith*
Smith

Sofian (SŌ-fē-an)
Arabic — *Devoted*

Sol (SAWL)
Latin — *Child of the sun*
**Sollie, Solly, Zollie,
Zolly**

Solomon (SAWL-ō-mun)
Hebrew — *Peaceful*
Biblical: King Solomon, builder of
   great temple, known for his
   wisdom.
Literature: Sholom Aleichem,
   storyteller; Sholem Asch,
   novelist.
**Salamone, Salmon, Salomo,
Salomon, Shalom, Shlomo,
Sholem, Sholom, Sol, Sollie,
Solly, Zollie, Zolly**

SKIP—*Shipmaster*

Somerset (SOM-er-set)
Old English—*Summer place*
Literature: Somerset Maugham,
novelist.

Songan (SON-gan)
North American Indian—*Strong*

Spark (SPARK)
English—*Happy*
Sparke, Sparkie, Sparky

Spencer (SPEN-ser)
English—*Dispenser of provisions*
Entertainment: Spencer Tracy,
actor.
Spence, Spense, Spenser

Sprague (SPRĀG)
French—*Lively*
Sprage

Stacy (STĀ-sē)
Latin — *Stable companion*
Entertainment: Stacy Keach,
  actor.
Stacee, Stacey

Stafford (STAF-erd)
Old English — *Of the landing place*
Staffard, Staford

Standish (STAN-dish)
Old English — *From the stony park*

Stanford (STAN-ferd)
Old English — *From the rock ford*
**Standfield, Standford, Stanfield,
Stanhope**

Stanislaus (STAN-i-slaws)
Polish — *Camp glory*
Stan, Stanislas, Stanislaw

Stanley (STAN-lē)
Old English — *From the rocky
  meadow*
Entertainment: Stanley Kubrick,
  filmmaker.
Sports: Stan Musial, baseball
  player.
Stan, Stanleigh, Stanly

Stanton (STAN-tun)
Old English — *From the stony
  dwelling*
Stanway, Stanwood

Stedman (STED-mun)
Anglo-Saxon — *Dweller at the stead*
Steadman, Steadmen

Stephen (STĒ-ven)
Greek — *Crown*
Famous: Stephen A. Douglas,
  Abraham Lincoln's opponent in
  political debates; Etienne Aigner,
  clothes designer.
Literature: Stephen Crane,
  Stephen Vincent Benet, Stefan
  Zweig, authors.
Entertainment: Stephen Stills,
  member of Crosby, Stills and
  Nash; Stephen C. Foster,
  songwriter and composer; Steve
  McQueen, actor.
**Etienne, Esteban, Estevan,
Stefan, Stefano, Steffen,
Stephan, Stephanus, Steve,
Steven, Stevie, Stevy**

Sterling (STER-ling)
Teutonic — *Good value*
Entertainment: Sterling Hayden,
  actor.
Sports: Sterling Moss, race-car
  driver.
Stirling

Sterne (STERN)
English — *Austere*
Stearn, Stearne, Stern

Steven (STĒ-ven)
See Stephen.
Entertainment: Stevie Wonder,
  singer; Steve Lawrence, Steve
  Martin, actors; Steven Spielberg,
  film director.
Sports: Steve Cauthen, jockey.
Steve, Stevie, Stevy

Stewart (STOO-art)
Anglo-Saxon — *Keeper of the state*
Entertainment: Stewart Granger,
  actor.
Stew, Steward, Stu, Stuart

Stiggur (STĒ-gur)
English — *Gate*
Stig, Stigger

Stillman (STIL-mun)
Old English — *Quiet man*
Stillmann

Strephon (STREF-un)
Greek — *One who turns*
Entertainment: Strephon, hero of
Iolanthe, by Gilbert and Sullivan.
Strep, Strephonn, Strepphon

Stuart (STŌŌ-art)
Old English — *Caretaker*
Literature: Stuart Chase,
economist.
Entertainment: Stu Gallagher, actor.
Steward, Stewart, Stu

Styles (STĪLS)
Old English — *From the stiles*

Sudi (SŌŌ-dē)
Swahili — *Luck*

Sullivan (SUL-i-vun)
Gaelic — *Black-eyed*
Sullie, Sully

Sultan (SUL-tun)
Swahili — *Ruler.*
Sulten

Sumner (SUM-ner)
French, Latin — *A summoner*

Sutherland (SUTH-er-lund)
Norwegian — *Southern land*
Sotherland, Sutherlan

Sutton (SUT-un)
Anglo-Saxon — *From the south town*

Sven (SVEN)
Norwegian — *Youth*
Svend, Swen

Swaine (SWĀN)
Teutonic — *Boy*
Swane, Swain, Wain

Sylvester (sil-VES-ter)
Latin — *Of the woods*
Literature: *Le Crime de Sylvestre
Bonnard,* by Anatole France.
Entertainment: Sylvester Stallone,
actor; Sly Stone, singer.
Silvester, Silvestre, Sly, Sylvestu

Tab (TAB)
English — *Drummer*
Entertainment: Tab Hunter, actor.
**Tabb, Tabbie,
Tabby, Taber, Tabor**

Tabib (ta-BĒB)
Turkish — *Physician*

Tabor (TĀ-bor)
Hungary, Turkish — *Fortified camp*

Tad (TAD)
See Theodore.

Tadeo (ta-DĀ-ō)
Spanish, Latin — *Praise*
Tadeas, Tades

Tadzi (TAD-zē)
Carrier Indian — *The loon*
Tadek, Tadzio

Tait (TĀT)
Scandinavian — *Cheerful*

Tal (TAL)
Hebrew — *Dew or rain*
Talor

Talbot (TAL-but)
Teutonic, French — *Valley shining*
**Talabert, Talbert, Tallie,
Tally**

Tales (TĀLS)
Spanish, Greek — *Flourishing*
Thales

Talman (TAL-mun)
Hebrew, Aramaic— *To oppress*
Talmon

Taman (TĀ-mun)
Serbo-Croatian— *Dark or black*

Tamas (TĀ-mas)
Hungarian, Greek— *Twin*
**Tammen, Thoma, Thomas,
Thumas, Tomasek, Tomasko,
Tomasso, Tomcio, Tomek,
Tomi, Tomislaw, Toms, Tonie**

Tammy (TAM-ē)
See Thomas.
Literature: *Tam O'Shanter,* by
Robert Burns.
Tam, Tammany, Tammie

Tanek (TAN-ek)
Polish, Greek— *Immortal*
Ateck, Tanis

Tanner (TAN-er)
Old English— *Leatherworker*
**Tan, Tann, Tanney,
Tannie, Tanny**

Taro (TAIR-ō)
Japanese— *First-born male*

Tarrus (TAR-us)
Zodiac— *Bull*
Tari, Taurin, Taurus, Tawrin

Tate (TĀT)
Teutonic— *Cheerful*
Tait, Taite

Tavish (TAV-ish)
Gaelic— *Twin*
Tav, Tavis, Tevis

Tawno (TAW-nō)
English— *Small*

Tayib (TA-ēb)
Indian— *Good or delicate*

Taylor (TĀ-lor)
Latin— *The tailor*

Teague (TĒG)
Celtic— *Poet*

Ted (TED)
See Theodore.
Famous: Teddy Roosevelt,
President; Ted Kennedy, Senator.
Sports: Ted Williams, baseball
player.
**Tedd, Teddey, Teddie,
Teddy, Tedman, Tedmund**

Temp (TEMP)
Old English— *From the town of the
temple*
Temple, Templeton

Terence (TAIR-ens)
Latin— *Smooth*
Literature: Terence Mulvaney,
hero in Kipling's *Soldiers Three;*
Terence Rattigan, playwright.
Entertainment: Terry Thomas,
actor.
Terencio, Terrence, Terry

Terrill (TAIR-il)
Teutonic— *Belonging to Thor or
martial*
Tirrell

Terry (TAIR-ē)
See Terence.

Tertius (TER-shus)
Latin— *The third*
Tertius, Tertus

Thaddeus (THAD-ē-us)
Greek— *Courageous*
Latin— *Praiser*
Biblical: One of the 12 apostles of
Christ.
Historical: Thaddeus Stevens
brought impeachment
proceedings against President
Andrew Johnson.
Literature: *Thaddeus of Warsaw,*
novel by Jane Porter.
**Tad, Tadd, Taddeo,
Taddeuss, Tadeo, Tadio,
Thad, Thaddaus**

THOMAS—*Twin*

Thaine (THĀN)
Old English—*A roofer*
Thacher, Thackeray, Thatch, Thaxter

Thayer (THĀ-er)
Teutonic—*Of the nation's army*
Thay

Theobald (THĒ-uh-bald)
German—*Bold for the people*
Ted, Tedd, Teddie, Teddy, Thebault, Theo, Thibaud, Thibaut, Tiebold, Tiebout, Toiboild, Tybalt

Theodore (THĒ-uh-dor)
Greek—*God's gift*
Literature: Theodore Dreiser, author of *An American Tragedy*.
Entertainment: Theodore Bikel, actor and folk singer; Ted Knight, actor.
Teador, Ted, Tedd, Teddie, Teddy, Teodoor, Teodoro, Theo, Theodor, Theodore, Tudor

Theodoric (thē-uh-DOR-ik)
Teutonic— *The people's ruler*
Historical: Theodoric the Great, king of the Ostrogath, an ancient civilization in Italy.
Derek, Derk, Derrick, Dieter, Dietrich, Dirk, Ted, Tedd, Teddy, Teodorico, Thedric, Thedrick, Theo

Theron (THAIR-on)
Greek— *Hunter*

Thomas (TOM-as)
Hebrew— *Twin*
Biblical: One of the 12 apostles of Christ; referred to as Doubting Thomas.
Famous: Thomas Edward Lawrence, known as Lawrence of Arabia; Thomas Jefferson, Thomas Woodrow Wilson, Presidents; Thomas A. Edison, inventor of the electric light bulb.
Literature: Thomas Hardy, Thomas Paine, Thomas Wolfe, authors.
Entertainment: Tommy Smothers, actor and singer.
Tam, Tamas, Tammie, Tammy, Thom, Thoma, Thomkin, Tom, Tomas, Tomaso, Tome, Tomlin, Tommie, Tommy

Thor (THOR)
Norwegian— *The thunderous one*
Mythological: Thor, the thunder god.
Thorbjorn, Thorin, Thorlief, Thorvald, Tore, Tove, Tyrus

Thornton (THORN-tun)
Anglo-Saxon— *From the thorny place*
Literature: Thornton Wilder, author and playwright.
Thorn, Thorndike, Thornie, Thorny

Thorpe (THORP)
Teutonic— *From the small village*

Thurlow (THUR-lō)
Old English— *From Thor's hill*

Thurston (THUR-stun)
Scandinavian— *Thor's jewel*

Tilden (TIL-den)
Old English— *From the fertile valley*
Tildan

Tilford (TIL-ford)
Old English— *From the good or fertile ford*
Tillford

Timothy (TIM-ō-thē)
Greek— *Honoring God*
Biblical: Timothy, one of the 12 apostles of Christ.
Famous: Timothy Leary, counterculture philosopher.
Literature: Tiny Tim, character in *A Christmas Carol,* by Dickens.
Tim, Timmie, Timmy, Timofei, Timoteo, Timothee, Timotheus, Tymon

Titus (TĪ-tus)
Latin— *The saved*
Tito, Titos

Tivon (TĪ-von)
Hebrew— *Naturalist*

Tobias (tō-BĪ-as)
Hebrew— *God is good*
Literature: Tobias Smollett, author.
Tobe, Tobiah, Tobie, Tobin, Tobit, Toby

Todd (TOD)
Scottish— *Fox*
Toddie, Toddy

Tom (TOM)
See Thomas.
Literature: *Tom Jones,* novel by
Henry Fielding; *Uncle Tom's
Cabin,* by Harriet Beecher Stowe;
The Adventures of Tom Sawyer, by
Mark Twain; *Sentimental Tommy,*
by James M. Barrie.
Entertainment: Tom Jones, pop
singer; Tom Tryon, actor.
Sports: Tom Seaver, baseball
player.

Tony (TŌ-nē)
See Anthony.
Entertainment: Tony Perkins,
Tony Randall, actors; Tony
Orlando, Tony Bennett, singers.
Toni, Tonnie

Torbert (TOR-bert)
Teutonic — *Glorious as Thor*
Bert, Bertie, Berty, Torebert

Torin (TOR-in)
Irish — *Chief*
Thorfinn, Thorstein

Torrance (TOR-uns)
Gaelic — *From the knolls*
**Tore, Torey, Torr,
Torrence, Torrey, Torry**

Townsend (TOWN-send)
Old English — *From the town's end*
Literature: Townsend Hope,
columnist.
Town, Towney, Townie, Towny

Tracey (TRĀ-sē)
Anglo-Saxon — *The brave defender*
Trace, Tracey, Tracie

Trahern (TRĀ-ern)
Celtic — *Stronger than iron*
Tray

Travis (TRAV-is)
French — *At the crossroads*
Literature: Travis McGee, hero of
John MacDonald mystery novels.
Entertainment: Travis
Edmondson, singer.
Traver, Travers, Travus

Tremain (tre-MĀN)
Celtic — *From the town of stone*
Tremayne

Trent (TRENT)
Latin — *Torrent*
Trant, Trante, Trenton

Trevor (TRE-vor)
Gaelic — *Prudent*
Entertainment: Trevor Howard,
British actor.
Trefor, Trev, Trevar

Tristan (TRIS-tun)
Welsh — *Sorrowful*
Literature: *Tristan and Isolde,* epic
poem by Thomas Malory;
Tristan, knight in King Arthur
legends.
Sports: Tristram E. Speaker,
baseball player.
Tris, Tristam, Tristram

Troy (TROI)
Gaelic — *Foot soldier*
Entertainment: Troy Donahue,
actor.

Truman (TROO-mun)
Old English — *Faithful man*
Literature: Truman Capote, author.
Trueman, Trumann

Tucker (TUK-er)
Old English — *Tucker of cloth*
Tuck, Tuckie, Tucky

Tully (TUL-ē)
Gaelic — *He who lives with peace of
God*
Tull, Tulley

Turner (TER-ner)
Latin — *Worker of the lathe*

Tyee (TĪ-ē)
North American Indian — *Chief*
Tyonek

Tyler (TĪ-ler)
Old English— *Maker of tiles*
Sports: Tyrus Raymond Cobb, baseball player.
Tiler, Ty

Tymon (TĪ-mun)
Polish, Greek— *Honoring God*
Tymek

Tyrone (TĪ-rōn)
Greek— *Sovereign*
Gaelic— *Land of Owen*
Entertainment: Tyrone Power, actor; Tyrone Guthrie, director and playwright.
Tie, Tynan, Tyrus

Tyson (TĪ-sun)
Teutonic— *Son of the Teutonic or German*
Tie, Ty, Tye

Udell (Ū-del)
Old English— *From the yew-tree valley*
Del, Dell, Udale, Udall

Uland (Ū-land)
Teutonic— *From the noble land*

Ulric (UL-rik)
Teutonic— *Ruler of all*
German— *Wolf ruler*
Alaric, Ric, Rick, Rickie, Ricky, Ulrich, Ulrick

Ulysses (ū-LIS-ēs)
Latin, Greek— *Angry or wrathful*
Famous: Ulysses S. Grant, President.
Literature: Ulysses, hero of Homer's *Odyssey;* novel *Ulysses,* by James Joyce.
Ulick, Ulises, Ulixes, Ulyzes

Unni (UH-nē)
Hebrew— *Modest*

Upton (UP-tun)
Anglo-Saxon— *From the hill town*
Literature: Upton Sinclair, novelist.

Urban (ER-bun)
Latin— *From the city*
Urbain, Urbane, Urbano, Urbanus

Uriah (ū-RĪ-uh)
Hebrew— *Jehovah is my light*
Biblical: Husband to Bathsheba.
Literature: Uriah Heap, character in Dickens' *David Copperfield.*
Urias, Uriel

Urian (ū-RĪ-un)
Greek— *From heaven*
Urien

Uriel (ŪR-ē-el)
Hebrew— *Flame of God*
Uri

Uziel (ū-ZĒ-el)
Hebrew— *A mighty force*
Uzziel

VACHEL — *Cowkeeper*

Vachel (VĀ-chel)
French — *Cowkeeper*
Literature: Vachel Lindsay, poet.
Vachell, Vachil

Vadin (va-DĒN)
Hindi — *Scholarly speaker*

Vail (VĀL)
Anglo-Saxon — *From the valley*
Bail, Bale, Vale, Valle

Valdis (VAL-dis)
Teutonic — *Spirited in battle*
Literature: Valdis Fisher, novelist

Valentine (VAL-en-tīn) or
(VAL-en-tēn)
Latin — *Strong, valorous or healthy*
Interesting: St. Valentine, patron
saint of lovers.
**Val, Valente, Valentin,
Valentino, Valerian,
Valerius, Valetijn, Valiant**

Valin (VĀL-in)
Hindi — *Monkey king*

Van (VAN)
Dutch — *From*
Entertainment: Van Johnson, Van
Heflin, actors; Van Cliburn,
pianist.

Vance (VANS)
Dutch — *Son of a famous family*
Literature: Vance Packard, author.
Van

Vancel (VAN-sel)
Hungarian — *Wreath or garland*

Vasilis (va-SIL-is)
Greek — *Kingly or magnificent*
Vasileior, Vasos

Vasin (va-SĒN)
Indian — *Ruler*

Vassily (VAS-i-lē)
Russian, German — *Unwavering
protector*
Vas, Vasilek, Vasya, Vasyuta

Vaughan (VAWN)
Celtic — *The small*
Vaughn, Von

Vere (VAIR)
Latin — *True or faithful*
Vered

Vernon (VER-nun)
Latin — *Growing green*
Lavern, Vern, Verne, Verney

Victor (VIK-tor)
Latin — *The conqueror*
Literature: Victor Hugo, novelist
and poet.
Entertainment: Victor Herbert,
composer; Victor Borge, pianist
and comedian; Victor Mature,
Vic Tayback, actors.
Vic, Vick, Victoir, Vittorio

Vidor (VĒ-dor)
Hungarian, Latin — *Cheerful*

Vigor (VĒ-gor)
Latin — *Vigor*

Vincent (VIN-sent)
Latin — *Conquering*
Famous: Vincent van Gogh,
painter.
Entertainment: Vincent Price,
actor; Vincent Minelli, film
producer.
Sports: Vince Lombardi, football
coach.
**Vin, Vince, Vincents,
Vincenty, Vincenz, Vinnie,
Vinny**

Vinson (VIN-sun)
Anglo-Saxon — *The conqueror's son*

Virgil (VIR-jul)
Latin — *Strange or flourishing*
Literature: Virgil, author of *The
Aeneid.*
Entertainment: Virgil Thomson,
composer and critic.
**Verge, Vergil, Virg,
Virge, Virgie, Virgilio,
Virginius, Virgy**

Vito (VĒ-tō)
Latin — *Alive*
Vite, Vivien

Vladimir (VLA-duh-mēr)
Old Slavic — *Powerful prince*
Literature: Vladimir Nabokov,
author.
Entertainment: Vladimir
Horowitz, pianist.
**Vladamir, Vladlan, Vladlen,
Waldemar, Wladimir**

Volney (VOL-nē)
Teutonic — *Most popular*
Volny

Waban (WAW-ban)
North American Indian — *The east wind*

Wade (WĀD)
Old English — *Advancer from the river crossing*
Wadsworth

Wainwright (WĀN-rīt)
Old English — *Wagon maker*
Wain, Wayne, Wright

Waite (WĀT)
English — *Guard*

Wakefield (WĀK-fēld)
Old English — *From the wet field*
Field, Wake

Wakiza (wa-KĒ-zuh)
North American Indian — *Desperate fighter*

Walbridge (WAL-brij)
Old English — *From the walled bridge*

Walcot (WAL-kot)
Old English — *Dweller in the walled cottage*

Waldemar (WAL-de-mar)
Teutonic — *Powerful and famous*
Valdemar, Wald, Waldo, Walley, Wallie, Wally

Walden (WAL-den)
Teutonic — *Mighty*

Waldo (WAL-dō)
Teutonic — *Ruler*
Literature: Ralph Waldo Emerson, essayist and poet.
Wald, Wallie, Wally

Waldon (WAL-dun)
Old English — *From the wooded hill*
Waldron

Walker (WOK-er)
Old English — *Thickener of cloth, fuller*
Walley, Wallie, Wally

Wallace (WAL-is)
Old English — *Welshman*
Literature: Wallace Stegner, novelist.
Wallache, Wallas, Wallie, Wallis, Wally, Walsh, Walt, Welch, Welsh

Walter (WAL-ter)
German — *Powerful warrior*
Famous: Walter Reed, discoverer of the cause of yellow fever.
Literature: Sir Walter Raleigh, Sir Walter Scott, authors.
Entertainment: Walter Cronkite, newscaster; Walt Disney, producer of children's movies; Walter Winchell, Walter Lippmann, Walter Matthau, actors.
Sports: Walter Camp, founder of All-American selection in football; Walter Johnson, baseball player; Walter Hagen, golfer.
Gauthier, Gualterio, Gualtiero, Wallie, Wally, Walt, Walther, Wat

Walton (WAL-tun)
Old English — *From the walled town*
Wallie, Wally, Walt

Ward (WARD)
Old English — *Guardian*

Ware (WAIR)
Anglo-Saxon — *Prudent, astute and wary*
Warfield, Warford

Waring (WAIR-ing)
Latin — *True*
Teutonic — *Heedful*

Warner (WAR-ner)
Teutonic — *Guarding warrior*
Famous: Warner Erhard, ESP theorist.

Warren (WAR-un)
German — *Protecting friend*
Famous: Warren G. Harding, President.
Entertainment: Warren Beatty, actor and director.
Sports: Warren Spahn, baseball player.
Ware, Waring

WARREN — *Protecting friend*

Warrick (WAR-ik)
Teutonic — *Strong ruler*
Aurick, Vareck, Varick, Warwick

Warton (WAR-tun)
Old English — *From the poplar-tree farm*

Washburn (WASH-bern)
Old English — *From near the overflowing brook*
Burn, Burnie, Burny, Wash

Washington (WASH-ing-tun)
Teutonic — *The acute or smart*
Famous: George Washington Carver, inventor of many uses for the peanut.
Literature: Washington Irving, author.
Wash

Watson (WAT-sun)
Anglo-Saxon — *Warrior's son*

Waverly (WĀ-ver-lē)
Old English — *From the meadow of quaking aspen trees*
Lee, Leigh, Waverley

Wayland (WĀ-lund)
Teutonic — *From the land by the highland*
Entertainment: Waylon Jennings, country-western singer.
Land, Way, Waylen, Waylon

Wayne (WĀN)
Anglo-Saxon — *Wagoneer*
Entertainment: Wayne Newton, singer and entertainer.
Waine

Webb (WEB)
Old English — *Weaver*
Weber, Webster

Welby (WEL-bē)
Scandinavian — *From the farm by the spring*

Weldon (WEL-dun)
Teutonic — *From the hill by the well*

Wells (WELZ)
Old English — *From the springs*

Wendell (WEN-dul)
German — *Wanderer*
Anglo-Saxon — *Dweller by the passage*
Famous: Wendell Phillips, abolitionist; Oliver Wendell Holmes, Chief Justice of the Supreme Court.
Sports: Wendell Scott, race-car driver.
Wendel

Wescott (WES-kot)
Teutonic — *Dwells at west cottage*
Wes

Wesley (WES-lē)
Old English — *From the western meadow*
Lee, Leigh, Wellesley, Wes, West, Westleigh, Westley

Westbrook (WEST-brook)
Old English — *From the western brook*
Brook, Brooke, Wes, West, Westbrooke, Westley

Weston (WES-tun)
Old English — *From the western estate*

Weylin (WĀ-lin)
Celtic — *Son of the wolf*
Waylan, Waylin

Wheeler (WĒL-er)
Old English — *Wheel maker*

Whitby (WIT-bē)
Scandinavian — *From the white dwellings of settlements*

Whitelaw (WĪT-law)
Old English — *From the white hill*
Whitford, Whitman

Whitney (WIT-nē)
Old English — *From the white island*
Whit

Whittaker (WI-tuh-ker)
Old English — *From the white field*
Whit

Wicent (WĪ-sent)
Polish, Latin — *Conqueror*
**Vincenty, Wicek, Wicenty,
Wicus, Wincenty**

Wichado (wi-CHA-dō)
North American Indian — *Willing*

Wilbur (WIL-ber)
Anglo-Saxon — *Beloved stronghold*
Famous: Wilbur Wright, inventor
of the airplane.
Wilbert, Wilburt

Wildon (WIL-dun)
Old English — *From the wooded hill*
Wilden, Willdon

Wiley (WĪ-lē)
Old English — *From the water*
Sports: Willie Mays, baseball
player.
Entertainment: Willie Nelson,
country-western singer.
**Willey, Willie, Wully,
Wylie**

Wilfred (WIL-fred)
Old English — *Resolute for peace*
Literature: Wilfred, hero in
Ivanhoe, by Sir Walter Scott.
**Wilford, Wilfrid, Will,
Willie, Willy**

William (WIL-yum)
Teutonic — *Determined guardian*
Historical: William Penn, founder
of Pennsylvania; William Tell,
Swiss national hero; William the
Conqueror, military leader.
Famous: William Henry Harrison,
William McKinley, William
Howard Taft, Presidents;
William Harvey, discoverer of
circulation of the blood.
Literature: William Blake, William
Wordsworth, William Butler
Yeats, William Faulkner, William
Buckley, Jr., authors.
Entertainment: William Holden,
actor; William Friedkin, director.
Sports: Willie McCovey, baseball
player.
**Bill, Billie, Billy,
Guglielmo, Guillaume,
Guillermo, Wilek, Wilhelm,
Will, Willem, Willi, Willie,
Willis, Willy, Wilmar, Wilmer**

Wilton (WIL-tun)
Old English — *From the farm by the
spring*
Sports: Wilt Chamberlain,
basketball player.
Will, Willie, Willy, Wilt

Winfield (WIN-fēld)
Old English — *From the friendly field*
**Field, Win, Winfred,
Winfrid, Winifield, Winnie**

Winslow (WINZ-lō)
Old English — *From the friend's hill*
Win, Winn, Winnie, Winny

Winston (WIN-stun)
Anglo-Saxon — *Friend or friendly
town*
Famous: Winston Churchill,
British Prime Minister.
**Win, Winn, Winnie,
Winny, Winstonn**

Winthrop (WIN-thrup)
Old English — *From the wine village*
Entertainment: Winthrop Ames,
producer.

Winward (WIN-werd)
Unknown — *My brother's keeper*

Wolcott (WAWL-kot)
Unknown — *Cottage in the woods*
Literature: Wolcott Gibbs,
playwright.
Walcot, Walcott, Wolcot

Wolfgang (WULF-gang)
Teutonic — *Advancing wolf*
Famous: Wolfgang Amadeus
Mozart, composer.
**Wolf, Wolfe, Wolfie,
Wolfram, Wolfy**

Woodrow (WOOD-rō)
Old English — *From the passage in
the woods*
Famous: Thomas Woodrow
Wilson, President.
**Wood, Woodie, Woodley,
Woodman, Woodward, Woody**

Worth (WERTH)
Old English — *From the farmstead*
Worthington, Worthy

Wright (RĪT)
Old English — *Carpenter*

Wuliton (WOOL-i-tun)
North American Indian — *To do well*

Wyatt (WĪ-at)
French — *Little warrior*
Famous: Wyatt Earp, old west
lawman and gunfighter.
Wiatt, Wyat, Wye

Wylie (WĪ-lē)
Old English — *Charming*
Lee, Leigh, Wiley, Wye

Wyman (WĪ-mun)
Anglo-Saxon — *Warrior*

Wyndham (WIN-dum)
Old English — *From the windy village*

Wynn (WIN)
Welsh — *Fair*
Winnie, Winny

Xanthus (ZAN-thus)
Latin — *Golden-haired*

Xavier (ZĀ-vē-er)
Spanish, Arabic — *Brilliant*
Entertainment: Xavier Cugat, band
leader.
Jaberri, Javier, Xever

Xenophon (ZĒ-nō-fon)
Greek — *Strange voice*
Xeno, Zennie

Xenos (ZĒ-nōs)
Greek — *Stronger*
Xenoz

Xerxes (ZER-sēz)
Persian — *King*
Interesting: Many Persian
emperors were named Xerxes.
Zerk

Ximenes (ZĪ-me-nēz)
See Simon.
Ximenez, Ximenia, Xymenes

Xylon (ZĪ-lon)
Greek — *From the forest*

Yadid (yuh-DĒD)
Hebrew — *Friend*

Yadin (yuh-DĒN)
Hebrew — *God will judge*
Yadon

Yakecen (YAK-sen)
Indian — *Sky or song*

Yakez (YAK-ez)
Carrier Indian — *Heaven*

Yale (YĀL)
Teutonic — *Payer; yielder*

Yancy (YAN-sē)
North American Indian —
Englishman
**Ioammis, Yance, Yancey,
Yank, Yankee, Yannakis**

Yarin (YAR-in)
Hebrew — *To understand*

Yasah (YĀ-zuh)
Arabic — *Wealth*

Yazid (yuh-ZĒD)
See Joseph.
Yusef, Zaid

Yeates (YĀTS)
Anglo-Saxon — *At the gates*

Yehudi (yuh-HOO-dē)
Hebrew — *Praise of the Lord*
Entertainment: Yehudi Menuhin,
violinist.

Yemon (YĀ-mon)
Japanese — *Guarding the gate*

Yeremy (YER-e-mē)
Russian, Hebrew — *Appointed by
God*
Yarema, Yaremka, Yerik

York (YORK)
Old English — *Estate of the boar*
Yorke, Yorker

Yucel (Ū-sel)
Turkish — *Sublime*

Yule (ŪL)
Old English — *Born at yuletide*
Entertainment: Yul Brynner, actor.
Ewel, Ewell, Yul

Yuma (Ū-muh)
North American Indian — *Son of a
chief*

Yvan (Ī-van)
See Ivan.

Yves (ĒVS)
French — *Little archer*
Famous: Yves Saint Laurent,
designer.
Entertainment: Yves Montand,
actor.
Ives

Zachariah (zak-uh-RĪ-uh)
Hebrew — *The Lord's remembrance*
Biblical: Zacharias, father of John the Baptist.
Famous: Zachary Taylor, President.
Entertainment: Zachary Scott, actor.
Zacarias, Zaccaria, Zach, Zacharias, Zacharie, Zachary, Zak, Zakarias, Zechariah, Zeke

Zahur (ZĀ-hur)
Swahili — *Flower*

Zak (ZAK)
Czech — *Schoolboy*
Zaki

Zamir (za-MĒR)
Hebrew — *A bird or a song*
Zemer

Zane (ZĀN)
Hebrew — *Ambush*
Literature: Zane Grey, author.

Zarek (ZAR-ek)
Polish, Greek — *May God protect the king*
Balte

Zebadiah (zeb-uh-DĪ-uh)
Hebrew — *Gift of the Lord*
Biblical: Zebedee, husband of Solome and father of apostles James and John.
Zebedee

Zebulon (ZEB-ū-lon)
Hebrew — *Dwelling place*
Historical: General Zebulon M. Pike, for whom Pike's Peak was named.
Zeb, Zebulen

Zedekiah (zed-e-KĪ-uh)
Hebrew — *God is mighty and just*
Biblical: Last king of Judah.

Zeke (ZĒK)
See Ezekiel.

Zelig (ZĀ-lik)
Teutonic — *Blessed*
Selig, Zelix

Zelimir (ZEL-i-mēr)
Slavic — *He wishes peace*

Zenas (ZĒ-nas)
Greek — *Jupiter's gift*
Zenos

Zephaniah (zef-uh-NĪ-uh)
Hebrew — *Hidden by the Lord*
Biblical: Prophet that lived at the time of Jeremiah.
Jeremiah, Zeph, Zephan

Zion (ZĪ-un)
Hebrew — *Fortress*

Ziven (ZIV-en)
Czech, Russian — *Vigorous and alive*
Ziv, Zivon

Zollie (ZAWL-ē)
See Saul.
Zolly

Zorya (ZOR-yuh)
Ukrainian — *Star*

INDEX

BABY-NAME WORKSHEET

First	Middle	Last

1. _____
2. _____
3. _____
4. _____
5. _____
6. _____
7. _____
8. _____
9. _____
10. _____

RANK NAMES IN ORDER OF PREFERENCE:

First: _____

Second: _____

Third: _____

BABY-NAME WORKSHEET

	First	Middle	Last
1.			
2.			
3.			
4.			
5.			
6.			
7.			
8.			
9.			
10.			

RANK NAMES IN ORDER OF PREFERENCE:

First: _____

Second: _____

Third: _____

BABY-NAME WORKSHEET

	First	Middle	Last
1.			
2.			
3.			
4.			
5.			
6.			
7.			
8.			
9.			
10.			

RANK NAMES IN ORDER OF PREFERENCE:

First: _____

Second: _____

Third: _____